MW01247819

Grotesque Touch

Grotesque Touch

*Women, Violence, and Contemporary
Circum-Caribbean Narratives*

Amy K. King

The University of North Carolina Press CHAPEL HILL

This book was published with the assistance of the Authors Fund of the University of North Carolina Press.

Set in Merope Basic by Westchester Publishing Services
Manufactured in the United States of America

The University of North Carolina Press has been a member of the Green Press Initiative since 2003.

Library of Congress Cataloging-in-Publication Data

Names: King, Amy K., author.
Title: Grotesque touch : women, violence, and contemporary circum-
    Caribbean narratives / Amy K. King.
Description: Chapel Hill : University of North Carolina Press, [2021] |
    Includes bibliographical references and index.
Identifiers: LCCN 2021026150 | ISBN 9781469664637 (cloth ; alkaline paper) |
    ISBN 9781469664644 (paperback ; alkaline paper) | ISBN 9781469664651 (ebook)
Subjects: LCSH: Women in popular culture—United States. | Women in
    popular culture—Caribbean Area. | Violence in women in popular
    culture—United States. | Violence in women in popular culture—
    Caribbean Area. | Slavery—History. | Plantations in literature. |
    Plantations in art. | Power (Social sciences)
Classification: LCC P94.5.W652 U6545 2021 | DDC 810.9/3522—dc23
LC record available at https://lccn.loc.gov/2021026150

Cover illustration: Lace pattern © Shutterstock.com/Sylvvie.

Portions of chapter 5 were previously published in a different form: "A Monstrous(ly-Feminine) Whiteness: Gender, Genre, and the Abject Horror of the Past in *American Horror Story: Coven*," in *Women's Studies: An Interdisciplinary Journal* (2017), reprinted by permission of the publisher (Taylor & Francis Ltd, http://www.tandfonline.com); and "'She Had Put the Servant in Her Place': Sexual Violence and Generational Social Policing between Women in Marie-Elena John's *Unburnable*," in *Reading/Speaking/Writing the Mother Text: Essays on Caribbean Women's Writing*, edited by Paula Sanmartin and Cristina Herrera (Demeter Press, 2015).

Dedicated to student activists at the
University of Mississippi and the
University of North Carolina at Chapel Hill.
For leading us into the future.

Contents

Acknowledgments xi

Introduction 1
Depicting Violence between Women in Circum-Caribbean Texts

CHAPTER ONE
Sensational Violence 22

CHAPTER TWO
Within and Beyond Sadistic Violence 44

CHAPTER THREE
Un-Silencing Sexual Violence 75

CHAPTER FOUR
Violent Denial in Post-Emancipation Households 102

CHAPTER FIVE
The Horror of Intimate Violence 142

Conclusion 174
Plantation Settings after 2016

Notes 185
Works Cited 203
Index 221

Figures

1.1 Henry Bibb, *Narrative of the Life and Adventures of Henry Bibb, An American Slave*, 1849 3

1.2 *The American Anti-Slavery Almanac for 1840* 5

1.3 *Negress Notes*, by Kara Walker, 1995 7

1.1 Cover art on plantation novels, 1969, 1978, and 1981 26

1.2 Cover art on two hardback editions of *Children of Kaywana*, 1952 and 1960 28

1.3 Cover art on *Children of Kaywana* pulp edition, 1976 29

1.4 Susan George as Blanche Maxwell and Brenda Sykes as Ellen in *Mandingo*, 1975 35

1.5 Mistress Epps, played by Sarah Paulson, in *12 Years a Slave*, 2013 39

1.6 Mistress Epps and Master Epps, played by Michael Fassbender, in *12 Years a Slave*, 2013 41

2.1 Gaite Jansen as Sarith and Yootha Wong-Loi-Sing as Mini-Mini in *Hoe Duur Was de Suiker*, 2013 69

2.2 Images of blood in *Hoe Duur Was de Suiker*, 2013 72

3.1 E'myri Crutchfield as Kizzy and Genevieve Hannelius as Missy in *Roots*, 2016 80

3.2 Front cover of the first edition of *The Black and White of It*, 1980 92

3.3 Front cover of the second edition of *The Black and White of It*, 1987 94

4.1 Rebecca Hall as Antoinette in *Wide Sargasso Sea*, 2006 132

4.2 Rowena King as Amélie, Karina Lombard as Antoinette, and Nathaniel Parker as Edward Rochester in *Wide Sargasso Sea*, 1993 135

4.3 Caroline Wilkins as Antoinette and Esther Henry as Tia in *Sargasso! A Caribbean Love Story*, 1991 139

5.1 Kathy Bates as Madame Delphine LaLaurie in *American Horror Story*, 2013 146

5.2 Angela Bassett as Marie Laveau in *American Horror Story*, 2013 153

c.1 *Bitch Planet*, Book One, by Kelly Sue DeConnick and Valentine De Landro, 2015 176

c.2 Katharine Leonard as Christine Turnfellow and Regina Hall as Ninny in *Insecure*'s show-within-a-show *Due North*, 2017 178

c.3 The Armitage family's house in *Get Out*, 2017 180

c.4 Georgina, played by Betty Gabriel, in *Get Out*, 2017 182

Acknowledgments

Writing these acknowledgments during the COVID-19 pandemic has been a bittersweet task for me. At the same time that I am thankful for the help, insight, and community from so many people over the years, I am also grieving for the time we should have spent together. With the knowledge that I cannot express my thanks enough, I owe the successes of this project to the following people.

This book is the result of conversations started in Tim Ryan's African American literature graduate seminar at Northern Illinois University (NIU). Moreover, Tim's generosity modeled the kind of mentorship I wish to extend to emerging scholars. I greatly appreciate Amy Newman's and Kathleen Renk's guidance during my short time there—my NIU family will always be close to my heart. Before graduate school, I was lucky enough to find faculty who would encourage my curiosity at Nacogdoches High School and Southern Nazarene University. Leann West, Peggy Poteet, Gwen Hackler, and Pam Bracken, especially, helped me have those first encounters with literature that started to dismantle what I thought I knew about the world.

I was fortunate to complete my PhD at the University of Mississippi with a committee that supported my interdisciplinary and expansive geographic and media interests, and I would like to thank Katie McKee and Leigh Anne Duck for continuing to encourage me in the years since. My project benefited from seminars with Adetayo Alabi, Deborah Barker, Martyn Bone, Jaime Harker, Sarah Lincoln, and Jay Watson, as each helped me put into conversation a variety of texts, narratives, and contexts. When I think of Oxford, Mississippi, I think of my community there—Mel Anderson, Emileigh Barnes, Pip Gordon, Tara McLellan, Sara Steffen, and Sara Williams are all family to me. I would not have fared as well in the "velvet ditch" without them. Similarly, at Georgia Tech as a postdoctoral fellow, I especially appreciated spending time with Nihad Farooq and Susana Morris; they both model how to navigate academia in ways that affirm and build. I am grateful for friends who continue to encourage me in ways I need, which usually means laughing at myself—thank you for being there, Court Carney, Lisa Hager, Emily Kingery, Nicole Lobdell, and Amy Montz.

I have developed sections of this book's argument through conversations at numerous conferences and symposia over the years. At the Futures of American Studies Institute, Elizabeth Maddock Dillon's seminar group provided generous feedback on an early version of my project. I appreciated the opportunity to present at the Black/White Intimacies: Reimagining History, the South, and the Western Hemisphere Symposium at the University of Alabama. Many thanks to Trudier Harris, Cassie Smith, and Andy Crank for organizing. I also presented a (at the time) "speculative" portion of my conclusion during the Plantation Modernity: A Global South Symposium at Clemson University, and I would like to specifically thank Jarvis McInnis and Sharon Holland for their comments, which helped me eventually bridge various analyses. Many thanks to Jonathan Beecher Field and Lee Morrissey for bringing us all together. I have also presented portions of this project at sessions for the American Studies Association, the Association for the Study of the Arts of the Present, the British Commonwealth and Postcolonial Studies Conference, the Modern Language Association, the Society for the Study of Southern Literature, the Society of Caribbean Research (Socare), the South Atlantic Modern Language Association, the Southeastern American Studies Association, the Southern Women Writers Conference, and the West Indian Literature Conference. I look forward to once again presenting alongside, sharing meals with, learning from, and continuing to conspire with Natalie Aikens, Michael Bibler, Katie Burnett, Maia Butler, Gina Caison, Frank Cha, Amy Clukey, Andy Crank, David Davis, Matt Dischinger, Norrell Edwards, Chris Eng, Shannon Finck, Katherine Fusco, Mikal Gaines, Sarah Gleeson-White, Allison Harris, Rebecca Hill, Anna Ioanes, Jina Kim, Katie Lennard, Ebony Lumumba, Molly McGehee, Monica Miller, Amy Monaghan, Will Murray, Mark Noble, Janelle Rodriques, Stephanie Rountree, Kelly Vines, Isadora Wagner, and Jeremy Wells.

This book would not have been possible without financial support from several institutions. I was able to complete chapter 3 at a summer institute sponsored by the National Endowment for the Humanities at Elon University. I would like to thank Ann Cahill and her collaborators for organizing a thoughtful schedule; the institute helped me see the pressing importance of approaching representations of sexual violence between women seriously and carefully. More recently, a postdoctoral research fellowship in the Center for the Study of the American South and Department of American Studies at UNC Chapel Hill gave me time, space, and resources to stitch together the project as a cohesive whole. Conversations with UNC staff, students, and faculty, along with participants in the Feminisms Here & Now Conference on campus, provided invaluable insights that influenced how I framed the book. Many thanks to Malinda Maynor Lowery for our encouraging and energizing conversations. I would also like to extend my thanks to Terri Lorant for helping my funding and conference travel go smoothly. At Auburn University, I received professional development funds to edit the final manuscript, and I thank the Department of English's chair Jonathan Bolton and administrative support associate Donna Kent for helping me secure this funding. I would also like to thank Lucas Church, Dylan White, and the editorial and production teams at UNC Press for streamlining the process and seeing the project through to publication. The anonymous readers for my project helped strengthen the argument, and I appreciate their constructive feedback generously given at multiple stages of the drafting and revising processes.

Writing and revising can be a lonely endeavor under any circumstances, and I appreciate the community I found in an online writing group, where Jill Anderson, Victoria Bryan, Thomas Bullington, Ren Denton, Heather Fox, and Susan Wood offered support. I am grateful for the time Jenna Sciuto took reading and responding to earlier chapter drafts; she helped bring a throughline to a chapter that felt scattered before. Many thanks for Whit Barringer's, Jessica Newman's, and Ashley Rattner's editing at various stages. Thanks also to Trevor Cokley for taking photographs for my project.

I could not have finished this book without Erich Nunn's support over the past five years. Thank you for telling me when my manuscript was good enough to stop revising; I appreciate that you made me dinner when I could not stop revising anyway. I am always grateful for my family's love and support—I love you, Mom, Dad, Emily, Jon, and Austen. And I wrote this book out of love, which for me means taking care with contexts and plainly addressing structures of power. With that in mind, I will be donating all proceeds I make as the author to the Emmett Till Interpretive Center in Sumner, Mississippi: "Racial reconciliation begins by telling the truth."

Grotesque Touch

Introduction

Depicting Violence between Women in Circum-Caribbean Texts

So you're writing about catfights?

This question, posed to me repeatedly over the years as I developed this project, speaks volumes about larger cultural stereotypes. It narrows women's physical violence down to an expression of jealousy—a "catfight"—a term that assumes women would *only* act in violence over the fear of losing a man's attention. In answering this question, I have had to admit that, yes, the performances of violence I write about include so-called catfights. As I show throughout *Grotesque Touch*, women's jealousies have long narrative histories in U.S. and Caribbean cultures. Even so, whether the people asking me about "catfights" knew it or not, they were categorizing women's actions as deviant and outside the strict parameters of acceptable "feminine" performance— passive, mild mannered, eager to please, middle to upper class, and white. As such, the question dehumanizes women. In this book, I ask a different question: What happens when we take representations of violent women seriously?

When we take these depictions of violence in written, visual, and audiovisual media seriously, we notice patterns and breaks in the patterns across time, space, genres, and types of relationships. When we take seriously the ways in which media depict women, we see how texts reflect and respond to cultural assumptions about women, violence, and power. We start to understand how violent moments reveal something about how these women claim a sense of themselves through violence. We see how physical touch might connect and separate women who experience different social positions. *Grotesque Touch* thereby asserts that when we look closely at representations of violence between women, we see how moments of violent touch act as pivot points in these women's identity development.

Grotesque Touch approaches this assertion by examining narratives of violence between women that originate in plantation slavery; thus this book sometimes draws on nineteenth-century tropes of enslavers and enslaved people.[1] Chapters 1, 2, and 3 discuss autobiographical narratives in some detail, for example. And, as we will see, several contemporary texts work to confront the violence of the historical archive, what Angela Naimou calls "a record of the violent erasure of its own contents," enslaved people (2). At every turn, *Grotesque Touch* recalls how, as Michel-Rolph Trouillot reminds us, "Power is constitutive of the story" of historical narrative (28). This book thereby makes clear how women's collusion with power structures originating in plantation slavery still affects how these structures shape identity formation in narratives today. Building on work by Elizabeth Christine Russ, George B. Handley, and Jessica Adams, *Grotesque Touch* considers how tropes form a *plantation imaginary* across time and media.[2] Taking depictions of women's violence seriously at the intersections of race, class, gender, nationality, ethnicity, skin tone, ability, and sexuality means delving deeply into an archive of narratives set on plantations, from nineteenth-century abolitionist depictions of plantation violence between women to twentieth- and twenty-first-century images, descriptions, and performances of violence.

I pause here to briefly juxtapose a nineteenth-century engraving and a twentieth-century painting to illustrate a recurring aspect of my argument: depictions of intimacy (and/or the lack thereof) in scenes of violence reveal a great deal about performances of identity and power. The first, an engraving that appears in Henry Bibb's *Narrative of the Life and Adventures of Henry Bibb, An American Slave* (1849), depicts an enslaver beating an enslaved woman with a household object (Bibb 113). The second image is a painting from Kara Walker's series *Negress Notes* (1995), in which an enslaved woman slits the throat of her enslaver. I argue that the engraving in *Narrative* connotes physical and social separation between the women via their race and class, while Walker's painting connotes intimacy via extreme violence. In both cases, the images counter popular representations of *good* white women, while Walker's painting additionally counters stereotypes about Black women's passivity.

The engraving that appears midway through Bibb's *Narrative* portrays the daily violence enslaved women endured at the hands of their enslavers (figure I.1). The engraving does not correlate to any singular scene Bibb describes in his written text. Rather, the engraving appears *alongside* Bibb's narrative and seems to offer an overview of enslaved women's experiences in the United States. The composition of the images (a white man poised to whip a Black woman on the left, a white woman ready to strike the same—or perhaps another—Black woman with a shovel or bedwarmer on the right) plainly pairs the acts of violence together while juxtaposing them in gendered locations. By showing the details of the men's faces (both the tor-

erned. He then commenced on this poor girl, and gave her two hundred lashes before he had her untied.

After giving her fifty lashes, he stopped and lec-

FIGURE I.1 Henry Bibb, *Narrative of the Life and Adventures of Henry Bibb, An American Slave*, 1849 (Madison: University of Wisconsin Press, 2001), 113.

turer and witness on the left), the engraving suggests that men who enslave are more likely to conduct their violence outdoors and in the public sphere. The engraving also suggests that women who enslave are more likely to conduct their violence inside the domestic sphere, away from the public eye. The white woman is faceless, anonymous in her violence. And yet, both images work together to ensure the totality and unavoidability of violence in the enslaved woman's life. Nowhere is she safe from bodily harm.

This engraving, like the narratives of formerly enslaved people in the eighteenth and nineteenth centuries, evinces how men's and women's physical violence were both part of the processes upholding slavery throughout the Caribbean and the United States. Still, if we look closely at the images of the enslaved woman in the engraving, we notice her anonymity as well. We are denied any certainty of the enslaved woman's emotions. Is she screaming, looking back at the man, looking up at the woman, looking upward appealing for mercy? We cannot know, because her facial features are blurred beyond a general expression of dismay. Even her motion and stance reflect her subjugation. Bound to a tree and suspended above the ground in one frame, falling back against a bed in the second frame, arms held up in both frames, her body passively receives violence. Whereas the enslavers' bodies connote action, the enslaved woman's body is acted upon.

Bibb's written narrative reiterates the anonymity and inaction of the enslaved woman: on the pages surrounding this engraving, Bibb recounts his experiences on a Louisianan plantation, where a deacon whipped a young mixed-race woman with two hundred lashes because she "displeased" the white woman who enslaved her (Bibb 112). Bibb goes on to describe the "inhuman manner" of the deacon's violence, as he stripped the woman naked and tied her up outside for her punishment, "exposed to the public gaze of all" (113–14). The scene and the engraving accompanying it at once create a narrative opening that suggests more violence inside the walls of the plantation house while reinforcing a stereotype of passivity.

Understanding the ways images circulated in abolitionist publications is essential to grasping the symbolic relationship between engravings and narrative explored here. In his study of visual representations of slavery in *Blind Memory*, Marcus Wood focuses on the "bizarre relationship between words and images" in Bibb's *Narrative*, since, "with the exception of the portrait [of Bibb] on the title page, few and maybe none of the engravings originally depicted Bibb or any of the characters in his work. The woodblocks used had already appeared in a variety of other publications, or had been adapted from earlier woodcuts and etchings in abolition literature" (118). The overall effect of viewing these images alongside Bibb's words is one of flattening out the experiences of Bibb, his family, and other enslaved people.[3] *Narrative*'s use of woodblocks thereby replicated larger patterns of U.S. and British representation, which, according to Maurie D. McInnis, entailed "the representation of the enslaved as victims awaiting salvation, rather than individuals capable of sorrow, resistance, and, most disturbing to the abolitionist cause, retribution" (29).[4] Briefly considering the wider context of this engraving in Bibb's *Narrative* offers a sense of how repetitions of these images in the nineteenth century limited audiences' perceptions of enslaved people's humanity by marketing them as helpless.

Nine years before Bibb printed his narrative, the woodblock engraving appeared in *The American Anti-Slavery Almanac for 1840*, opposite information about postage rates and the almanac's calendar for January (figure I.2). As Teresa A. Goddu indicates, these almanacs "were consistent bestsellers, selling upwards of a hundred thousand copies a year by 1839" ("Antislavery Almanac" 132), and employed a sophisticated blending of visual technologies

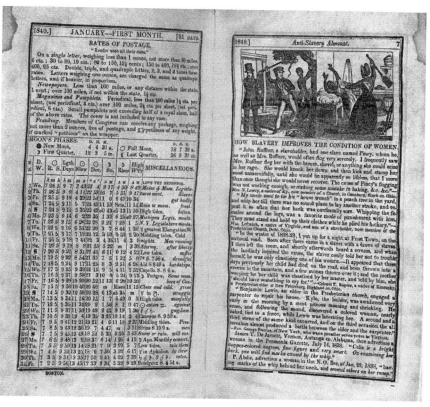

FIGURE 1.2 *The American Anti-Slavery Almanac for 1840* (New York: American Anti-Slavery Society; Boston: J. A. Collins), 6–7. Calendar pages for January. Courtesy of the David M. Rubenstein Rare Book & Manuscript Library, Duke University.

(charts and graphs, for instance) to reach a wide audience through a recognizable genre (the almanac), which many people used to forecast weather patterns and other phases of natural phenomena.[5] Unlike in Bibb's *Narrative*, these violent images in the 1840 almanac additionally feature a title, "HOW SLAVERY IMPROVES THE CONDITION OF WOMEN" (*American Anti-Slavery Almanac* 7). If the disjunction between the title and these images confused a reader, then the subsequent testimonials from people who claimed to have witnessed Black women suffering under their enslavement makes clearer the cruel inverse of the title: slavery does not improve the condition of women, Black or white.[6]

For example, the first quote, from a Mrs. N. Lowry ("a native of K[entucky], now member of a Church, in Osnaburg, Stark co. Ohio"), details the torture of an enslaved woman named Piney endured at the hands of her enslavers, John and Mrs. Ruffner (7). The woman who enslaved Piney would "flog her with the broom, shovel, or anything she could seize in her rage. She would knock her down and then kick and stamp her most unmercifully, until she would be apparently so lifeless, that [Mrs. N. Lowry] more than once thought she would never recover" (7). Given that this quotation appears directly under the engraving and title, it is possible to see the images as illustrating Piney's experiences, which provides a bit more contextual specificity than the engraving's appearance in Bibb's *Narrative*. Still, the images themselves tend to anonymize the enslaved woman's face, as if the woodblock itself never was able to show the woman's expressions—her facial features are even more blended in this 1840 almanac than in Bibb's 1849 book.

Many of the thirteen woodblocks that appear in this volume of the *Almanac* visualize physical torture that enslaved people experienced (branding, burning, hanging, and hunting with dogs, for instance) alongside the phases of the moon and other almanac facts. The *Almanac* thereby merges horrific violence with the everyday cycles of the earth—at once inviting audiences to gaze upon tortured bodies and go about their daily lives (and possibly tie guilt to the actions of their everyday lives).[7] Considering these pages within the scope of popular imagery depicting enslaved people as passive reveals how the images replicate, in Martha J. Cutter's words, "the idea that the pained body and psyche of the enslaved is a low, unfinished, disabled, child-like, or in some way inferior entity that needs the help and mediation of the white viewer, who is separated within the text or artwork from the viewed" (10). So, while antislavery publications "aggregated" these images "to reveal slavery's horrors to be systemic rather than singular" (Goddu, "Anti-Slavery's Panoramic Perspective" 15), we can also understand that the images, taken together, perpetuate racist narratives even as they try to advocate for emancipation.

I consider Kara Walker's painting from her series *Negress Notes* here to illustrate the concerns of *Grotesque Touch* further (figure I.3). Specifically, this contemporary painting shows the artist's powerful re-visioning that diverges from popular images of Black women, such as the depiction in the almanac's engraving and portrayals on pulp novel covers, as we will see in chapter 1. The painting features an enslaved woman slitting the throat of her enslaver, to the extent that the white woman's head appears to be severed from her neck. Upon closer examination, we see a book dropping from the enslaver's gloved hands, perhaps signifying the white woman's (willed) de-

FIGURE 1.3 Kara Walker, *Negress Notes* [detail], 1995, collage, ink, gouache, and watercolor on paper, 6 × 9 inches. Artwork © Kara Walker, courtesy of Sikkema Jenkins & Co., New York.

tachment from the realities of her society. The enslaver does not "dirty her hands" with reality.

This painting departs from Walker's well-known style of creating silhouetted murals to depict this scene of violence through gentler strokes of watercolor on a smaller scale. Because of the soft lines and diffuse, warm colors of the painting, Walker's scene is ironically romantic and avoids stereotypical images of and connotations about Black women: the enslaved woman's body is not made available to the viewer's consumptive gaze—she is neither Mammy nor Jezebel.[8] We also notice that while the enslaved woman acts with a look of determination on her face, her right hand holds the knife, and her left hand more softly holds, or caresses, her enslaver's shoulder. In this painting, Walker combines an image of extreme violence with familiarity between women to illustrate that they exist in a relationship of false intimacy with each other that, at its very core, is violent. In this way, Walker's painting achieves through different aesthetics what Christina Sharpe sees in Walker's more familiar panoramas: "Walker's silhouettes depict the centrality of what passes as the underbelly of and vestibular to the plantation romance; she exposes the relationships that construct us all" (159). The enslaved woman's act of violence thereby takes advantage of false intimacies to explode the women's roles within the plantation household, and in doing so, she shatters the lingering imagined plantation of finery predicated on invisible labor. Walker's painting centers women's violent intimacies to tear down this mythos.

While texts that depict violence between enslavers and enslaved women frequently show the women enacting violence via instruments (a whip or a machete, for example), violence through touch (skin-on-skin contact) suggests moments of questioning and—sometimes—change. Minrose C. Gwin sees a complex interplay between touch, power, and connection in William Faulkner's *Absalom, Absalom!* (1936) when Clytemnestra (Clytie), a mixed-race woman, touches the arm of Rosa Coldfield, a young white woman: "Clytie's touch, frozen in Rosa's consciousness and in our own, seals black woman to white in one epiphanic gesture" (Gwin 4). Rosa understands that touch has the potential to undo the very hierarchical thinking of her Mississippian society: "But let flesh touch with flesh, and watch the fall of all the eggshell shibboleth of caste and color too" (Faulkner 139). In order to uphold their social separation, Rosa returns Clytie's touch years later, this time as "a full-armed blow like a man would have," according to the narrator Quentin Compson (369). Clytie calling her "Rosie" catalyzes Rosa's efforts to separate herself personally and socially from the formerly enslaved woman (Gwin 127). While the first touch showed how unstable their social separation is, the second touch—one of outright physical violence—attempts to enforce their separation.

Of course, not all unmediated physical touch between women signals the possible destabilization of hierarchies. We can find one well-known exception in Margaret Mitchell's *Gone with the Wind* (1936). Scarlett O'Hara's "violent blood" (Mitchell 640) is always boiling just below the surface and provides evidence that violence is essential to her white supremacist society in Georgia before, during, and after the Civil War. Tellingly, her violent outbursts are limited to the enslaved woman Prissy. According to Tim A. Ryan, "Mitchell's narrative and rhetoric demonize Prissy as they demonize no other black character" so that Prissy becomes a stand-in for racialized class anxieties (43).

Separating the women even further socially, the popular film adaptation released in 1939 obviously plays up Scarlett's violence against Prissy for laughs in the tradition of U.S. minstrel shows (apparent in Butterfly McQueen's portrayal of Prissy).[9] Another recent example of such violent touch that separates enslaver from enslaved people appears in Lalita Tademy's *Cane River* (2001), where, in the novel's first sentence, the enslaved child Suzette's life changes in 1834 Louisiana due to her enslaver's physical touch: "On the morning of her ninth birthday, the day after Madame Françoise Derbanne slapped her, Suzette peed on the rosebushes" (3). This slap warns Suzette's mother that Madame Derbanne no longer considers Suzette a harmless child; instead, her "little-girl days are done" (12), and soon after this scene a white man rapes Suzette. Madame Derbanne's violence thereby ushers Suzette into the physically damaging realities of enslavement—a system that attempts to make people into things. And yet, Suzette persists in her assertion of selfhood.

My close readings of the engraving (in Bibb's *Narrative* and *The American Anti-Slavery Almanac for 1840*) and the painting by Walker, combined with a survey of oft-cited texts (Faulkner, Mitchell) along with a novel cited less often (Tademy), signal my method of constellation-making throughout this book. *Grotesque Touch's* collection of texts is messy, expansive, and persistent, as I bring into conversation specific scenes of violence from a variety of media and genres over time. To do this, I contextualize each trope of violence with various written texts including novels, short fiction, poems, and autobiographies, but I understand that such a conversation about iconography must consider visual and audiovisual media, such as films, television shows, paintings, and book cover artwork. Images of violent women—which are as influential, if not more influential, in cultural memory (compared to depictions in novels) due to their persistence in film and television—necessitate careful study to uncover the intricacies of what they are telling, and retelling, about power. Therefore, my primary texts are diverse in terms of media and time period; much of my project's contextualization relies on texts produced in the nineteenth century.[10] In grouping together texts in this way, I do not intend to imply an exact correlation between genres, media, and modes; indeed, to say that abolitionist-promoted images in the nineteenth century are *just like* the images on twentieth-century pulp novel covers flattens out the cultural and historical contexts in which these images are produced and circulated.

Grotesque Touch mainly focuses on how some tropes originating in plantation slavery echo through fictional texts produced in the twentieth and twenty-first centuries. While each chapter (including this introduction) takes a long historical approach to themes of violence between women, I find that placing temporal distinctions on my primary texts is essential. The texts I focus on were produced or published after 1960 and reflect (or react to) a cultural milieu of decolonization throughout U.S. and Caribbean cultures.[11] As such, primary texts tend to respond to (or reinforce) colonial racism, classism, ableism, and sexism. In this sense, I build on Arlene R. Keizer's premise in *Black Subjects*: "Rather than using representations of slavery primarily to protest past and present oppression—this is how slavery had figured in most African-American and Caribbean works up through the early 1960s— black writers have begun to represent slavery in order to explore the process of self-creation under extremely oppressive conditions" (11). At the heart of *Grotesque Touch*, then, is a concern for how women in certain texts in the twentieth and twenty-first centuries attempt to gain positions of power through violence that echoes back to plantation slavery. Each chapter examines the theme of "self-creation" in scenes of violence between women on and beyond plantation settings to show, in a personal sense, each woman's identity formation via acts of violence. Still, it bears repeating that each text (whether film or novel or painting) was produced at a certain time and place. This means that *Grotesque Touch* traces themes of violence from firsthand accounts of plantation slavery up to our contemporary moment via themes of mediated, skin-to-skin, sadistic, retributive, sexual, silenced, and abject violence. At the same time, chapters consider how each text's cultural milieu influences the politically progressive or conservative nature of that depiction of violence and self-making in eras of twentieth- and twenty-first-century decolonization and neo-colonialism.[12] Thus, this conversation is purposefully more expansive than many studies, for it breaks out of dichotomous thinking concerning race, ethnicity, region, and nation, as I draw from a variety of texts that depict U.S. and Caribbean characters and settings.[13]

Opening up this conversation beyond U.S. settings is essential to trace repetitions and transformations of popular tropes. My methods (and title) are thereby inspired by Christina Sharpe's *Monstrous Intimacies*, for I also believe that pursuing the legacies of grotesque touch across plantation imaginaries means "articulating a diasporic study that is attentive to but not dependent upon nations and nationalisms and that is linked, in different forms during slavery and into the present freedoms, by monstrous intimacies, defined as a set of known and unknown performances and inhabited horrors, desires and positions produced, reproduced, circulated, and transmitted, that are breathed in like air and often unacknowledged to be monstrous" (3).[14] As such, *Grotesque Touch* draws on the approaches exemplified in Sharpe's work but more specifically focuses on how power circulates through *hemispheric* narratives of grotesque physical touch.

Consequently, I use the term "circum-Caribbean" to connote hemispheric movement and performances around and through Caribbean and U.S. settings.[15] Whereas chapters 1 through 3 of *Grotesque Touch* feature plantation settings during slavery, chapters 4 and 5 extend beyond physical plantation settings to examine the resonances of colonizing violence after emancipation. While my project builds on earlier work by Handley, Valérie Loichot, and Russ, I find that "circum-Caribbean" reflects the movement (circum-) of iconography and ideas throughout the hemisphere, throughout time.[16] The depictions of violent women I analyze in *Grotesque Touch* come from writers', artists', and directors' replications or imaginative revisions of *monstrous* and *grotesque* gender, class, racial, national, and sexual norms circulating even today. Thus, my project is inherently interested in avoiding conventional cultural, regional, geographical, and national divides. In doing so, I foreground fruitful—if also difficult—conversations that have been happening over time between texts depicting Caribbean and U.S. settings, ranging from Haiti, to Louisiana, Jamaica, Suriname, Illinois, Cuba, and beyond.[17] Each chapter of *Grotesque Touch* incorporates media from various settings; furthermore, the chapters build on each other and gradually spiral further outside of conventional southern U.S./Caribbean pairings so that, taken as a whole, the conversation lies outside of simple geographic distinctions.[18]

Hence, this project implicitly—and sometimes explicitly—highlights the tensions of dichotomous thinking about the United States, "the South," and the Caribbean.[19] *Grotesque Touch* sees what Édouard Glissant does—that "history travels with the seas," so to speak (29)—for the plantation imaginary travels throughout the hemisphere and echoes through texts and their contexts into the present day.[20] As such, *Grotesque Touch* goes beyond any other study to date to examine the intersections of race, gender, class, sexuality, ethnicity, skin tone, ability, and nationality in circum-Caribbean depictions of violence between women in the wake of slavery.[21] For example, this study picks up where Paul Gilroy in *The Black Atlantic* leaves the stories of Margaret Garner (the self-emancipated woman whose life Toni Morrison reimagines in *Beloved*) and Mrs. Hicks (an enslaver who murdered Frederick Douglass's cousin—her property—for not keeping a baby in her charge quiet at night). Although Gilroy identifies that these women's stories "raise complex questions about the mediating role of gender categories in racial politics and in particular about the psychological structures of identification facilitated by the idea of maternity," he also acknowledges "it is impossible to explore these important matters" in his book (68). I take up where Gilroy leaves considerations of women and violence. Moreover, I argue that representations of violent women illuminate and problematize aspects of *the grotesque* enacted on and continuing beyond the actual setting of the plantation.

In using the term "grotesque," this book means to focus both on bodily performances of violence *and* how these performances mirror a corrupt sense of self-formation in the legacies of slavery. This book thereby employs Patricia Yaeger's sense of the grotesque in *Dirt and Desire*, which has become a mainstay of studies of women in southern U.S. cultures. Yaeger's project urges closer examination of the grotesque — "figures of dirt, monstrosity, the throwaway, gargantuan women, old children, and the problem of arrested systems of knowledge" (8) — to uncover what was frequently present, yet somehow ignored, in American literature at large. Specifically, Yaeger asserts, "These fictions ferret out subsemantic obsessions about race and gender that invite a rethinking of some of the most basic categories that we use to think about American literature" (8). My approach in this book is likewise attuned to how texts call into question what we frequently take for granted in terms of identity and representation — here, in depictions of violent women. Departing from Yaeger's argument in *Dirt and Desire*, my archive expands beyond literatures written by women in the southern United States to more fully (though not completely) examine repetitions of grotesque identity formation across the hemisphere.[22] As such, my project focuses on multiple performances of violence between women that shock readers and viewers into acknowledging the logical outcomes of a system that granted — and still does grant — some people total power over others' bodies.[23] *Grotesque Touch* at once challenges readers to take women's violence seriously and to consider how these scenes of violence reflect much larger structures of power in the wake of plantation slavery. The violent scenes in this study are not exceptional; instead, they emphasize how pervasive the imbalances of colonizing power are, and have always been. Contextualizing contemporary texts' performances of violence between women via plantation structures helps us see how the intertwining of violence, intimacy, and power persist into the present. Furthermore, *Grotesque Touch* shows how easily people use these performances to shape their identities. It is my hope that readers will realize that we still have much work to do to uncover, untangle, and articulate how specific grotesque themes speak to each other across circum-Caribbean genres, media, and contexts.[24]

One slice of the much larger conversation at hand addresses the patterns connecting violence in many of these texts. The study of violence in media has become increasingly popular in U.S. and Caribbean scholarship, but to explore the tropes of violence—and the violence of tropes—about these cultures is a daunting task, given that their histories, realities, and representations are saturated with the brutality of colonization, slavery, and neo-colonialism.[25] Focusing on the details and descriptions of scenes of violence risks further desensitizing readers to this violence, as Saidiya V. Hartman argues in *Scenes of Subjection*.[26] I read scenes of violence between women closely, not to casually replicate them but to show readers what is at stake when we take these instances of violence seriously.[27] When we look closely at twentieth- and twenty-first-century representations of violence between women, then these representations indicate much larger circum-Caribbean currents of iconography and revision. Furthermore, scholars have long argued that the violence of decolonization is a response to colonial violence. Speaking from the context of the Algerian War of Independence, for example, Frantz Fanon, in his oft-cited chapter "Concerning Violence" in *The Wretched of the Earth*, makes clear why anticolonial violence operates as it does: "The violence of the colonial regime and the counterviolence of the [colonized] balance each other and respond to each other in an extraordinary reciprocal homogeneity" (88). Building on Fanon's theorizing of decolonization as "always a violent phenomenon" (35), because it ushers in a timeline unlike that which preceded it, Nick Nesbitt questions if we in the twenty-first century can condemn anticolonial violence of the past. Our subject-positions are not like theirs, which were forged *through* and *in spite of* enslavement and torture (Nesbitt 214–15). These concerns foreground the depictions of retaliatory violence in chapter 2, as contemporary texts wrestle with the implications of showing enslaved people's physical violence against their enslavers. Moreover, in looking closely at scenes of violence and contextualizing them within their cultural moments, *Grotesque Touch* considers how persistent stereotypes about *exceptional* violence obscure structures of power. In Nesbitt's and Deborah A. Thomas's responses to patterns of violence in Caribbean cultures, for example, they gesture toward the grotesque systems put into place in the past that still affect how Caribbean peoples and places are perceived in popular cultural representations at home and elsewhere.[28] These narratives that marginalize people as Other extend beyond people's imaginations to affect how they act in relation to each other, which means that popular cultural representations help ensure the continuation of colonizing systems that harm people.[29]

More specifically, as my analysis of Walker's painting emphasizes, I am particularly interested in instances of violence wherein women's physical contact with other women tells us something about the nature of their identities at the intersections of multiple, interlocking identity vectors. Walter Johnson's work on antebellum slave markets is instructive here, as the scenes I examine do not necessarily "chart . . . a map of foreordained conclusions" (9). Instead, as Johnson argues, the performances of the slave market—for enslavers and enslaved people—relied on "the contingent perspective of each of its participants," and Johnson strives "to assess their asymmetric information, expectations, and power" (9). Central to the "rituals of the slave pens" is how they "taught the inexperienced" enslaver "how to read black bodies for their suitability for slavery, how to imagine blackness into meaning, how to see solutions to their own problems in the bodies of the slaves they saw in the market. Gazing, touching, stripping, and analyzing aloud, the buyers read slaves' bodies as if they were coded versions of their own imagined needs" (149). Johnson's work on how knowledge was built via touch in U.S. slave markets is an important precursor to *Grotesque Touch*. Enslavers and enslaved people learned to perform their respective social roles during their physical interactions, and, as we will see, many texts feature women who learn what it means to wield power over others through touch. Time and again, these texts reveal enslavers' "imagined needs," to borrow Johnson's term, through women's violent interactions with other women. *Grotesque Touch* thereby shows, first, how women who are enslavers attempt to assert physical dominance over enslaved women's bodies in order to claim a sense of control inside their homes and in their societies (see chapters 1, 2, and 3). However, my argument does not end with representations of women who enslave: extending Johnson's claims, *Grotesque Touch* shows how enslaved women have also learned the lessons of performing power through violence (chapter 2) and how women in post-emancipation settings continue to attempt to wield the plantation's hierarchies on other women's bodies (chapters 4 and 5).

Many circum-Caribbean texts that feature violence between women (as enslavers and enslaved women, employers and domestic servants, rivals, and lovers) reveal the often-overlooked intricacies of power, identity formation, and intimacy. These aspects come to light through an intersectional feminist analysis of representations of race, class, gender, sexuality, ethnicity, skin tone, ability, and nationality. While it is true that intersectionality is often, as Vivian M. May argues, "treated as a gesture or catchphrase . . . used in a token manner to account for a nebulous, depoliticized, and hollow notion of 'difference'" (8), I employ an intersectional feminist lens in this project for two reasons: first, intersectionality as a sociological framework helps us understand how humans experience privilege and oppression according to the simultaneous, inextricable interactions of multiple identity vectors; and second, it exposes and uproots the lies colonizing culture tells us about women's exceptionality via racist, classist, and sexist narratives.[30] If I were to use conceptual tools that do not examine how sexism, racism, classism, ableism, and nationalism intersect with and mutually reinforce each other, then I would be analyzing but one node of how power works.[31] One method of examining power in this way is to scrutinize what Patricia Hill Collins calls "controlling images," which "are designed to make racism, sexism, poverty, and other forms of social injustice appear to be natural, normal, and inevitable parts of everyday life" (69). The abundance of controlling images in literature has not gone unnoticed; Barbara Christian's groundbreaking essay "Images of Black Women in Afro-American Literature" shows, for instance, the overwhelming influence of controlling images on depictions of Black women in U.S. literary narratives. More recently, work such as Kimberly Juanita Brown's *The Repeating Body* takes on the thematic repetitions of Black women's bodies across modes. Specifically, Brown's study focuses on "the repetitive qualities of the black Atlantic that hover somewhere between the past and the present" as they provide "insight into the visual, material, and gendered iterations of slavery's indelible memory" (13).[32] Through centering Black feminist methods, I hope to uncover how narratives distort perceptions of women. I gather images, scenes, and performances of violence between women to show how they reflect and reinforce women's allegiances to and struggles against structures that colonize. I do this to acknowledge the harm of persistent narratives about women's exceptionality.[33] Working against such narratives means acknowledging how they hide realities of power imbalances, including how we are conditioned to internalize the grotesque lessons of what it means to wield power over others—to dehumanize, silence, and exploit.

One of the main myths that appears again and again across genres and media is one about women's inherent goodness, as if the gendered category of "woman" exists outside of the relational categories of "race," "class," and "nation"—as if women, if they were given the social and political power to lead the world, would create peaceful societies without war, poverty, racism, rape, and other kinds of violence. However, this book mobilizes an intersectional feminist methodology that, like in work by Marisa J. Fuentes, bell hooks, and Anne McClintock, shows that women are very much embedded in how colonial societies determine power — through domination.[34] Indeed, this departure from a utopian outlook about women is at the heart of many circum-Caribbean texts that portray violence between women. Across its chapters, *Grotesque Touch* works against narratives of white women's "goodness" to see the grotesqueness in their subject formations. I frequently pause to point out how white women's own insecurities have often, and still, pose direct and lethal harm to women of color. *Grotesque Touch* also goes further to show how women from various national, ethnic, racial, class, and sexual backgrounds learn from these grotesque displays of white supremacy to inflict physical pain on other women in order to assert power.[35]

To do so, *Grotesque Touch* examines texts ranging from obvious exploitation (pulp novels) to more complex, yet also sensationalistic, productions (the film *Mandingo*) to radical revisions of plantation violence between women in contemporary novels and films. Focusing on how scenes of violent touch between women use intimacy to expose power relationships on the plantation (i.e., both violence that is mediated with a weapon and directly applied, skin-to-skin), this study makes clear how the grotesque violence of U.S. and Caribbean plantation slavery comes to bear on contemporary images and performances.[36] Collectively, chapters in *Grotesque Touch* argue that popular imagery (such as violent enslavers on pulp novel covers) and subversive performances (where skin-to-skin touch complicates social categories) exist on a continuum of sensational representations throughout the hemisphere.

Chapter 1 begins with salacious representations of women's violence in pulp novels, which helped popularize depictions of plantation violence in the second half of the twentieth century. Surveying a variety of pulp novel covers and their publication histories, I argue that violence inflicted by white women and mediated with instruments of torture in pulp novel cover artwork in the 1960s and 1970s maintains violence as a tool of separation. As such, the covers allow white audiences to see their base desires play out in the torture of Black bodies while keeping social categories safe from questioning. These pictorial depictions of white women as they prepare to inflict violence (or have just inflicted violence) on enslaved people suggest social separation in two senses of the term: first, white women's posturing on the covers connotes their racialized class positions above enslaved people; second, because these images appear on pulp novel covers, they signal to readers aberrant social performances. Consequently, the artwork on these pulp covers "other" violent white women, which distances readers from social critique. Then, chapter 1 continues to examine stereotypical depictions of women in the exploitation film *Mandingo* (Richard Fleischer 1975). I read closely a scene of violence between an enslaver and an enslaved woman to illustrate a conservative depiction of a white woman's power that plays up sensationalistic stereotypes. In *Mandingo*, a white woman attempts to grasp white men's power through enacting her own violence; however, the film expels her deviancy in the final act to reestablish misogynistic social order. Though *Mandingo* is not a revolutionary film, it provides a sense of how characters *perform* power, thereby exposing some of the fault lines of sadistic violence. Finally, chapter 1 provides a counterpoint to exploitative stereotypes via the film *12 Years a Slave* (Steve McQueen 2013), in which the woman who enslaves actually increases her power on the plantation by manipulating the system's economies of grotesque, corrupted intimacies through briefly employing violent skin-to-skin touch. As will become evident in this first chapter, I see visual and filmic representations of violence between women on plantation settings as existing on a continuum—on one end appear the most decontextualized, salacious, and (sometimes) romanticized performances, and on the other end appear contextually sensitive adaptations conversant in generic and filmic conventions. And yet, the degree of adaptation (how much the writers, directors, and producers change the source text, and for what purposes) also factors into this continuum.

Chapter 2 shows how contemporary texts that further complicate themes of sadistic violence, intimacy, and power also might fall into narrative traps of sensationalism and/or romantic ideals. Still, each text in chapter 2, from Madison Smartt Bell's novel *All Souls' Rising* (1995) to Marlon James's novel *The Book of Night Women* (2009) and Jean Van de Velde's film *Hoe Duur Was de Suiker* (2013), illustrates how violent touch enacted by women who enslave and women who are enslaved can reflect their plantation regime's paradoxical performances of law and order. Key scenes in the novels show how depictions of extreme violence—enacted by a woman who enslaves in Saint-Domingue (*All Souls'*) and an enslaved woman in Jamaica (*Night Women*)—have the potential to uproot racialized, gendered, and classed social norms. Because the women attempt to form subject-positions within plantation regimes where sadistic violence is codified and normalized, these novels' scenes of grotesque touch show the bitter ironies and impossibilities of attempting to claim stable identities under such conditions. In chapter 2, my argument expands beyond the experiences of white women to more fully explore how women who are enslaved experience, process, and react to the sadistic violence of plantation regimes. In doing so, chapter 2 considers how contemporary texts show enslaved women's retributive violence to be a complex endeavor, one that might replicate the plantation regime's sadism. Chapter 2 concludes with an analysis of how the Dutch film *Hoe Duur Was de Suiker* further expands performances of touch, intimacy, and violence through an enslaved woman's narrative of agency that avoids depicting her retributive violence. The film is progressive in that it shows how an enslaved woman's interactions with white women's violence in Suriname affect her identity; however, the film ultimately perpetuates a harmful romance plot when an enslaved woman becomes her enslaver's lover. Though *Hoe Duur Was de Suiker* shows the enslaved woman choosing not to enact her own violence shaped by the sadism of plantation systems, the film continues to contain her through persistent romantic narrative tropes that embed her further in her (former) enslaver's home as a means of narrative resolution.

Indeed, romantic narratives about women and their relationships within a context of slavery continue to enact harm by silencing enslaved women's experiences. Chapter 3 extends this discussion into representations and performances of sexual violence between women. While blatant sexual violence between a woman who enslaves and an enslaved woman is less common in texts (especially due to assumptions about the kinds of violence white women are capable of), chapter 3 examines how instances of such violence reveal racialized class, gender, and sexual norms that circulate in the plantation imaginary. By setting their narratives in the United States during slavery, the latest miniseries adaptation of Alex Haley's *Roots* (2016), Valerie Martin's novel *Property* (2003), and Ann Allen Shockley's short story "The Mistress and the Slave Girl" in *The Black and White of It* (1987) demonstrate how thoroughly corruptible positions of power are when they come from the racialized sexual economies of slavery. Then, Shockley's story "Women in a Southern Time" (1987) reveals how the enduring legacies of slavery likewise affect women's same-sex desires in a Jim Crow setting. Shockley's stories expose a continuity between the oppressions of slavery and post-emancipation domestic labor, because white women act through violently coded sexual touch that silences Black women inside the white women's homes. As in previous chapters, chapter 3 is also attuned to how (and to what extent) each text contextualizes violence between women. Building on chapter 1's analysis of plantation pulp novels, for example, here I explore how the covers and front matter of Shockley's paperback editions for her collection *The Black and White of It* (1980, 1987) factor into our readings of her stories that depict continuities of sexual violence between women from the nineteenth century into the twentieth. The ways the 1987 edition of Shockley's collection expand the author's reach across time, along with the front matter's advertising of the collection via titillation characteristic of erotic paperbacks, deepen the implications of *Grotesque Touch*'s continuums of representation. Indeed, Shockley's stories and the book that houses them also put forth a thesis about the complexities of audience desire.

Chapter 4's discussion of post-emancipation settings builds on this examination of audience desire in two main ways: first, chapter 4 interrogates how some popular narratives privilege a sense of "sisterhood" across racialized class borders in segregated societies; second, chapter 4 questions the efficacy of narratives that decontextualize violence between women in post-emancipation settings. In an era of decolonial struggles across the United States and Caribbean, many narratives perpetuate a sentimental fiction about women that forgoes white women's complicity in systems of power. This chapter thereby explores how the denials of structural oppression and physical violence in domestic labor are common to popular fictions and some twentieth-century feminist rhetorics alike. In these examples, denials of white women's participation in violent systems *silence* the experiences and viewpoints of women of color in order to privilege sentimental narratives of "sisterhood" that center the (supposed) "goodness" of white women. Then, chapter 4 reveals how progressive texts use violent outbursts between women of different racialized class positions to show how the grotesqueness of the plantation past persists into present conditions of employment. In doing so, the chapter exposes the continuance of racist, sexist, ableist, and classist systems of violence from slavery well into the twentieth century in some circum-Caribbean texts. Specifically, this chapter explores how Ellen Douglas's novella *Hold On* (1963), set in Mississippi; Toni Morrison's novel *Tar Baby* (1981), set in an imaginary Caribbean location; and the novel and filmic legacy of Jean Rhys's *Wide Sargasso Sea* (1966, 1991, 1993, and 2006), set in Jamaica and Dominica, reveal or obfuscate social realities in moments of violent touch. In its violent scene, *Hold On* illustrates the fragility of sentimental narratives when a middle-class white woman enacts her racist, sexist society's violence on the body of a Black woman who once worked as her maid. The violent scene starkly depicts the inequities of their relationship and the white woman's own feelings of superiority, realities she tries to deny. Morrison's *Tar Baby* takes a different approach, as the novel portrays two-way violence between a white woman and a Black woman from the United States. By depicting this violence in a Caribbean setting, Morrison's novel effectively connects their dynamics to national and hemispheric contexts of domestic and migrant labor in the twentieth century. In the chapter's final section, issues of titillation reappear in my analyses of the filmic adaptations of *Wide*

Sargasso Sea. As I will show, merely featuring a scene of violence between a white woman and a Black woman does not automatically shed light on the women's relationships within a context of domestic labor. Instead, the two studio-produced adaptations of *Wide Sargasso Sea* depict Caribbean women as exotic/erotic Others, thereby creating colonizing narratives. This final section of the chapter asserts the importance of cultural and narrative context when producing a film about Caribbean places, cultures, and peoples; otherwise, as the filmic legacy of *Wide Sargasso Sea* shows, Caribbean women become less-than-human stereotypes.

Throughout *Grotesque Touch*, I dissect stereotypes about women that popular cultural narratives have perpetuated and circulated over time—specifically, that violent women must be aberrant and *monstrous*. Chapter 5 shows how these tropes come to bear on contemporary settings. In chapter 5, women's violence as lovers or rivals in twentieth- and twenty-first-century settings literalizes the grotesque social legacies of plantation slavery. The chapter first considers more obvious performances of women as abject monsters, such as in the third season of the television show *American Horror Story* ("Coven" 2013–14). In the "Coven" season, the show revises some of the racist tropes of horror and exploitation cinema to show how an enslaver (brought into the show's present, the 2010s) signals the "undead" nature of the nation's violent, racist past. However, "Coven" neatly resolves these conflicts when the racist, violent white woman from the past finally dies, erasing her "monstrous femininity" and (apparently) racism in general. Chapter 5 then shifts to more nuanced depictions of women's violence in the novels *Unburnable* by Marie-Elena John (2006), set in Dominica, and *Memory Mambo* by Achy Obejas (1996), set in Chicago. In these novels, the systems of colonizing violence from the past break through into the present, as women must deal with how dominant classes label them as monstrous. All these texts use the vocabularies of abjection as horror to depict violence between women as rivals or lovers, and each text draws on a variety of popular monstrous figures, including witches, voodoo practitioners, zombies, and vampires. However, by depicting women engaged in intimately grotesque scenes of abject violence, these texts show that the violence between women is symptomatic of their violent societies at large, societies that employ sadistic colonizing oppression in the aftermath of plantation slavery.

Each chapter showcases sensational aspects of representations of violent women alongside the revolutionary re-visioning of this violence in a multitude of written, visual, and audiovisual media. In this way, *Grotesque Touch* models a vigorously intermedial, cross-cultural project, as it shows how these scenes of violence between women create a constellation of images and performances across the hemisphere. As readers progress through *Grotesque Touch*, they will see how many texts draw from and revise shared circum-Caribbean iconography in the wake of plantation slavery. Overall, *Grotesque Touch* indicates that women's violence against other women is not impossible or merely tantalizing; instead, looking closely at scenes of women committing violence against other women can lead to a fuller understanding of how performances of gender, sexuality, class, race, ability, and nationality circulate—and can be reimagined—throughout the hemisphere.

CHAPTER ONE

Sensational Violence

> But the rage of the white ladies still pursued them with redoubled
> fury, for what is so violent as female jealousy?
> —LEONORA SANSAY, *Secret History; or, The Horrors of St. Domingo*, 96

In Leonora Sansay's epistolary novel *Secret History; or, The Horrors of St. Domingo* (1808), white Creole women and Black women order violence against each other out of jealousy, which ends in death, during the Haitian Revolution. Sansay relates scenes of violence that predictably "other" all the colony's inhabitants, describing a white Creole woman as demonic in Letter II for ordering an enslaved person to behead her husband's (suspected) Black lover and leave the head on a platter, where her husband would see it (70). Later in Letter IX, the novel describes a Black woman who was "a very devil" throughout the revolution, as she ordered the murders of white women whom her husband, a chief of some social standing, pursued (92). While this woman apparently stabbed a white man, which prompts the narrator to call her "fury in female form" (92), the novel does not describe her physically inflicting violence on white women. Sansay's novelization of the end of French rule in Saint-Domingue paints a chaotic picture of a culture disordered by its Caribbean locale. Sansay, a writer from an emerging United States, gives her audience a salacious model against which to define themselves, a trope that continues in U.S. popular culture and political discourses.

This chapter begins with Sansay's novel because it makes titillating the violence of "female jealousy," one of the catalysts for women's violence across all chapters in *Grotesque Touch*. As the historiography of women's experiences under enslavement shows, white women's constrained social place has traditionally framed how historians discuss violence. According to Deborah Gray White, for example, white women in a southern U.S. context "were powerless to right the wrongs done them, but some did strike back, not always at Southern patriarchs, but usually at their unwitting and powerless rivals, slave women" (41). The obsessions, deceptions, and resulting violence wrought by white women feature in autobiographies of formerly enslaved women and fictional texts alike.[1] However, in its portrayal of jealous women's murderous ire, *Secret History* stays within certain social expectations for women at the time. In both descriptions of white and Black women's violence inflicted on other women, they order someone else to enact it; these women avoid physically touching their female foes who belong to a different race and (racialized) class. The women are, in effect, removed from this violence due to a strict logic of gendered social place. Sansay's novel is an early example of women using their social positions to remove themselves from some physical acts of violence. *Secret History* thereby demonizes white and Black women in a Caribbean locale while, at the same time, the novel upholds a sense of the women's gendered place in society. The women's actions maintain a gendered line that presupposes that men, and men alone, would have the power to physically inflict pain and death.

Moving into twentieth-century texts, this chapter examines narratives that continue to "other" the women involved in scenes of violence, as in Sansay's novel. I look beyond the recurrent trope of jealousy to examine more closely the dynamics and limits of power and intimacy in scenes when white women lash out against enslaved women. Throughout these depictions (including the most tantalizing), white women claim identities *through* physically enacting violence with a weapon. To pick up a whip, or any other instrument of torture, admits agency in that act of violence; in doing so, women who commit such acts mirror the prerogatives of men who enslave. In this chapter, I specifically examine tropes of sadistic white women in plantation pulp novel cover artwork and exploitation films of the 1960s and 1970s, as these women enact physical violence via a whip to gain white men's power. Closely reading a scene of violence between women as enslaver and enslaved, this chapter uses the exploitation film *Mandingo* (Richard Fleischer 1975) to illustrate a conservative depiction of a white woman that plays up sensationalistic stereotypes.[2] Then, the chapter provides a counterpoint to these stereotypes in the film *12 Years a Slave* (Steve McQueen 2013), in which a woman who enslaves actually increases her power on the plantation by manipulating the system's economies of grotesque, corrupted intimacies. Throughout, I sketch a constellation of violent scenes between women to show how visual, written, and audiovisual texts depict white women negotiating power structures in order to claim their sense of agency in plantation regimes.

Popular plantation pulp novel covers from the 1960s and 1970s commonly feature a white man (or, more rarely, a white woman) wielding a whip and standing above an (assumed) enslaved person. Here, I focus on those images that feature a violent white woman, as this trope (white woman with whip in hand) mixes taboos of interracial sex and gendered violence. Building on

Thavolia Glymph's *Out of the House of Bondage*, I assert that while depictions of violent white women "contradicted prevailing conceptions of white womanhood—and still do" (5), this sensationalized trope removes an enslaver from intimacy with enslaved people. These pulp covers forgo depicting skin-to-skin touch (and the personal connections that touch implies) to instead deal in suggestion, desire, and separation.

As Susan Stryker says more generally about pulp paperbacks in the mid-twentieth century, they were "born from a seamless fusion of form and function" and "became near-perfect commodities—little machines built to incite desire at the point of purchase, capture it, and drive it repeatedly into the cash nexus at 25 cents a pop" (8).[3] Although the plantation pulps I examine were published in the United States and United Kingdom after the so-called golden age of pulp publication—and they likely cost a dollar or more instead of a quarter—their cover artwork markets the novels in the same manner, here using *the plantation* in U.S. and Caribbean settings as shorthand for unnatural desires. Indeed, Ramón E. Soto-Crespo theorizes such twentieth-century narratives as revolving around a "circum-Atlantic trash subject"; he claims this "large archipelago of island sagas" acts as an "archive of trash forms [which] covers a region made of separate yet connected spaces" ("Archipelagic Trash" 303). These plantation pulp novels were popular in the 1960s, and editions were reissued in great quantities in the 1970s, as series upon series were churned out following the popularity of the television miniseries *Roots* and studio-produced exploitation film *Mandingo*. John Harrison says in his catalogue of "hip pocket sleaze" that plantation pulps produced in the 1970s combined "with elements from the blaxploitation film genre" and resulted in "a politically incorrect hotbed of racial lust and violence which would not (and most certainly should not) survive in today's climate" (182).[4] Yet, these volumes sold, and continue to sell—if not for the formulaic plots, then for the imagery they circulate.[5]

Plantation pulp novel covers, as a rule, imply taboo identities and activities, and as Jessica Adams briefly notes in *Wounds of Returning*, pulp fictions used "taboo sexuality as a primary element of what got people interested in the plantation" (56). I explore here how a selection of covers connotes power, as the trope of the enslaver wielding a whip indicates separation (both physical and social) because she does not have to physically touch enslaved people to inflict pain. These pulp covers that feature a white woman holding an instrument of torture, then, suggest interracial sex and gender-bending identities, but her stance ensures that the audience understands her social separation. The enslaver remains aloof, detached from enslaved people.

Although examinations of pulp novels have gained popularity in cultural studies, the planation pulp novel subgenre is still undertheorized. This could be due to the pulp publication process itself, which repackages a hardback novel in low-quality paperback binding, a process that makes a novel more accessible to a general reading audience and tends to ensure a series's continuation (and generic transformation) in paperback form. For instance, U.S. writer Kyle Onstott's quasi-historical-novel-turned-infamous-exploitation-film *Mandingo* first appeared as a hardback in 1957, whereupon its life as a pulp novel (as people likely remember it today) began in the 1960s. Furthermore, the Falconhurst series (of which *Mandingo* was the first novel) morphed over the years as a paperback novel series set in the United States and Caribbean until its conclusion in the late 1980s, when the paperbacks were repackaged as romance novels. Plantation pulps published after the filmic adaptation of *Mandingo*, such as the Dragonard series by Caribbean-born author Rupert Gilchrist (with Caribbean and U.S. settings), more easily fit inside a sexploitation plantation subgenre. In this series, sadistic sex meets racist and sexist dialogue at every turn, though the 1987 B-movie film adaptation of the first novel (*Dragonard*) dilutes these tropes. Overall, the convoluted publication histories of these series (and any hardcover-to-pulp publication trajectory) complicate publication research. Indeed, probably the most curious trend in the lifespan of such series is that some were reprinted near the end of the twentieth century as collectors' hardbacks, complete with the sensationalized pulp cover artwork appearing on the dustjackets.

For example, covers on the novels *Falconhurst Fancy* and *Dragonard Blood* display various iterations of the trope of a white woman wielding a whip, from the late 1960s to the early 1980s (figure 1.1). Enslavers appear within a range of authority on these covers, which insinuates a mixture of danger and power to audiences. Nevertheless, they seem to have it both ways: the covers imply sexual misconduct, while they also reaffirm that white women merely adopt white men's power. Moreover, there is no mistaking a woman's stance as indicating close relationships with enslaved people. These covers specifically feature a variety of poses as half-dressed Black men square off against or succumb to the white women's whips. The evocation of interracial sex is here, but also the covers masculinize the enslaver, especially as she cross-dresses and wields a whip on covers for *Dragonard Blood* (1978 and 1981). Of note is the fact that the artists who painted these and other pulp covers most likely did not read the narratives; instead, according to Jaye Zimet, artists relied on salacious depictions of physically dominant and predatory masculinized women, as were popular on earlier lesbian pulp covers

FIGURE 1.1 *(Left to right)* Cover art on plantation novels *Falconhurst Fancy* (Pan pulp edition, 1969) and *Dragonard Blood* (Corgi pulp edition, 1978; Bantam pulp edition, 1978; Souvenir Press Ltd hardback edition, 1981).

in the 1950s and 1960s (23). The cross-dressing woman on the Dragonard covers—Imogen—does take on a masculinized identity in the novel, as she cuts her hair and dresses in pants while managing her father's plantation. These covers, however, do not accurately convey Imogen's appearance—the narrative describes her during a whipping scene as "a mad woman, a china doll with unkempt black hair and blazing blue eyes," not a buxom blond woman in revealing clothing (Gilchrist 18). However, she does whip enslaved men to enact revenge because, in her words, they are "so manly" (29), and later she dresses in men's clothing and takes an enslaved woman as a lover. These narrative elements point to the novel's conclusion that Imogen is *unnatural*. Therefore, in a novel that features many permutations of sex—mostly coerced—Imogen's own performances of race, gender, and sexuality take center stage on the covers, as pulp covers notoriously suggest the taboos novels commit within their pages. In a world made abhorrent and titillating by slavery, as the Dragonard series repeatedly implies, her identity is supposedly the most shocking, the most perverse, the most likely to attract readers.

To illustrate this trope further, consider the transformation of cover art when hardback novels became pulp productions. The popularity of Guyanese novelist Edgar Mittelhölzer's *Children of Kaywana*, initially published in 1952, ensured more hardback editions in the 1960s and, soon after, pulp paperback editions (figure 1.2). I mention the hardback publication dates of *Children of Kaywana* to stress that later pulp covers differ dramatically from the earlier editions. *Children of Kaywana* is a sweeping novelization of European colonialism in Guyana (the Kaywana series moves from the 1600s all the way to the twentieth century), and the series (like Falconhurst and Dragonard), is sure to include sensationalistic depictions of sadism.[6] These earlier hardback jackets for *Children of Kaywana* do feature women: the cover on the left brings a light-skinned woman to the forefront, while the second cover showcases the character Kaywana, a mixed-race woman whose parents were an Englishman and Indigenous woman. In the novel, Kaywana's enslaver-class progeny regard her as the ancestor they should emulate. Of note is the fact that the 1960 cover shows a silhouetted whipping scene in the background, yet the perpetrator of the whipping is — by all appearances — a man wearing breeches and a jacket. While the hardcover does not share the aesthetics of pulp cover artwork, this image does peddle the book according to the stereotypical imagery of a topless, wild Indigenous woman in a violent Caribbean setting. Thus, the novel's cover art has always advertised its narrative in ways that distance readers from this wayward enslaver-class family, a narrative that Soto-Crespo claims ultimately "show[s] how some subjects are despised, untrainable, and unassimilable" in the midst of movements for independence and nation-building throughout the Caribbean (*White Trash Menace* 66). Through depicting enslaver-class people as such both in the novel and on hardback covers, *Children of Kaywana* was primed for pulpy replications.

If pulp novel covers are meant to lure readers by hinting at gender-bending spectacle and suggesting "abnormal" sexualities within the novel, then the 1976 Bantam Books pulp cover of *Children of Kaywana* fits the bill (figure 1.3). The cover specifically circulates an image of a white woman that has remained taboo, for Western cultural norms dictate that white women should not act with such lusty violence, especially against other women. Here we see an enslaver (again, with whip in hand) towering above a scantily clad enslaved woman while a shirtless man watches in the background, presumably holding the reins of his enslaver's horse. The enslaved woman, whose clothing barely covers her body, averts her eyes from her enslaver's disdainful gaze. Interestingly, the enslaver dresses more conservatively here than on the pulp

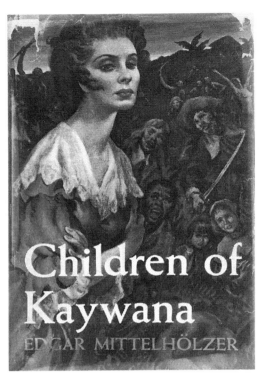

FIGURE 1.2 Cover art on two hardback editions of *Children of Kaywana* (The John Day Company, 1952; Secker and Warburg, 1960).

novel covers I have previously examined in this chapter; still, her masculinized stance connotes physical power and the threat of sexual violence against another woman, which seemingly advertises more explicit transgressions within the novel's pages.[7] The image presumably is of the enslaver Hendrickje, a direct descendant from Kaywana's line who sadistically lashes out against her masochistic husband and whips enslaved people (Mittelhölzer 227–28, 233, 255). She also oversees the tarring and feathering of recalcitrant enslaved people and assists in the act of burying elderly enslaved people alive (354, 393). Furthermore, Hendrickje proclaims the motto for her enslaver-class family, "Only by brutality can we ever attain to the heights—to power!" (398). The novel obviously characterizes Hendrickje in a manner that shows her subverting gendered norms via her violence and (violent) sexuality; yet, the scene on the pulp novel's cover does not actually occur in the novel.

Although the scene depicted on this cover does not appear in Mittelhölzer's novel about enslavers in seventeenth- and eighteenth-century Guyana,

Children of Kaywana
by Edgar Mittelhölzer

✦ ✦ A savage novel of slave rebellion—of
untamed sex and unspeakable violence.

FIGURE 1.3 Cover art on
Children of Kaywana pulp edition
(Bantam Books, 1976).

this "fact" does not matter in the currency of images that this cover art draws from and contributes to. The image obviously plays on customers' expectations of race and gender to lure them into purchasing the novel. Here, the enslaver threatens to subvert her position of class, color, and gender to enact violence against an enslaved woman herself. Also, the cover art suggests—in a tantalizing manner—that the enslaver is about to subvert sexual boundaries as well. In these ways, the 1976 cover art for *Children of Kaywana* blatantly perpetuates *the plantation mistress* as a titillating plantation pulp novel staple.

Despite their obvious pandering to an audience lured by images of (often) scantily clad white women holding whips and threatening Black people with violence, these pulp novel covers also present audiences with an implied power differential between the enslaver and enslaved people. This fraught relationship between enslavers and enslaved women has long provided writers with an opportunity for fictional and critical re-vision. Most frequently, white women "transform sexual jealousy into perverse cruelty" (Gwin 50), which novels integrate into their narratives to imagine—or reimagine—the relationships of power on the plantation. For example, Nanny's story of her life under slavery that she tells Janie in the early pages of Zora Neale Hurston's *Their Eyes Were Watching God* (1937) depicts violence between a white woman and an enslaved woman in a predictable way: she strikes the enslaved woman out of jealousy for giving birth to a mixed-race child, but she does not inflict further punishment via a whip herself. In Nanny's retelling, the enslaver ironically wipes her hands after slapping the enslaved woman and says she would not "dirty [her] hands" (18). Instead, the enslaver orders a man—the overseer—to whip her until she bleeds (18). The white woman's use of her classed, racialized, and gendered position ensures that her hands are "clean" while still planning to inflict grotesque, socially sanctioned violence upon a Black woman's body.

White women's violence was, and still is, denied by people who believe gendered assumptions about enslavement. As Drew Gilpin Faust puts it, "rationalized, systematic, autonomous, and instrumental use of violence belonged to men," while "a contrasting yet parallel ideology extolled female sensitivity, weakness, and vulnerability" (63, 64–65). Still, many texts feature women who enslave threatening such violence, as in Kate Chopin's fin de siècle short frame story "La Belle Zoraïde" (1894), set in Louisiana. Even in a collection of "local color" stories, Chopin includes a brief interlude in which Madame Delarivière, a white woman, verbally threatens violence against Zoraïde, an enslaved woman who has a light skin tone. When Zoraïde wants to marry a man with darker skin and her enslaver responds negatively, the young woman asks, "Am I white, nénaine [aunt/godmother]?" (154). For her supposed presumption, Madame Delarivière responds, "You white! Malheureuse [unhappy woman]! You deserve to have the lash laid upon you like any other slave; you have proven yourself no better than the worst" (154). Madame Delarivière in effect *keeps her hands clean* in the story, as she threatens violence that does not come to fruition. More recent novels, such as Edward P. Jones's *The Known World* (2003), imaginatively revise this trope of a white woman keeping her hands clean, as one narrative sidebar reveals that a jealous enslaver does not receive the last word in the fate of her enslaved rival, Ophelia (40). The local African American community ascribes Ophelia's abrupt disappearance to her ascension into heaven, which consequently takes away the enslaver's agency and values Ophelia's life. Her community's folktale extracts Ophelia and saves her—at least in their memory—from experiencing her enslaver's violence. Even though the enslaver most likely murdered Ophelia, the narrative purposefully leaves the last word about her disappearance to her community. There are numerous narrative techniques to show a white woman keeping her hands clean of violence against enslaved women, ranging from enslavers relying on gendered norms (and ordering others to enact such violence) to narratives featuring enslaved peoples who can reimagine or overpower enslavers' dominant narratives. These fictional stories I have mentioned distance the enslaver from the action of whipping (or murdering) an enslaved woman.

Depictions of violence between an enslaver and an enslaved woman that feature a woman of a higher class dirtying her hands with violence are less common; however, when the white woman picks up an instrument of torture to enact violence on an enslaved woman's body, these narratives often focus on the sadistic pleasure she enjoys.[8] There has been some debate about interpreting enslavers' personal accounts concerning such acts of violence. The historian Marli F. Weiner suggests that women who enslaved participated in violence less enthusiastically than many works of literature portray: "Whether mistresses applied the whip themselves or caused a surrogate to do so for them, it was for many women an immediate solution to a distressing problem, used in anger and often accompanied—or followed—by uncertainty" (284). Yet, Glymph identifies how drawing this conclusion distorts our vision of relationships under enslavement because "scholars seem to be of two minds about the role mistresses played, at once judging them violent and good" (23). Historical work that idealizes white women based on gendered assumptions undermines a full consideration of women's positions of power as enslavers. Glymph asserts that "violence on the part of white women was integral to the making of slavery, crucial to shaping black and white women's understanding of what it meant to be female, and no more defensible than masters' violence" (5). As Stephanie E. Jones-Rogers argues in *They Were Her Property*, "Formerly enslaved people also remembered their female owners as powerful disciplinarians who used a variety of techniques that resembled those of male slave owners" (60). Time and again, the texts in *Grotesque Touch* echo Glymph's and Jones-Rogers's findings. In the rest of this chapter, some fictional depictions offer spaces to rethink gendered, classed, racialized, and sexualized assumptions about white women as they attempt to find pleasure and power through violence against enslaved women.

Up to this point, I have mentioned the presence of sadism and torture on plantation pulp novel covers, a trope that resonates throughout genres and media in *Grotesque Touch*. I see these depictions of sadistic torture on a continuum—on one end appear the pulp covers that entice via sexual, gendered, and racial taboos, and at the other end (and somewhere between) are those texts that show *how* plantation societies themselves relied on daily outpourings of sadistic violence.[9] In other words, plantation torture in narratives can be sadistic and titillating, while at the same time such violence can be everyday and instrumental; the convergence of these narrative elements helps to shape the grotesque nature of violence in each text. Hence, extreme violence plays into the everyday practices of circum-Caribbean plantations, as Octavia Butler's protagonist Dana realizes in *Kindred* (1979) when she is transported from the 1970s back in time to antebellum Maryland and sees the almost blandness of torture: "Like the Nazis, ante bellum [*sic*] whites had known quite a bit about torture—quite a bit more than [she] ever wanted to learn" (117).

Elaine Scarry's claims about the place of torture in a regime's embodiment of power can help chart how narratives illustrate the grotesque nature of plantation structures via violence, including women's violence. According to Scarry, a regime acts out the pain of torture in an "obsessive, self-conscious display of agency," which is "built on these repeated acts of display and ha[s] as its purpose the production of a fantastic illusion of power" (27, 28). Torture, then, "is a grotesque piece of compensatory drama" (28). These performances of power are manifest throughout the archives of slavery; for example, DoVeanna S. Fulton makes the connection between torture, touch, and slavery clear, as she illustrates how Scarry's descriptions of torture and power characterize relationships in nineteenth-century slave narratives (43). Furthermore, in Edward E. Baptist's *The Half Has Never Been Told*, the chapter "Seed" chronicles how white masculinity became defined through violence and the torture of Black bodies during slavery's expansion west, when "white men's code of masculinity shaped all lives on slavery's frontier: shaped the costs of being black, the benefits of being white, the costs of being female" (217). Performing plantation violence is thereby coded as masculine in many texts (such as in *Secret History* and in the pulp novels I have already discussed). In the remainder of this chapter, I show how two films stage such grotesque violence between women—via instrument and touch—to explore the very shakiness of, to borrow Scarry's term, the plantation regime's "compensatory drama."

In a move that might at first appear to counter my aims, I focus on Richard Fleischer's film *Mandingo* here. The film brought plantation exploitation tropes to the big screen in a major U.S. studio release. *Mandingo*'s popularity spawned a slew of plantation pulp novel series and low-budget movies that obviously capitalize on the sadistic sexuality inherent to plantation societies, such as *Mandinga* (a dubbed 1976 Italian film supposedly set in Louisiana) and ever-persistent *Mandingo*-themed (Black/white) erotica and pornography.[10] With such an infamous cultural legacy, one mainly influenced by the proliferation of low-budget knockoffs, *Mandingo* is sometimes remembered as a throwaway film not worthy of contemporary contemplation. I argue, though, that the film more complexly depicts violence between women than the one-dimensional tropes of pulp novel cover artwork. Analyzing women's violence in *Mandingo* encapsulates *Grotesque Touch's* argument at large, as the film both sensationalizes violence between women and exposes plantation structures. Here, these structures prevent women from claiming agency. More than mere celluloid trash — as movie critics and scholars have tended to frame the film — *Mandingo* shows how a white woman's actions to claim power categorize her as deviant, not only to the characters in the film but also to audiences who expect her to be passive.[11]

Mandingo portrays a white woman's attempt to gain power on a Louisianan plantation through sexualized, sadistic violence, which (in the film) is a white man's prerogative. When a white woman, Blanche Maxwell (played by Susan George), whips her husband Hammond's enslaved lover, Ellen (Brenda Sykes), she ostensibly selects Ellen as her victim because she is Hammond's clear favorite. In the film, Hammond Maxwell (played by Perry King) rejects Blanche's body because her sexual appetite (i.e., her lack of virginity due to incest and her presence of sexual longing) makes her "a strange kind of white lady" to him. As such, the social mores depicted in the film reflect what the historian Anne Firor Scott finds in *The Southern Lady*: "The accepted belief was that only men and depraved women were sexual creatures and that pure women were incapable of erotic feeling" (54). Blanche does not fit inside any of the prescribed roles for white women in her society; neither sex worker nor lady, she has no place. Yet, her attempts to obtain pleasure and agency underscore the film's depictions of grotesque social codes. The whipping scene between her and Ellen shows how strictures of gender, class, race, and sexuality have cornered her inside the plantation house, where she supposedly has power as a white woman of the enslaver class.[12] The dark, dingy interior spaces of the plantation house reflect Blanche's lack of power in any space.

While it would be easy to read this whipping scene in terms of Blanche expelling her sexual frustration via inflicting violence on Ellen, the scene more complexly portrays Blanche's position on the plantation. She begins by ordering her handmaid to "bring [her] that wench Ellen." Upon the enslaved woman's inaction, Blanche exclaims, "You heard me! Fetch her!" Even though Blanche is the only white person present on the plantation because her husband, Hammond, and his father, Warren (James Mason), are attending a slave fight in New Orleans, the handmaid implicitly knows Blanche has no real power; indeed, the elder Maxwell entrusted the plantation's well-being to the cook Lucrezia Borgia (Lillian Hayman) before they departed. Underscoring these realities, Blanche's appearance hints at sexual depravity, as she teeters inside her room, intoxicated, hair disheveled, and sparsely dressed in her corset and petticoat. Contextualized with Valerie Steele's study *The Corset*, Blanche's appearance would signal "feminine erotic beauty" to some in the nineteenth century and would connote deviancy to audiences in the 1970s (114, 120, 166). Blanche's state of undress in the scene thereby insinuates her abnormal sexual nature, especially when she hurriedly searches her chest of drawers for a riding crop and then strikes furniture with the instrument.

The scene's composition continues to depict Blanche's precarious subject-position. The camera initially foregrounds Blanche near her massive, unmade bed; yet, as Ellen moves into the room upon Blanche's order, the camera tracks around to be nearer to Ellen (figure 1.4). When the shot composition puts the women on equal footing, Blanche interrupts Ellen's seemingly superior air to order her to "take all of [her] clothes off." Still, Ellen does not move, nor does she speak, but the handmaid interjects that Ellen is "knocked," pregnant. Because of the handmaid's comment, Blanche's impetus for calling Ellen into her room shifts; not only will she whip Ellen for being Hammond's favorite, but she will, in her words, "whup that sucker [child] right out" of Ellen's body. Jealousy, rage, and a craving for power bring Blanche to action as she strikes a fully clothed Ellen with the whip while yelling "Pig! Filthy! Dirty dirty pig!" When Ellen falls down to the floor and cries out, Blanche continues to circle her, shouting insults while her whip's lashes rain down.

Blanche's performance of physical power in her bedroom does not allow her a release, however. Although the audience has already witnessed Blanche's brother, Charles (Ben Masters), use a young enslaved woman's body for his own sadistic pleasure when he whipped her with a belt, the film prevents Blanche from reaching any kind of climax through using a whip. Instead, she merely strikes at Ellen until someone stops her. Lucrezia, true to her position as the keeper of the house, rushes in to prevent a serious crossing of boundaries as she shouts, "Oh no, Miss Blanche! Please!" Foiled in her attempt to appropriate a white man's pleasure via a torture instrument,

FIGURE 1.4 Susan George as Blanche Maxwell and Brenda Sykes as Ellen in *Mandingo* (Paramount, 1975).

Blanche does not allow Ellen to escape unscathed. Blanche resorts to using her hands and the very architecture of the plantation house—her supposed domain—to assert some agency by pushing Ellen down the stairs. Smiling and breathing heavily while looking down on Ellen's prone body, Blanche has the posturing of orgiastic triumph after the force of her hands and gravity on Ellen's body have physically separated the women, as enslaver and property. Evinced in her attitude while she looks down on Ellen, Blanche believes she has achieved the status of "master." This feeling of power, though, is short-lived and illusory.

However sensational the film's portrayal of U.S. plantation cultures might be, *Mandingo* places the sadistically violent plantation society under scrutiny. The film reveals that Blanche inflicted serious harm when Warren Maxwell and the audience see whip marks on Ellen's back. While Warren believes keeping the incident a secret from his son is paramount, he still lectures Blanche on her behavior, calling her actions "zany" and asking her, "Ain't you got no pride?" Though the film avoids portraying Blanche as a helpless child, a counter to Onstott's depiction of Blanche as infantile—in the novel she is "caught" by Lucrezia Borgia (spelled as "Lucretia" in the novel), then lies down on her bed while kicking her feet into the air in a tantrum (448)—the film also makes clear that men's expectations constrain her. Still, it is worth noting that the film, consistent with exploitation genres, oversimplifies the more complex relationship between Blanche and Ellen in the novel. Onstott's novel provides a glimpse into Ellen's thoughts about her enslaver: "Jealousy she admitted to herself, but never hatred. Now she hated. Now she willed Blanche injury, illness, abortion, death. To murder her would alienate her white lover and defeat her purpose. If she could poison her secretly! There could be no rivalry—the other was white. Murder was the only solution" (378). While Ellen does not act on these impulses in the novel, the film's exclusion of Ellen's thoughts—violent or otherwise—is curious. Furthermore, Ellen's darker skin tone and afro hairstyle in the film contrast with the description of Ellen as having a lighter skin tone in the novel. Why does Ellen in the film look like a figure of Black Power, and yet she does not divulge violent thoughts of retribution, or much agency at all? Indeed, the film sets Ellen up to be pitied, whereas Blanche is the only woman capable of disrupting the flow of the plantation system, albeit briefly, and at the expense of Ellen's body. Here and elsewhere in *Grotesque Touch*, I see a white woman's efforts echoing myopic liberation efforts in the twentieth century. In light of this interpretation, I argue that the movie does not solely rely on sensationalistic iconography; although the depiction of Blanche and Ellen's relationship in the film is not radical, the film grants Blanche enough agency to greatly harm Ellen, thereby showing the white woman to be an active agent in the plantation structure, despite white men's insistence that she is not. Ultimately, the fallout from Blanche's efforts provides a means of critiquing the plantation system that the film portrays.[13]

More than merely inviting audiences to gaze upon the punishment and undress of enslaved people (which the film does repeatedly), the scene of violence also sets Blanche on a path of self-destruction; the film makes clear that she cannot claim a white man's dominion for herself. According to the gendered strictures of her society, then, Blanche's claim on Mede, whom his enslavers call a "Black Mandingo buck," is far outside of her social reach as a white woman of the enslaver class. Viewers should realize, however, that Blanche merely mirrors white men's prerogatives when she rapes Mede (played by Ken Norton). In the end, when Blanche gives birth to a mixed-race child, Lucrezia's observation that Blanche is (in her words) a "white nigger" evinces Blanche's place in this society. Her attempt to claim a white man's position renders her an error to be eradicated and forgotten. In *Mandingo*, social mores deem Blanche deviant, not only through her overt sexuality but also via her attempts to seize power through violence, including sexual violence. Blanche does not, and cannot, fully embody the subject-position that belongs to wealthy white men. True to exploitation film genres, *Mandingo* expels the deviant woman in order to return to a misogynist social equilibrium. In the end, the film reveals more about producers' and audiences' desires in the 1970s than how white women benefited from planation structures.

Steve McQueen's *12 Years a Slave* (2013), which won the Academy Awards for Best Picture and Actress in a Supporting Role, is the first Hollywood studio production since *Mandingo* to feature onscreen violence between a white woman and an enslaved woman. The thirty-eight-year gap between the releases of *Mandingo* and *12 Years a Slave* is a remarkable span of time. This timeline demarcates the temporal reaches of my primary texts (mid-twentieth century to 2010s); more importantly, the gap of (nearly) four decades highlights the absence of women's violence in studio depictions of plantation settings. What is it about *women* acting violently *against other women* that makes studio writers, producers, and directors so reluctant to feature this violence on plantations, especially since—as I have noted—historians and novelists purposefully include women's violence against women in their studies and narratives to provide a fuller idea of the structures of power on plantations throughout the hemisphere? My reading of *12 Years a Slave* offers an entry point into answering this question, for the film's depiction of a violent enslaver in Louisiana uproots centuries of lies about white women that negate their complicity in slavery.

Although the film continues the trope that this violence between women grows from jealousy on U.S. plantation settings—the enslaver Mistress Epps (played by Sarah Paulson) focuses her ire on an enslaved woman, Patsey (Lupita Nyong'o), whom her husband rapes—12 Years a Slave does not display the woman's violence in the same sensational manner as Mandingo. Instead, the film more consistently implies her motivations: Mistress Epps uses violent touch to assume—and keep—her power inside and outside the plantation house. Moreover, the film shows Mistress Epps making violent skin-to-skin contact with Patsey, which is uncommon in written texts and films alike—because it shows a woman who enslaves employing her body as a weapon, which is most often framed as a white man's prerogative. The film adaptation shows a white woman's violence as reflecting her society's grotesque ideals of power, which are very much in line with Scarry's theorizations of a regime's performances of torture. In this way, Mistress Epps performs ritualized torture to "prove" her power. Jones-Rogers sees this process in the narratives of people who were enslaved: because "the abuse and murder of enslaved people . . . affirmed a slave-owning woman's power," enslavers sometimes forced enslaved people to view "ritualized performances . . . as a way of further convincing them of that power" (79). The film thereby expands and revises the depiction of Mistress Epps in Solomon Northup's autobiography (1853), in which she appears with less agency. In its adaptation, the film more fully shows a woman actively choosing to embrace the regime's violent order. Audience members watch a woman hemmed in by some social parameters, and yet she successfully uses the grotesque intimacies of the plantation in her search for power.

When audiences first see Mistress Epps, they are likely to believe she will remain in a stereotypically passive role, as she stands silently behind her husband while he reads and extemporizes on a biblical passage to a group of newly purchased enslaved people. As Master Epps (Michael Fassbender) struggles through the passage (which he says is about "masters" having the authority to beat their human property "with many stripes"), the audience notices a glimpse of confusion on his face, signaling the man's shaky literacy and thinking skills as he stretches the meaning of the scripture's words to fit his message. Just as Master Epps reaches the part about "many stripes," the audience notices Mistress Epps's form behind him, which connects her image to the words. Although the camera focuses on Master Epps, his wife's presence is unmistakable, and this sets the tone for her character in the film: she is a shadowy, ever-present figure who also threatens the violence that Master Epps speaks about.

While Master Epps's violence is random, loud, and—frequently—fueled by drunkenness, Mistress Epps deals out her violence with cold calculation

FIGURE 1.5 Mistress Epps, played by Sarah Paulson, glancing at her hands before entering the plantation house in *12 Years a Slave* (Twentieth Century Fox, 2013).

that weighs the costs and benefits of physical touch. In a subsequent scene that portrays the implicit violence of looking in the context of slavery, the audience sees Patsey fashioning dolls out of cornhusks as she pleasantly hums to herself while sitting in grass; she is the epitome of innocent youth when she situates the dolls in a circle so that they appear to dance together. In a reverse shot, however, the audience sees the enslaver looking down on Patsey from her second-story veranda (figure 1.5). Mistress Epps's gaze intrudes upon Patsey's fleeting moment of leisure, and while she does not seem to show any emotion while doing so, Mistress Epps wipes her hands before walking inside the plantation house, as if watching Patsey in this intimate moment has sullied her in some way. Already, the audience recognizes that Mistress Epps in the film differs from Northup's written account when he says she "was not naturally such an evil woman, after all. She was possessed of the devil, jealousy, it is true, but aside from that, there was much in her character to admire" (130). In the film, Mistress Epps's spying on Patsey foreshadows the enslaver's later violence, for she violates Patsey's sense of comfort with her gaze; the enslaver's acts of looking and then brushing off her hands, in other words, hint that her cultural milieu thoroughly shapes the enslaver's character. Mistress Epps, even in this moment, shows that she wishes for the power to violate any sense of personal comfort and safety that enslaved people might experience.

The next scene amplifies this intrusion. After Master Epps drunkenly commands enslaved people to dance inside his home for his enjoyment, Patsey dances in the middle of the group, moving with liveliness that the other exhausted enslaved people do not show. At the same time, Master Epps stares at her. Then, Mistress Epps strides in front of her husband—from the scene's background to the foreground—when she grabs a decanter and throws the heavy object at Patsey's face, which causes the young woman to collapse. The enslaver takes this opportunity, in front of the other enslaved people, to command her husband, "You will sell the negress," and then more forcefully, "You will remove that black bitch from this property." Master Epps, while not attending to Patsey's injury, maintains his position of power as he replies to his wife that he will "rid" himself of her before he sells Patsey. Then, some enslaved people drag Patsey from the dance floor as the music returns. Although Master Epps does not show any feeling for Patsey when Mistress Epps injures her, Patsey's presence in the house reveals the white woman's tenuous position, for she may be usurped by the enslaved woman.

Unsurprisingly, Mistress Epps doubles her efforts against Patsey after her husband rapes the enslaved woman. Whereas she used the decanter as an instrument to commit violence against Patsey before, now Mistress Epps employs her own fingernails to scrape the skin off Patsey's cheek. In a subsequent dancing scene, Master Epps sits in a stupor while his wife arrives with an enslaved person to serve pastries. She purposefully skips Patsey, and she says to her husband that Patsey has given her a "look of insolence" that is "hot" and "hateful." Though her husband gained the upper hand in their previous confrontation, now Mistress Epps tells him that he is "man-less" because of the way he deals with his property. When she cannot get him to respond to her words, she walks over to Patsey and scratches her face. Patsey, reacting to this injury, screams and shrinks to the ground, while Mistress Epps yells, "Beat it from them!" This act of violence and authority apparently stirs her husband, for Master Epps takes Patsey from the room, presumably to inflict further violence on her body.

The scene that I have described is significant, not only because Mistress Epps uses her husband's feelings of guilt and weariness to her advantage but also because she makes skin-to-skin contact with Patsey. After bullying her husband, Mistress Epps looks down at her fingers, as if contemplating the moment of violence between her and Patsey that she inflicted with her body (figure 1.6). In this way, *12 Years a Slave* portrays violence between women in a more reflexive manner than *Mandingo*: Mistress Epps's pause creates an (albeit brief) opening in which the enslaver might consider the humanity of the enslaved woman. Ultimately, though, viewers can connect the scene in which Mistress Epps spies on Patsey from the veranda to this one, for just

FIGURE 1.6 Mistress Epps glances at her fingers as her husband, played by
Michael Fassbender, stands (Twentieth Century Fox, 2013).

as she dusts off her hands when she is through looking at Patsey, so does
the enslaver disregard the moment of intimacy in her violent touch. The
white woman uses her body as a weapon against Patsey, and the film rules
out any connection between the two women other than that of enslaver and
enslaved person, owner and property. At the conclusion of this scene, Mistress Epps commands *her* enslaved people to eat and then continue dancing; she has supplanted her husband in terms of prestige, and she does so
through inflicting violence with her body, which is commonly framed as
the prerogative of white men.

Whereas Master Epps's power seems to diminish after he assaults Patsey,
Mistress Epps's control of her husband increases when she inflicts pain on
the enslaved woman. After Solomon (Chiwetel Ejiofor) returns from a season working at another plantation, the audience sees the evidence of this
struggle for power marked on Patsey's body: now her face bears scars from
the decanter and her enslaver's fingernails, as well as a bloodshot eye. Then,
in the following extended whipping scene, which Solomon describes in his
autobiography as "the most cruel whipping that ever [he] was doomed to
witness—one [he] can never recall with any other emotion than that of horror" (Northup 168)—the audience notices how Mistress Epps influences Master Epps's actions against Patsey to a previously unseen degree. Believing
Patsey to have left the plantation to seek a sexual relationship with his neigh-
bor Master Shaw (though she went to Shaw's for soap because Mistress
Epps does not allow her any), Master Epps is so enraged upon Patsey's return

that he orders her to be stripped and tied up so that he can whip her. However, upon hearing Mistress Epps's cold encouragement as she stands off-camera to the side of him—"Do it. Strike the life from her"—he cannot work up the courage to perform the deed himself. Master Epps instead forces Solomon to whip Patsey while the camera follows him as he moves with a jittery walk over to his wife. In this scene, the camera's movements and framing of Master and Mistress Epps and Patsey create a fluid sense of their triangulated relationship—and the camera is as restless as Master Epps appears to be. While Master Epps fidgets in this scene, Mistress Epps calmly voices criticisms about her husband's shortcomings (he is "a fool for the taking"). When she eventually gets through to her husband, he takes the whip from Solomon and inflicts a series of lashes on Patsey's back. Upon exhausting himself, Master Epps drops the whip, and he and his wife turn to enter the house together, thereby dusting off their hands concerning Patsey. Thus, *12 Years a Slave* shows that violence on the plantation requires the participation of both enslavers. Unlike in the exploitation film *Mandingo*, *12 Years a Slave* does not depict Mistress Epps's violence as exceptional. Here, the audience sees for the first time a white woman calculating what her violent touch will bring her—supremacy on the plantation.

I also want to suggest, however, that Master Epps's anxieties about Patsey's visitations to the Shaw plantation are not entirely unwarranted. The film shows Patsey having tea—complete with her wearing a bonnet and enjoying a formal tea service—with Mistress Shaw (played by Alfre Woodard), a formerly enslaved woman. Mistress Shaw does not romanticize her position to Patsey or Solomon when he shows up to retrieve the enslaved woman for Master Epps; instead, she lets the two know that she reached this position because of her enslaver's sexual desire, and she says, "Where once I served, now I have others serving me." Mistress Shaw adds, though, that she can foresee the crumbling of the enslaver class, and she tells Patsey to "take heart." As Patsey sits, dressed in her finest clothing, the audience notices the markings from Mistress Epps on her face. This exchange hints at insurrection as well; although she does not encourage Patsey to take action against her enslavers, Mistress Shaw's comments suggest a narrative that could have been quite radical, for mainstream cinema has not yet shown an enslaved woman who enacts revolutionary violence against a woman who enslaves her. Indeed, Patsey resumes the subjugated position she has known, and the film forecloses the possibility that she could have acted in retaliation. The film—remaining true to Solomon Northup's autobiography—leaves Patsey behind crying in the dust when Solomon is rescued from the Epps plantation.[14]

In McQueen's *12 Years a Slave,* audiences see how plantation violence relies on a white woman's performance of what is commonly configured as a white man's prerogative—inflicting violence on an enslaved woman via skin-to-skin touch. This depiction of a woman's calculated physical violence goes beyond the sensationalized iconography of plantation pulp novels and exploitation films like *Mandingo* because it shows the enslaver benefiting from this violent system. The film thereby depicts a white woman afforded the privileges of race identified by recent historians. In the next chapter, I will show how novels and films set on Caribbean plantations deepen this discussion of violent touch and intimacy through two-way violence. In these narratives, enslaved women attempt their own insurrections against their enslavers, which reveals how all women are shaped by the plantation's sadistic norms.

CHAPTER TWO

Within and Beyond Sadistic Violence

> I live within the sword
> within rage and outrage
> I live beyond the sword
> I contemplate horror
> because it is there
> in memory and anticipation
> in the details of days
>
> . . .
>
> I had taken my machete
> to my mistress
> made cane of her
> motives of insult
> —GAYL JONES, "The Machete Woman," 50

Gayl Jones's "machete woman," enslaved in the New World, cuts down her enslaver to end her many abuses. This chapter illustrates a range of violent relationships between enslavers and enslaved women embodied in Jones's speaker—women who "live within the sword" and those who begin to "live beyond the sword" when they contemplate what violent actions represent. Building on chapter 1's movement from sensational representations of violence between women to texts that more carefully contextualize such violence on plantations, this chapter traces a trajectory of consciousness akin to Jones's "machete woman." Here, I show how narratives frame enslaved women's insurrections (via mediated violence, skin-to-skin touch, or nonviolent actions) with white women's sadistic violence. As in Jones's poem, the "horror" of plantation systems is in the relentless "details of days," the grotesque intimacies evident in violent contact. At every turn, these narratives illustrate the instability of power, as violent touch between women threatens to subvert the colonial hierarchies it supposedly enforces. Through their violent intimacies, the texts in this chapter thereby take the examples in chapter 1 to their logical limits, as moments of women's grotesque touch reflect plantation regimes' elaborate, contradictory, and unstable performances of law and order. Undermining self/Other distinctions at important moments, these narratives moreover create openings for revolutionary thought.

This chapter examines the relationships between intimacy, touch, and violence in two novels, Madison Smartt Bell's *All Souls' Rising* (1995) and Marlon James's *The Book of Night Women* (2009). Key scenes in these novels illustrate how depictions of extreme violence enacted by a woman who enslaves in Saint-Domingue (*All Souls'*) and an enslaved woman in Jamaica (*Night Women*) have the potential to uproot racialized, gendered, and classed social norms. While these texts ultimately contain white and Black women within their plantation societies' strictures, the novels offer glimpses of what it means to look at the sadistic norms of slavery head-on, what it means—in other words—to "live within the sword" (to form a sense of self via violence in such a culture), or to attempt to "live beyond the sword." My contemplation of women's violence in Jean Van de Velde's film *Hoe Duur Was de Suiker* (2013) brings this conversation back into the realm of audiovisual representation, for the film complicates previous performances of touch, intimacy, and violence through an enslaved woman's narrative that is ultimately shaped by violence perpetrated by white women in Suriname. Though the film creatively situates an enslaved woman's identity in the context of enslavers' violence, it also culminates in an unimaginative romance plot between the enslaved woman and a man who enslaves. Even so, this chapter ultimately argues that some narratives that include violent touch between women (however imperfect or difficult these representations might be) shift their focus to create more space for enslaved women's experiences and perspectives. Consequently, this chapter departs from chapter 1's more simplistic depictions of violence to dwell on how these texts (politically revolutionary and conservative alike) uncover contexts and implications of sadistic plantation violence.

In sketching such a (seemingly) contradictory trajectory here, I attend to how these contemporary texts call into question what Jenny Sharpe refers to as "the complicity of our readings with the documents on which we rely for imagining what transpired in the past" (xiii). In this way, I am not particularly interested in digging down to try to uncover a means of "true" (or in some way uncomplicated) resistance that does not replicate plantation violence. Instead, I am pursuing how this selection of texts set in Caribbean locations offers ways to consider the intertwining of violence and intimacy in the making of "an agency that was precariously balanced between acting and being acted upon" (xxv). Whether the texts sensationalize and/or romanticize enslaved women's individual actions is an important concern in this chapter; however, my argument evinces how a text's pandering to audiences' desires (those who want to see "the violent Caribbean" and those who want to see interracial love "against all odds" on plantations) does not necessarily foreclose readings of how the text also shows enslaved women grappling with the violence of slavery that intends to dehumanize them. Here, I am reminded of Elena Machado Sáez's argument in *Market Aesthetics*, that the Caribbean diasporic authors whose historical fiction she traces have a "pedagogical task . . . responsive to the decontextualization of the Caribbean and offer . . . counternarratives that educate the amnesiac reader" (32). Such "historical novels affirm the relevance of the Caribbean to European and American histories, particularly as a space where the seeds of globalization were planted during New World imperialist enterprises." I believe it is instructive to see each text in this chapter as offering narratives that speak back to the sadistic violence of plantation slavery. I ultimately argue here, then, that texts need not be ideologically cohesive to give us innovative glimpses into women as characters who (in either the briefest scenes or via sustained characterization) come to the realization that daily plantation violence reflects much larger (and contradictory) hemispheric systems of power.

Depictions of circum-Caribbean cultures have long featured manifold scenes of violence. Texts that offer multiple examples of grotesque violence portray colonial and neo-colonial histories and cultures that are, at their root, violent—what Patricia Yaeger calls "the stunning, violent abundance of a world made from the excess of Europe's circum-Atlantic trade" in her essay "Circum-Atlantic Superabundance" (770–71). Yaeger begins this essay by citing U.S. author Madison Smartt Bell's novel *All Souls' Rising* as an example. She asserts that the dismemberment, torture, and murder of enslaved people by their enslavers in the novel is "excess [that] looks exactly like verisimilitude—like brutality surfeited with the real"—in a culture in which "flesh and commodity seem forever commingled" in a circuitous spiral (769, 770). Yaeger's point is essential here, for Bell's novel about the Haitian Revolution makes a temporal and geographic jump from the settings of *Mandingo* and *12 Years a Slave* in chapter 1, yet the texts are undeniably involved in a dialogue about contemporary circum-Caribbean representations of power. Specifically, *All Souls' Rising* follows my discussion of these films because Bell's novel describes in a scene of brutality an enslaver (Claudine) enacting what the novel frames as a white man's (i.e., masculinized) power over the body of an enslaved woman (Mouche). Unlike the brief ex-

amples of violence between women acted out in chapter 1's filmic representations, Bell's novel describes sadistic violence in a lengthy scene. Indeed,
All Souls' provides an interesting turning point in my analysis because the
novel's tendencies to relay the details of torture like crucifixions and evis-
cerations, just to name a couple, aesthetically mirror exploitation productions that feature scene upon scene of outlandish torture. According to at
least one reviewer when *All Souls'* was published, this kind of representation of violence "threatens to numb by repetition into a handbook of splat-
terpunk," "to become mere slush, the sentimentality of gore" (Vernon pars.
6 and 7). As Kathleen Gyssels indicates, the scenes of "whipping and raping,
torturing and castrating are pictured in graphic, at times cinematographic
writing, which has a deliberately unpleasant and discomforting impact on
the reader" (114). And yet, scholars typically do not engage with these
scenes or the discomfort therein.

I argue that Bell's novel leads readers through Claudine's consciousness
as she attempts to claim agency in a colonial society rooted in sadism via this
"graphic" and "cinematographic" scene of extreme violence against an enslaved woman. The grotesque, unsettling specifics of this scene are key to
my argument, and I uncover the nuances of power that lie within the scene's
language (that makes readers uncomfortable). As in chapter 1, this violence
(predictably) begins with a feeling of jealousy; moreover, the scene quickly
becomes one in which Claudine uses violent touch to shape her subject-
position in this plantation society. Unlike chapter 1's representations of violence that physically and mentally separate white and Black women in pulp
cover artwork and *Mandingo*, however, in this chapter mediated touch gives
way to intimate, skin-to-skin touch, through which Claudine perceives a connection with Mouche. Still, the script of violent self-making she follows
forecloses a sense of shared humanity. In this way, my argument follows Gyssels's claims that *All Souls' Rising* "can be read as historiographic metafic-
tion" in its parody of Enlightenment thought, "deliberately setting the
tragedies and turmoil, the inequalities between men and women, the total
incomprehension and even annihilation of the women as subjects, their insanity and self-destructive behaviour, against the [Enlightenment's] putative
gallantry, 'refinement' and 'delicacy'" (112). As *All Souls'* suggests in this scene
of extreme violence, a white woman's ability to claim a stable subject-position
in this society is paradoxical: to achieve a position of mastery means that
white women lose themselves.

Colin Dayan's *Haiti, History, and the Gods* further elaborates this tie between the Enlightenment and slavery in circum-Caribbean cultures, as she

traces a hemispheric preoccupation with racialized sentimentality: "Out of the ground of bondage came a twisted sentimentality, a cruel analytic of 'love' in the New World: a conceit or counterfeit of intimacy" (189). Dayan illustrates this topsy-turvy logic of the French Code Noir, which ostensibly curbed extremely violent punishments. As Dayan indicates, this baffling document of law shows the business of making people into things; the code "designates slaves only to negate them" as "slaves exist legally only insofar as they disobey: no juridical mention is made of obedience. Recognition is granted only as a prohibition or corrective for insubordination" (209). Since "slaves" are categorized as "things," it follows that "no amount of amputation, torture, or disfiguring can matter" (204). Making people into things is, of course, a hallmark of the Marquis de Sade's popular fictions, which Dayan connects to the French Antillean slave trade; Sade's *The Hundred and Twenty Days of Sodom* "revealed the truth at the heart of the traffic in slaves: not only economic gain, but the tempting and pleasurable reduction of human into thing" (212). Sadism, then, lies at the heart of slavery, which is entrenched in Enlightenment thought. Moreover, the code—enacted in slavery and reflected in Sade's catalogues of torture (214)—evinces that slavery relies on patterns of corrupt intimacies. Thus, as Nick Nesbitt summarizes from Baron de Vastey's writing following the Haitian Revolution, the very systems enslavers operated under were unjust and illegitimate (Nesbitt 185). The Haitian Revolution, Nesbitt synthesizes, "was emphatically the destruction of a normative world-system, one that legitimized the enslavement, debasement, and torture of millions of Africans in New World slavery. It was no expression of unreflective, barbaric savages, but the expression of the radical enlightenment in its highest and most far-reaching manifestation, under the categorical imperative of universal justice as equality" (161). This kind of legitimate, revolutionary violence (in Frantz Fanon's words) springs forth "precisely at the moment" the colonized person "realizes [their] humanity" (Fanon 43). The ways sadism both reflects and creates a delegitimized social structure in slavery—and the violence necessary to remake the world—are the themes Madison Smartt Bell picks up in his late-twentieth-century novel.

This social milieu shapes the character Claudine Arnaud, a French woman displaced in the colonial realm of Saint-Domingue, and the deep contradictions of Enlightenment thought prime her mental state—so much so that her "insanity" reflects the norms of plantation slavery. Claudine, in other words, does not merely lash out at her husband's infidelities; she mirrors what is acceptable for white men in her society.[1] In doing so, the novel highlights the grotesqueries of the colonial project in Saint-Domingue, what

Doris Garraway calls "a genocidal state of affairs maintained by an astound-ing rate of slave consumption . . . which extracted on average ten to fifteen years of labor from captive men and women before they were driven to death" (240). *All Souls'* begins with a scene of torture and "slave consumption" as Doctor Antoine Hébert approaches Habitation Arnaud in 1791 and finds a recently pregnant enslaved woman crucified upon a post. The enslaver Mi-chel Arnaud explains to Hébert his justification of the murder: this en-slaved woman killed her newborn, his property, with the very nail that pins her hands to the post. After her prolonged death, Arnaud personally severs her wrists, ankles, and neck, to him a mutilation of already-wasted property because he has lost his money that he paid for her body as "breed-ing stock" (Bell 20). Hébert, newly from France, questions the white Creole man's justification because "one does not ordinarily torture animals" (20). Torture, however, *is* a mainstay of the plantation economy that has made people into things, and after calling Hébert both a "sentimentalist" and "Ja-cobin," Arnaud tells the traveler, "You have lost your way" (20). All roads in Saint-Domingue lead to horrific scenes of mutilation and murder, and readers learn this alongside the doctor.

Interestingly, Claudine does not intend to murder Mouche when their scene begins later in the novel; she acquires her husband's shaving razor to, apparently, feel the sensation of the blade barely marking her skin. Because of "the merest scratch" the blade leaves on Claudine's skin, "the arm seem[s] more fully hers than it had before" (87). Extended periods of loneliness, in-toxication, and powerlessness characterize Claudine's life on the plantation as she daily encounters her husband's mixed-race children, while she remains childless, reminiscent of Blanche in the film adaptation of *Mandingo*. In *All Souls'*, the scene jumps from Claudine's masochistic marking of her own skin to her sadistic lashing out against an enslaved woman's body. Claudine finds her excuse to punish Mouche when she spills her coffee service; the sheathed blade "shift[ing] uncomfortably between her breasts" spurs Claudine on, re-minding her of its presence and access to her husband's power via an instru-ment of pain (87). Spilled coffee and sugar (the wasted, superabundant products of this plantation economy) bring Claudine to action when she de-stroys Mouche's body (both a product and producer of the plantation). She does so with her husband's blade, which represents (in this novel) mascu-line power.

The scene continues to follow a pattern set by the enslaver and enslaved woman, one characterized by unquestioned domination and submission. When Claudine leads Mouche to a shed by her ear, the narrator reveals the power dynamic that the women's performances repeatedly showcase: "Of course Mouche was much stronger than she, but they had played this scene together often enough before that the black girl knew her only choice was submission" (88). Another player in this scene is the enslaved man Isidor, whom Claudine depends on to tie Mouche's wrists. Because of her position of authority above enslaved people, Claudine does not have to perform every task of punishment. As enslaver, her prerogative is to decide which aspects of the process she will act out. Isidor, however, senses a difference in today's playacting: it has become too real, and "anxious sweat" covers him as he realizes the supporting role he must play (88). He is not in attendance during the beating to bear witness, though, because Claudine immediately commands Isidor, "Leave us," so she may conduct the violence and savor sadistic pleasure (88).

Left alone with Mouche, Claudine's imagination intrudes, and she thinks that Mouche's garment was torn "perhaps from Arnaud's greedy hand that morning" (88). Though jealousy impels Claudine, the narration divulges more about her motivations while she strips away Mouche's dress and commences striking her with a riding crop. Mouche's reactions do not placate Claudine's desires, and she wants to inflict more pain via a larger instrument, in her thinking, to "flay the bitch to the bone": "Anything to change the timbre of her insincere cries so they no longer would remind her of the self-same moaning Mouche had given up when she was covered by Arnaud" (88–89). Sexual jealousy appears to be at the heart of Claudine's actions, but such language gives way to Claudine's feelings of "insufficiency" because Mouche's cries lack sincerity (89). The scene, acted out by the women numerous times before—as evidenced by the patterns of old and new whip marks on Mouche's back—suddenly is not *real* enough for Claudine. The usual instruments of torture (rope and whip) prove insufficient.

When Claudine's eyes meet Mouche's, the rules for the scene change, and she involuntarily remembers how her parents "sold" her into marriage because they assumed Arnaud, a Creole enslaver, would be rich (89). This connection with Mouche—over the women's ostensibly shared experiences as chattel that men exchange—is "intolerable" to Claudine (89). She thinks "the strokes of the crop must wear it away, but they would not, and still their eyes were locked" (89). Despite their presumed shared experience, Claudine believes that her class position has ultimately sealed her fate of uselessness, for her dowry was not made of anything tangible, while the trade of enslaved people yields objects that are "real to the touch and to use" (89). In this moment, though, Claudine does not realize or admit that she profits from the buying and selling of enslaved people. Claudine instead desires *to be acknowledged as real* in the only way she knows how; embodying the violence of enslavers seems to drive her actions.

The narration indicates that this "crackling connection" between the women brings them "to a communion larger than themselves," as "all over the island masters and slaves were expressing their relation in similar ways" in moments of torture and murder (89). This moment of recognition—between women as women in this specific time and place—makes an instance of ineffective punishment into something more; the novel transforms this moment into a microcosm of superabundant sadistic violence found throughout the island, as "all these were as sacraments, body and blood" (89).[2] Yet, the sacramental aspect of ritualized violence should not overshadow applications of Elaine Scarry's concept of torture as "a grotesque piece of compensatory drama" (28); enslavers enact such violence continuously to stage the total power they so desperately want to embody. Even though Claudine *individually* acts out a scene of torture in hopes that her power will be acknowledged, the narration clearly shows how her thoughts and actions fall into a prescribed social script. The rest of the scene thereby illustrates Claudine's use of a racist, classist, and sexist society's sanctioned means of torturing enslaved people. For example, when the impossibility of finding satisfaction via the whip frustrates her, Claudine discards the instrument, and flesh meets flesh as Claudine claws at Mouche's exposed, whipped back. "Scoring the flesh with her nail points" (Bell 89), Claudine makes physical contact with Mouche, which is very different from but also intimate like Claudine's initial feeling that Mouche "anticipated a touch of love" (88). Though Mouche utters a "shout of surprise at this" pain, the enslaved woman's reaction is "still . . . not all [Claudine] wanted" (89). The violent intimacy of this scene reveals how Claudine expects to gain power in this society. While Claudine may appear to be "driven insane" and thus commit "insane acts of violence" (Gyssels 117), I argue that Claudine's extremely violent acts in this passage put her in close communion with a society supersaturated with violence: Claudine's "insanity" merely mirrors the corrupt logics of her society at large.

Just as Claudine's slight marking of her skin with the blade signaled her agency via pain, making painful contact with Mouche's body when she bites off a fingernail—that she tore while clawing Mouche's back—solidifies (in the moment) her subject-position: "Exhausted from the encounter, Mouche breathed on that same sighing pattern. Claudine thought that while her power over the girl was absolute, Mouche did not fully recognize this truth.

Yet she would make her know it" (Bell 89, emphasis mine). Here, she feels her husband's sheathed razor between her breasts, and Claudine asserts her power when she orders enslaved people to open the storeroom. To Isidor she says, "You will take your orders from me," and after she slaps the enslaved woman Marotte, she declares, "The master is gone. . . . I will be obeyed. Do you hear me? Fetch a pry bar" (89, 90). The narration—filtered through Claudine's mind—divulges that her husband also used Marotte for his sexual pleasure, like an unnamed enslaved woman before her who fled from the plantation and her mixed-race children (90). Once again, the passage indicates how cruel repetition marks Claudine's—and the enslaved women's—lives: Claudine is constantly reminded of her husband's infidelities, while the enslaved women cycle through the enslaver's bedroom as he repeatedly rapes and discards them over the years. "The shock of palm on cheek [is] sweet" to Claudine when she strikes Marotte's face (not for the first time); the enslaver asserts her dominance over—and separation from—yet another woman, again, via her own body (90). With the razor tucked between her breasts, and enslaved people apparently under her thumb, Claudine breaks into the storeroom to indulge in the white brandy Arnaud keeps hidden from her. Claudine's desire for power leaves her, like the liquor, "transported," albeit briefly, for she can know no stable position of authority in this narrative (90).

Mouche's assertion of her personhood through song, through her voice, jerks Claudine out of her euphoria and spurs her to follow through with sadistic mutilation. What Claudine hears as "a singular liquid sound, like a long wave rippling all the way back to Guinée," the novel describes as an articulation of Mouche's "essential African self," and Claudine realizes that her violence has not touched Mouche's identity (91). Mouche's assertion of self undermines Claudine's position as subject: Claudine realizes that she has no power to alter Mouche's inner being, and this realization infuriates her. Frustration and anger renew Claudine's efforts. The narration shows her obsessive urge to have Mouche "know" her place as enslaver, and Claudine attempts to separate the two women into the actor and the acted upon, forever (91). With calculated certainty, Claudine begins a script that she believes will correct her and Mouche's positions and relations toward each other:[3] "Mouche sang on, unaware of her, until Claudine took her shoulder with a certain gentleness and turned her so her back was to the wall. Her eyes rolled open an instant before the voice ceased, as Claudine let the razor decline through a slow curve and come to rest against the point just below the sternum where the taut rise of the belly began. Mouche's throat worked, silently now, and

Claudine saw her eyes widening and saw that she *had* understood, at last"
(91, emphasis in original). Embracing her role as an enslaver, Claudine can
forsake whipping and clawing for a calmer, almost "gentle," action as she asserts her power over Mouche. Resting the blade on Mouche's pregnant ab-
domen, Claudine claims the same calculated cruelty that her husband knows
as his right. Just as he matter-of-factly nailed an enslaved woman to a stake
to punish her for killing her child (his property), Claudine can coolly assert
her right over the enslaved woman's pregnant body. Remarkably, Claudine
claims this agency with a blade, which is not only associated with her husband but also characterized as the weapon of necessity used by enslaved
people. Just as they cut down the cane fields with machetes, they use these
farm instruments to cut down their enslavers, like Gayl Jones's "machete
woman." Claudine, however, does not recognize such associations while her
hand acts out the logical, violent outcome of her quest for power.

What happens next shows that the mechanisms of sadistic power cannot
be stopped once they are put into motion, because "when Mouche s[ees]
there [i]s no limit, that truly nothing could stop [the enslaver] now, Claudine could no longer stop herself" (91). Claudine's body, now seemingly at
one with her social conditioning, plays this scene out to its logical—
grotesque—conclusion. Claudine's hand bearing the blade cuts "Mouche's
body open" (91). The detached narrator describes disembowelment with a
tone fitting the cruel action Claudine (aspiring to mastery) commits, as if she
performs a perfunctory act on the plantation. An "awful scream," however,
rises from one or both women, possibly showing that they are finally connected via this terrible act; yet, Claudine cannot tell which woman screamed,
"for Mouche was singing again now, and that was what Claudine could not
bear" (91–92). The script of sadistic torture Claudine has followed ultimately
does not change anything, for Mouche's voice makes her selfhood clear.
Mouche's vocalization is reminiscent of the form of agency Marisa J. Fuentes speaks of in reference to the historical archive: "Perhaps resistance to the
violence of slavery is survival, the will to survive, the sound of someone wanting to be heard, wanting to live or wanting to die. But the struggle against
dehumanization is in the *wanting*. And sometimes, we can hear it" (143, emphasis in original). Mouche's resistance, her "wanting to be heard," "mad-
dens" Claudine, and her actions again reflect the frenzied woman readers saw
earlier in the scene: Claudine "sw[ings] wildly at the neck, spinning herself
half around," and severs Mouche's artery with the blade (Bell 92). Whether
calculated or frantic, none of Claudine's actions can erase Mouche's inner
self, a personhood separate from the plantation regime. In this moment,

Claudine fully embodies the "horror" of "the details of days," described by Jones's "machete woman." Again, Claudine's reactions to Mouche's resilience mirror the mores of people who belong to her social class, who constantly inflict horrific torture on enslaved people's bodies in an effort to prove their power. In doing so, Claudine's actions ironically reflect the delusional thinking required to maintain systems of enslavement in the (seemingly incongruous) age of Enlightenment.

Despite the violence Claudine inflicts upon Mouche's body, she does not touch, much less destroy, the enslaved woman's self. The novel evokes this idea by describing what Claudine sees when she stands back from the gore. Claudine notices two things: first, Mouche's fetus in its embryonic sack lying on the floor; and second, the abundance of Mouche's blood covering her clothing and surroundings. The flittering life "pulsing inside" its embryonic sack signals to Claudine that she ultimately does not, nor cannot, discover Mouche's true self (92). Claudine now seems to acknowledge defeat, for she observes and touches Mouche's blood in a catatonic state: "She dabbled two fingers in it, noting that Mouche's blood was just the color of her own, precisely. She made a print, an oval dot, over the place where she'd nicked herself that morning, then stroked a double line down her cheek with her two fingers" (92). Despite Claudine's efforts to force Mouche to recognize her position as a powerful subject, Claudine seems to realize that she is indeed connected to Mouche via how the plantation economy classified them as women, as reproductive bodies. Claudine embraces her class position via spilling an enslaved woman's blood on a whim; yet, just as the bodies of both women bleed when they menstruate, so are the women reduced to what their bodies can produce on the plantation.

Unlike her husband, Arnaud, Claudine's act of violence psychologically haunts her: apparitions of Mouche's mutilated corpse and the fetus follow her and tell "her that the work of destruction she'd begun would be unending" (92). Moreover, both Isidor and Marotte run away and join the ranks of Maroons waiting for their time to strike, and the narrative leaves open the possibility that, perhaps, Claudine's act of violence spurs the initial attacks on the plantations. In this reading of the Haitian Revolution, a white woman's violent actions against an enslaved woman serve as the final straw for the enslaved and self-emancipated people of Saint-Domingue. This reimagining of the revolution supposes that Claudine's actions were the *worst* acts of violence that had ever occurred. However, according to Baron de Vastey in his 1814 chronicles of the torture enslaved people experienced in Saint-Domingue, violence ordered or physically inflicted by white women was a "matter of common knowledge" (123).[4] Likewise, viewing Claudine's violence as exceptionally brutal (so much so that it started a revolution) replicates how enslavers themselves insisted, according to Michel-Rolph Trouillot, that "resistance did not exist as a global phenomenon. Rather, each case of unmistakable defiance, each possible instance of resistance was treated separately and drained of its political content" (83). Still, the novel confirms that sadism serves as the backbone of the plantation system; furthermore, the formerly enslaved people's actions during the Haitian Revolution show how all people carefully study—and then perform—such violence.

No violence is isolated in Saint-Domingue, as Claudine quickly realizes. Her circular thoughts turn her into a ghostly figure who believes she should "face whatever [i]s there" in the shed, "but she d[oes] not go" (Bell 94). Instead, Claudine flees to the Flaville plantation, where the memories of her actions still haunt her: "To imagine that on that day itself she'd thought her situation was unbearable, that thought seemed laughable now" (152). Again, Claudine's thoughts are ironic, for there was no "day of innocence" Claudine could have escaped to; even if she had remained in France, she would have been caught up in the tumult of the French Revolution. Claudine begins to understand that violence is intrinsic to Saint-Domingue society when self-emancipated people attack the plains (including the Flaville plantation), murdering and raping as they go. This realization saves her life when she meets a group of self-emancipated men on the road. Because she unflinchingly cuts off her ring finger to give to the men, they do "not know what to do about her anymore" (176). Unlike Blanche in *Mandingo*, Claudine's separation from society comes from her realization that she (and everyone she knows) is caught in the circular, violent performance of power. Having discovered this reality, Claudine now does not "fit" within her gendered social class; she is outside looking in.

More like a seer than what the self-emancipated man Riau calls a "whitelady," Claudine in 1792 can no longer live inside the myopic homes of the white elite. When she visits a priest to confess her actions, her society's refusal of her agency confronts her. Claudine admits, "Oh, the power I had over her . . . It was absolute. How could I make you understand it? No one can know" (338). The priest replies, "You must sacrifice your pride" (338). The priest operates on gendered assumptions: a "whitelady" could not have such power. Although Claudine's mutilation of Mouche's body was socially sanctioned violence because enslavers could do with their property as they liked, this same society in the novel still claims that a white woman would not, could not, have *absolute* power over another. Her society's unwillingness to see her as a subject, one capable of grotesque violence, drives Claudine to cloister herself. In these ways, Claudine embodies the illogical drives of enslavement; her performance of sadistic violence does not grant her a stable place in this society. Instead, Claudine's story evinces that, as in the words of Julietta Singh's *Unthinking Mastery*, "the narratives of mastery are always fragile, threatened, and impossible" (18). As the novel repeatedly reveals, enslavers' reliance on sadistic demonstrations of power proves how such systems cannot endure.

All Souls' continues to show the contagion of sadism during the Haitian Revolution as people of all racialized classes perform the cruelty they learned from the ruling white elites. They, in the words of Jones's "machete woman," "live within the sword / within rage and outrage" (50). Dr. Hébert's observations of the revolutionaries' camps later in the novel—while they are gradually shifting from guerrilla conflict to military regiments because of Toussaint L'Ouverture's influence—reveals how self-emancipated people have internalized white enslavers' methods of exerting power. In one scene, Hébert witnesses Marotte in the camp when she strikes the white captive Hélène for ruining a chemise while laundering it, "weakly, meaning to shame her more than to do real physical hurt" (Bell 248). The doctor realizes that "these [a]re the caprices of Madame [Claudine] Arnaud which Marotte [i]s reenacting, as [i]s strictly natural, certainly—as chains of being bound her to do" (248). This "impersonal" act of violence between women belonging to different racialized class positions—here reversed in the camp—reveals, along with numerous other examples, the way such violence perpetuates social control. Likewise, self-emancipated people marching under the leadership of Jeannot carry the banner of impaled infants before them. As Riau reflects, "I knew this was a thing the whitemen had done before," which signals how the grotesque violence of enslavers dictates the ways self-emancipated people attempt to achieve power in the novel (176).

The doctor realizes what is at stake in the revolution when he witnesses Choufleur, a mixed-race man, skinning his white father alive: "he was seeing what it meant to be human" and "who, in the final analysis, would be allowed to be one" (237). Toward the end of the novel, Riau understands that Toussaint changes his troops' tactics (away from sadistic acts of torture and murder) because he does "not want [them] to go to be with the dead any longer"; he does not want them to be caught in the spiraling performance of sadistic violence (376). Claudine, though, is still "with the dead" because this plantation society will not acknowledge her reality. Claudine is cloistered with Les Ursulines in Le Cap when self-emancipated people invade and destroy the city in 1793. Years after her act of violence against Mouche, Claudine has internalized the scene, and her posturing reflects her inner conflict: "She stood on tiptoe, her head thrown back and to one side, resting on her collarbone, bare scorched breasts lifting and her muscles strained as if she were depending from a hook somewhere above her. Arnaud recognized her posture but without knowing why" (493–94). Arnaud, arriving to save his estranged wife, neatly demonstrates what has so haunted Claudine: he does not recognize her stance as that of the murdered Mouche, whom he believed was killed by the Maroon forces when they ransacked the plantation. The enslaver class in the novel, then, always overlooks Claudine because of her gendered position. Despite her attempts to assert her agency via instruments of torture and her body, she has no place in this society because white men do not recognize her actions, due to her gender. Moreover, Claudine's scene of violence departs from the women who enslave in chapter 1; Claudine wavers between identifying with Mouche—especially after skin-on-skin touch—and wanting to force Mouche to conform to a subjugated position as Other. This glimpse of intimacy between women amid horrific violence makes Bell's novel noteworthy, for Claudine cannot attain a stable subject-position through this violence.

In Jamaican novelist Marlon James's *The Book of Night Women*, these tropes of sadistic violence—the effects of "living within the sword" in Gayl Jones's poem—expand to Jamaican plantation society. Like *All Souls' Rising*, James's *Night Women* depicts white enslavers participating in sadistic actions normalized by law. Trevor Burnard and John Garrigus likewise draw a historical comparison between Jamaica and Saint-Domingue, as both colonial cultures practiced the de facto lawfulness of enslavers' violence: "There were effectively no constraints in Jamaica limiting slave owners' behavior toward enslaved people. Saint-Domingue, in contrast, had a comprehensive slave law, the Code Noir of 1685, which theoretically governed relations between slaves and masters in the French colonies. In practice, however, the Code Noir was rarely used to punish masters. Throughout the eighteenth century Saint-Domingue's planters claimed the right to control and punish slaves as they saw fit. In many ways, the attitudes and claims of Saint-Domingue's planters resembled those of their Jamaican counterparts" (17). James's novel pays special attention to how women internalize these violent social norms, adding an imaginative companion piece to Christine Walker's historical study *Jamaica Ladies*, which "explores how the gendered dimensions of female slaveholding—its small-scale and intimate nature—shaped the lives of enslaved people in ways that are not well understood" (21). In

Night Women, the young white Creole woman Isobel and her mother, Mistress Roget, rely on the sadistic use of torture instruments to maintain "control" over enslaved people. Moreover, the novel explores how the young mixed-race woman Lilith learns what it means to wield such power, as Lilith forgoes using instruments of torture (such as a whip or knife) to employ her body as a weapon against her enslavers. Through her embodiment, she realizes what it means to have power to destroy—thus, to have power to make her self in this culture.

The Book of Night Women appears in a genealogy of resistance narratives that shows how, in Fanon's words, colonial and decolonial violence "balance each other and respond to each other in an extraordinary reciprocal homogeneity" (88). From the enslaved women who would covertly use poison against their enslavers in C. L. R. James's groundbreaking work *The Black Jacobins* (16) to women who enact more direct physical insurrection, resistance from enslaved women represents a wide spectrum of actions in circum-Caribbean texts. The fin de siècle U.S. novel of manners *Iola Leroy* by Frances E. W. Harper (1892), for example, does not avoid depictions of enslaved women performing retaliatory violence. As told by Aunt Linda (a woman who was formerly enslaved), a mother was sold away from her son because she struck back during a whipping by Miss Nancy, her enslaver. According to Aunt Linda, Miss Nancy constantly whipped enslaved people and sold at least one mother away from her child (159). The story evinces the enslaved woman's strength and individuality: she stands up to Miss Nancy to prevent her enslaver from whipping her. In doing so, the enslaved woman made her enslaver afraid of her. Likewise, Sherley Anne Williams's novel *Dessa Rose* (1986) reveals white people's fears of an enslaved woman who physically lashed out against a woman who enslaved her. While a white man who wishes to write an account of her crime interviews her, Dessa's mind keeps replaying the scene of near-murder, and she wishes her actions had been successful (58–59). This radical trope of physical violence is evident even in some nineteenth-century slave narratives. For example, DoVeanna S. Fulton's *Speaking Power* frames the slave narrative *Sylvia Dubois* (1883) in terms of Sylvia's "unprecedented" use of violent touch to retaliate against her enslaver, Mrs. Dubois (53). Complicating Elaine Scarry's theories of torture, Fulton claims that the enslaver "using her hand" against Sylvia "removes the mediating device Scarry discusses and changes the torturer/prisoner relationship. Mrs. Dubois's hand personalizes the abuse and Sylvia responds in kind" (53). I build on Fulton's argument to assert that narratives that feature such violent touch between women leave more room for identification with

58 CHAPTER TWO

the other woman, whether Black or white, than works that feature women using instruments of torture. *The Book of Night Women* explores this very complexity of relationships.

Born in 1785 on the Montpelier Estate in Jamaica, Lilith physically experiences violence from an early age. In James's novel, for example, Black women repeatedly strike Lilith because they deem her (in their words) "uppity" and "too spirited" when she does not understand that her actions are unacceptable to her gender, race, and class (4). However, the novel itself values Lilith's and other enslaved people's voices. Told through a third-person narrative style, the novel filters the events and the thoughts of enslaved characters through the speech cadences of patois, which—by its very writing style—upholds Lilith's resistant (and then defiant) voice. According to Machado Sáez, the novel's tone often "symbolizes the tension that James imagines between the objectives of his historical fiction and the demands of his audience, between the historical contextualization of the enslaved who have been erased from history and the commodification and decontextualization of such narratives within the book market" (113). To bridge these concerns, *Night Women* "imagines an economy of knowledge that situates the reader as a student seeking information from the narrator" (113), wherein the reader learns alongside Lilith what it means to try to carve out a "self" amid plantation violence. For instance, James's novel shows that when she was young, Lilith "couldn't understand when the wet nurse slap her and say that a good girl was supposed to make [white] manchild win," and after this "Lilith cuss and ask if manchild can't win if girl don't lose and she get another slap" (M. James 4). This exchange foretells Lilith's strength and individuality as a young woman, but it also marks the beginning of a long string of repeated, and unheeded, lessons at the hands of women about her place in society. Early in the novel, Homer, an enslaved woman who runs the household, slaps Lilith's face when she does not understand that a young white girl has outgrown her attentions as a playmate (6). Yet, no one bothers to explain to Lilith why she receives these violent reactions from others. Many enslaved people accept the caste system on the plantation as natural, although they have learned and internalized it, and they deem Lilith's initial ignorance of the system unnatural, merely worthy of a slap or two to correct her deviant nature.

The young Lilith, however, does not accept her social position (to be taken at will by men), and she murders a Johnny-jumper (a Black slave driver) because he attempts to rape her. Lilith's inner monologue tells of her strength, as she cuts the Johnny-jumper to pieces with his own machete: "That was the first time she feel the darkness. True darkness and true womanness that make man scream. She shudder and she feel 'fraid and proud and wicked and she feel good. So good so that she get more 'fraid" (16). Lilith's power, made evident through violent action, shows early in the novel that she is at odds with the status quo, which her adopted mother, Circe, voices: Lilith is "too spirited" (18). To Circe, the Johnny-jumper "was just goin' cut [Lilith] down a notch. Get rid of that damn pride. She just a nigger girl" (18). In the face of multiple threats of violence, Lilith begins to "live within the sword," like Gayl Jones's "machete woman," a subject-position necessitated by her drive to survive in an environment that intends her bodily harm at every turn.

Rejected by her adopted mother and ignorant of how she should act in her social position, Lilith struggles to reconcile what she believes is her due—a privileged position in the household because of her lightly colored eyes—and what physical violence tells her body. The narrator explains the complex rankings of enslaved people on a plantation, based on color and labor: "Truth be told, slaves in Jamaica have more ranking among themself than massa. In this place two thing matter more than most, how dark a nigger you be and where the white man choose to put you. One have all to do with the other" (32). When Homer brings Lilith into the kitchen to work inside the house after she murders the driver, Lilith interprets this as her innate specialness for her skin and eye color. She thereby fantasizes about what the owner of the plantation, "Massa" Humphrey, could do for her: "There be two things that a white man can do at once. A white man can save her from the Johnny-jumpers and put her above other negrowomens. A white man like Massa Humphrey can also take her and hold her with [a] gentle hand" (80). Evident here and elsewhere, such as when Lilith physically attacks Andromeda, a young enslaved woman, in the kitchen and then has her poisoned so she can serve at the plantation's ball (46–47), Lilith has internalized the hierarchical system of the plantation and lacks the critical lens to scrutinize it. To learn her place, however, means almost total destruction.

Although a sense of guilt haunts Lilith because her desire to supplant Andromeda resulted in her death, the prospect of catching Humphrey's eye at the ball overshadows these feelings. Nevertheless, the young white Creole woman Isobel's entrance into the story (when she plans the ball) portends a violent fate for Lilith's aspirations to rise above her place in the kitchen. Isobel relishes the punishments of enslaved people, and she has learned torture's necessity to keeping order. When people find Andromeda dead from what they believe is "the flux," Isobel steps in to boldly declare that she died from "Obeah" worked against her, and that the solution is to "make [the whites'] own Obeah seem greater" than that of enslaved people (112). Here, Isobel attempts to increase her power through appropriating Obeah, African diasporic cultural and folk beliefs and practices that include a justice-making ethos for enslaved persons. To use these beliefs to the enslavers' advantage, Humphrey employs Isobel's suggestion to place candles within eyesight of enslaved people who labor in the fields, and they order any enslaved person who attempts to put out the flame (for fear of spells worked on them) to be tortured and murdered as a lesson to others. Isobel chooses to "watch the whole thing from the terrace even after Massa Humphrey say he had seen enough" (115), which shows that she unabashedly savors such punishment. Unlike Mistress Epps, who seems reserved about her role in plantation violence when she initially spies on Patsey in *12 Years a Slave*, Isobel seems primed to seek enjoyment in colonial Jamaica's system of enslavement. The society's penchant for sadistic violence spills out of Isobel during these scenes of torture.

Despite Lilith's imaginings that the ball will elevate her standing, events solidify her social position as an enslaved woman. Already accustomed to brutality in disciplining Humphrey's slaves, Isobel dictates Lilith's punishment when Lilith accidentally spills hot soup on Isobel's chaperone. Once the mechanisms of power have been set into motion, there is no room for compassion or understanding, as Lilith discovers when several white drivers severely beat and rape her as the first stage of punishment. Much like Claudine's final interaction with Mouche in *All Souls' Rising*, punishment knows no bounds; thus, drivers whip Lilith regularly, merely to keep reminding her of her subordinate social position whenever Isobel calls on Humphrey.

Knowing that even the most severe beatings will not break Lilith's spirit, Isobel arranges to send Lilith to her family's plantation, Coulibre, where Isobel's mother "will teach her some social graces" (176).[5] Ironically, Isobel tells Lilith, "I shall make a little lady of you," though "lady" is a social position beyond Lilith's racialized class (176). Here, Isobel infers that Lilith is too dangerous to be around Humphrey until she has been broken. Because Lilith "failed" to catch Humphrey's eye, "it will be [Isobel's] task to remind [her] of that failure. And of [her] place" (177). Isobel continues this speech by saying that Lilith "will be [Isobel's] shadow" because she has "decided to keep [Lilith] closer than a brother. Very close" (177). Isobel thereby takes the initiative to ensure Lilith will never be a sexual temptation for Humphrey. In doing so, Isobel hopes to secure her own position within his household; as a white woman, she has little social power unless she is married into the plantation. The historian Barbara Bush's findings about white women in the context of British Caribbean plantations are relevant to Isobel's position in the novel, for even if she does marry well, "in this matrix of power, where patriarchal structures intermesh . . . with basic economic structures of labor exploitation, the position of white women [i]s ambiguous" (194). Isobel's subordination is increasingly apparent in *Night Women*, for her social position becomes entirely unmoored after her family perishes in a fire and Humphrey refuses to marry her. The context for Isobel's actions is consequently made clear, for her unstable social position mirrors that of Blanche in *Mandingo* and Claudine in *All Souls' Rising*. Moreover, in this narrative, the reader sees the genealogy of sadism through Isobel's mother, Mistress Roget.

Lilith's compulsory movement to the plantation Coulibre emphasizes a continuum of violence in circum-Caribbean texts. Unlike in many texts previously discussed in *Grotesque Touch*, Mistress Roget has strict control over the punishment of enslaved people. In an extended scene in which Lilith details the torture and murder of fellow enslaved woman Dulcimena (for leaving a goat pen open), Mistress Roget actively participates in the sadistic violence of torture, and she "wield[s] the cart whip herself . . . as hard as she c[an] flog" (199–200). When the enslaver tires, the whip passes to enslaved people's hands; torture relies on forcing enslaved people to enact violence against each other, as in *12 Years a Slave*. *Night Women* mediates this violence through Lilith's perspective, though, as the violence of the white Creoles does not go unanswered.

While Lilith's time at Coulibre—her so-called seasoning—could make her numb to daily plantation violence (such as Dulcimena's torture and death), Lilith develops the desire to enact her own violence against her oppressors. Immediately following the murder of Dulcimena, visions of torturing and mutilating white flesh consume Lilith's mind. The strength—"spiritedness"— Lilith has always known becomes an all-encompassing hatred: "Lilith start to imagine what white flesh look like after a whipping. What white neck look like after a hanging and what kinda scar leave on a white body after black punishment. She think of the little Roget boy, Master Henri, of tying and hanging the boy up by him little balls and chopping him head off. She make the thoughts of white blood work into a fever" (200). Even before Lilith enacts violence against the Rogets, her imagined violence against them sets this narrative apart from others in *Grotesque Touch* because Lilith seems consumed by "liv[ing] within the sword / within rage and outrage," like the "machete woman" in Gayl Jones's poem (50). When the family inflicts violence on her body once Humphrey gives them permission to whip her, Lilith tips over the edge to act on her impulse (M. James 206). The narrative describes this violence against Lilith (done ostensibly for her own good to eradicate "disturbing spiritedness that must be tamed") in terms of the sadistic torture already evident in the family's treatment of Dulcimena: "Lilith get whip and hit so much that she could tell just from the sound what a nigger was getting beaten with. . . . Lilith know the difference between the smart of the rope, cowskin, cart whip, bullwhip, slap with wedding-ring finger, punch, box, and hot tea throw on her dress" (206). As is to be expected in this narrative, "most of the whipping, pinching, hiding, scraping, cutting, thumping and punching Mistress Roget do herself," even though she has recently given birth (206). This depiction of violence on a plantation reveals that the enslaver not only considers brutally beating her enslaved property as an obligation, but she relishes these interactions as well. In this way, *The Book of Night Women* reimagines narratives such as Mary Prince's depictions of slavery in Bermuda in *The History of Mary Prince* (1831). Prince likewise catalogues how the woman who enslaved her "caused [her] to know the exact difference between the smart of the rope, the cart-whip, and the cow-skin, when applied to [her] naked body by [the enslaver's] own cruel hand" (14). Moreover, whether Mistress Roget mediates violence against Lilith with an instrument of torture or carries out violence with the briefest flesh-to-flesh touch, she means this violence to convey a sense of their permanent separation via racialized class. Though, in this reimagining of commonplace violence between women on plantations (as in Prince's account), the enslaved woman inflicts her own physical violence in retaliation.

Lilith's thoughts of vengeance against the Rogets follow suit: visions of "fire," "darkness," and so much "blood spraying and flesh tearing" crowd her mind so that she cannot sleep (M. James 206). Once she visits Homer and the older woman finally confides in Lilith about her own history of losing her children to the auction block, receiving "the worst whipping ever in Montpelier," and then experiencing a loss of identity, Lilith springs to action (216). Although Lilith premeditates her retaliatory violence during her obsessive thinking, her actions still take her by surprise. Lilith's use of her own body as an instrument of retribution shows how she has internalized the violent society around her; according to Sam Vásquez, this society has made her body "become . . . a political site of cultural memory for the violence and sexual abuse she suffers and negotiates" (52). As such, she fully embodies Gayl Jones's "machete woman." In James's novel, Lilith turns to action, and the narrative shows how only physical violence can make Master Roget "look . . . at her with black man fear on him face" as she holds him under water to drown him during his bath (M. James 223).

Now that she has murdered the head of the plantation household, Lilith believes she knows what the dark apparitional woman who appears to her wants: "Blood. The woman want blood" (224). Just as Claudine and Isobel commit acts of torture against enslaved people that seem to follow a script, so do Lilith's actions of revenge play out. When Lilith notices Mistress Roget at the door witnessing the drowning, Lilith chases the screaming woman down: "Lilith catch up to Mistress Roget by the stair balcony and push her hard. Matraca [the family's enslaved nursemaid] coming up the stairs and scream. Two scream, but Mistress Roget's scream get cut when she burst over the wood balcony and fall to the marble floor and crunch her neck. Blood spread from under her back like two red wing" (224). Shoving the woman with her hands—the same hands that just drowned Master Roget—and then burning the house down (with the Roget family's children locked in the nursery with Matraca), Lilith shows how her body is a weapon seasoned by the lessons of her enslavement. Moreover, her body proves to be capable of bringing down the Coulibre plantation and the family it sustains.

As Lilith flees the plantation house, however, the fire she set almost claims her as well, which symbolizes the perils of retaliatory violence: "She run down the rest of the stairs and trip and fall to the floor and get up to find her shoulder and chest soak with the mistress' blood. The fire coming after her, hopping down from step to step like a impudent pickney. Lilith run" (225). This image of Lilith soaked in the enslaver's blood and fleeing the fire essentially frames the novel's conclusion. By acting on the violence that her body learned from enslavement, Lilith understands that violence marks all and destroys all, utterly. Lilith subsequently discovers that her remarkable sense of self and the bodily harm she inflicts on her socially sanctioned superiors caught Homer's eye; because of this, the main portion of the novel depicts Homer attempting to include Lilith in her plans for insurrection. Yet, what Lilith discovers through her violent actions against the driver (with a machete) and the Roget family (with her hands) is that violence against others does not help her realize her true self. At this point, like Jones's "machete woman," she begins to live "beyond the sword" and "contemplate horror" in her actions, which reflect enslavers' violence (G. Jones 50). Lilith knows that if this internal flame is actually "true darkness and true womanness that make a man scream, . . . then she don't want it no more. Mayhaps true womanness was to be free to be as terrible as you wish. Like a white woman" (M. James 236). Lilith arguably acted against these social superiors to cling to her sense of self, the kind of legitimate self-formation Nesbitt posits "redeem[ed] the violence of those subject to slavery and torture *for them as subjects*" (215, emphasis in original). However, Lilith's own thoughts reiterate that the violence she has relished makes her more like the white woman Isobel than Lilith would like.

Making this point clear, the narrative increasingly features Isobel's ramblings and threats of violence after her family dies. Suspecting Lilith of the violence against her parents and siblings, Isobel says, "I wish I had the bare hands to choke you or a knife to cut your tongue out. I wish I wasn't a lady or a woman, but a nigger like you," and she asks, "Can you imagine that? Can you imagine me envying a wretched nigger like you?" (M. James 235). Despite the enslaver-class woman's cries of difference based on racialized gender stereotypes, the narrative has already proven Isobel's participation in the compensatory, sadistic torture of enslaved people. Isobel's insistence of her difference from Lilith is most likely a response to the cultural belief that people of color influenced whites' degeneration in the Caribbean.[6] As Omise'eke Natasha Tinsley claims in *Thiefing Sugar*, "white women's emulation of nonwhites troubled many observers" in the Caribbean as early as the eighteenth century (81). Still, Lilith sees her own retaliatory actions as mirroring Isobel's and the enslaver class's violence. Isobel invites the comparison repeatedly, as she later calls both herself and Lilith "colonial creatures" (M. James 299). Lilith is thereby trapped between two realities: either she lives as her own person or she will always be caught up in performing the cycles of plantation violence, which she perceives in Isobel's character.

James's novel evinces how retaliatory violence enacted by enslaved people can spiral out of the plantation's wellspring of sadism. Because of this realization, Lilith is reluctant to join the enslaved women who plan a violent insurrection on the Montpelier plantation. These women, led by Homer, are responsible for the deaths of other enslaved women, mostly out of fear that they will reveal their plots, as the deaths of Lilith's adopted mother Circe and, later, Iphigenia show (293, 368). Lilith discovers from murdering the Roget family that "killing too easy. . . . Is like when you see what two hand can do, you just want to do more. It just come over you like anointing" (318). Lilith does not wish to enter the pact with the other enslaved women, "'cause [she] probably won't stop" killing once she starts (319). At stake for Homer and Lilith are their very selves. Homer asks Lilith, "You think you is woman?" Not wishing to participate further in plantation violence, Lilith asserts to Homer, "Me think me is Lilith" (341). Consequently, the novel shows Lilith claiming an identity of her own—even though she is pulled in various directions because she feels a sense of loyalty to her fellow enslaved women and her new lover, the white overseer. At the same time, Homer's sense of self slips away.

During the insurrection on Montpelier, then, Lilith acts to preserve her self, while Homer and other enslaved people lose themselves in the battle because revenge motivates them. Homer, for example, enters her elderly enslaver's door and says, "Me goin' deal with you special" (393). She carries a personal vendetta against her enslaver—Humphrey's mother—for allowing men to rape her repeatedly and then selling her children "just 'cause [she] don't want [Homer] to have or love nothing but [her]" (392). Homer goes about torturing her elderly and disoriented enslaver to the extent that she can hardly stand up: "The mistress face punch up and bloody. Homer swinging wild and for a instant the two women looking like they holding each other up" (395). While the women's momentary postures suggest the intimacy of their relationship, theirs is a false closeness that has always relied on violence, which reflects the twisted sense of intimacy Colin Dayan identifies in slavery during the Enlightenment. Furthermore, Homer's violence is siphoned and then exhausted as she strikes out against her enslaver; she acts out of a desire for personal retaliation instead of contributing to a larger effort that might bring down the plantation system. This point is reminiscent of Kara Keeling's criticisms of the film *Sankofa* (1993) for constructing an enslaved woman's individual retaliatory violence against her enslaver's sexual abuse in such a way that it "implies that such [sexual] violence is individuated, rather than systemic, and even sanctioned by [the enslaved woman] Shola herself, because, until she (finally) fights back . . . , she tolerates rather than resists being raped" (Keeling 65). Homer's actions against her enslaver are likewise individuated, and the enslaved woman seems to merely endure the oppressions of enslavement until she acts out—against this one enslaver. The novel thereby posits that this violence, focused on a single person, is not the violence of revolution, which "remain[s] open to new ideas and echoes from the world outside" (Fanon 70). Homer's violence reflects that of the plantation system, now performed via her acts of sadistic torture.

When the insurrection ends as troops arrive, Homer has only tortured and murdered Humphrey's mother, and the other remaining rebels are placed inside cages dangling from trees (M. James 408). If James's novel suggests that this particular insurrection is a waste because of its limited focus on revenge (both against enslaved people and enslavers), then what methods lead to freedom? Having survived by not participating in the insurrection, Lilith lives to teach her own daughter—born from her (coerced) union with the white overseer — to write. *Night Women* offers a possible answer in its final chapter: Lilith's daughter Lovey Quinn has written this entire book from her mother's recollections. In the end, it is "time to give account of the league of women" (412), and Lovey summarizes the stories of each enslaved woman in the novel: "Homer didn't die by gunfire at the mistress window. Homer die the day she get word 'bout her pickneys. . . . Then [her enslaver] grow to need Homer and hate her even more. There was a quilt of scar on Homer back too and some of that the mistress leave herself. But Homer bide her time. Homer watch, Homer wait and Homer plot" (415). Remembering the women of Montpelier is Lovey's task. She asks, "What can me do but tell the story?" (416). She answers, "For somebody must give account of the night women of Montpelier. Of slavery, the black woman misery and black man too. And me goin' sing the song and me mother goin' sing it. . . . We goin' sing once, then no more" (416). Giving voice to the enslaved women of Montpelier proves to be the novel's main task, but Lovey's words also echo the final section of Toni Morrison's *Beloved* (1987): "It was not a story to pass on" (323). By "singing once," Lovey hopes to voice the women's stories in such a way that ends the cycle of plantation violence. Upon its conclusion, the novel implies that violence cannot revolutionize a grotesque system through individuated, sadistic actions of revenge.

While Isobel's frequent contact with enslaved women might lead readers to hope that she eventually forms a bond with these women, her social position demands that she exert power over them. *Night Women* makes plain the necessity for these social divisions due to Isobel's unstable position as an unmarried white Creole woman. Likewise, the Dutch film *Hoe Duur Was de Suiker* shows how the social pressures, pleasures, and privileges of whiteness manifest for women who enslave in a Surinamese plantation context.[7] Director Jean Van de Velde's filmic adaptation of Cynthia McLeod's best-selling 1987 Dutch novel, which most literally translates into English as "How Costly Was the Sugar," is set in mid-1700s Suriname. Remarkably, the film adaptation shifts the novel's narrative to show "the cost of sugar" through an enslaved woman's perspective, as the film frequently features Mini-Mini's voiceovers about her life. The film depicts the complicated intimacies of a plantation household in Suriname: for example, the two main characters (the enslaver Sarith and enslaved woman Mini-Mini) are likely half-sisters. While the film forgoes any possibilities of a cross-racial bond between the women that would undo social hierarchies and barriers, it does not represent enslaved women as the "mules of the world," which is how *12 Years a Slave* depicts Patsey.[8] The film also avoids presenting Mini-Mini (played by Yootha

Wong-Loi-Sing) as the constant victim of Sarith's (Gaite Jansen) ire. Unlike the novel, which frequently mentions that Sarith strikes Mini-Mini so that "a twisted ear or a push in the back was almost the order of the day" (McLeod 96), the film complexly depicts touch, intimacy, and violence between women.[9] Furthermore, Mini-Mini's narrative voice connects Sarith's violence to the greater violence of circum-Caribbean plantation slavery, inherent to the sugar trade. In the end, however, the film abandons its more radical messages about women's intimacies and violence to enclose Mini-Mini in a loving relationship with a man who was her enslaver. While these narrative features allow Mini-Mini to "live beyond the sword" of plantation violence, the remainder of this chapter will explain how these elements create a deceptive narrative, politically conservative at its core.

Tellingly, the first scene depicts Mini-Mini as a child witnessing the whipping of an enslaved man in 1747, while the enslaver Rachael and her daughter Sarith look on. Rachael orders the whipping and demands that the enslaved man say, "Thank you, Misi"; at the same time, the young Sarith hides her face in Rachael's dress, which shows she is still inexperienced in the processes and pleasures of exerting power. In this and subsequent scenes, Mini-Mini implicitly frames the narrative of her life through her interactions with white women's violence. The audience discovers that Mini-Mini is writing the story of her life in Dutch, not the creolized language Sranan Tongo required of enslaved people at that time, and she continues by saying, "My story begins with a plantation." Therefore, her story begins with the violence enacted by a white woman on a plantation, and the film continues to show how white women influence Mini-Mini's understanding of her self, all while she tells this story via her appropriation of her enslavers' language.

Mini-Mini's narration continues while the audience witnesses scenes from her mother's life, such as when a white man (Rachael's husband) and his teenage son raped her mother, Kwasiba, when Kwasiba was fourteen years old. Mini-Mini is the product of this sexual abuse, and Kwasiba becomes the wet nurse for "Misi" Rachael's daughter, Sarith. Mini-Mini and Sarith thereby grow up together, and they share several childhood scenes, such as when they peer into the sickrooms of the young and older white men. The men's deaths lead Rachael to seek a new living situation on Hébron Plantation, where the Fernandez patriarch was left a widower. The film's focus thereby departs from the novel's, for the novel primarily shows Sarith's relationship with her white stepsister, Elza Fernandez. The film more consistently focuses on Mini-Mini and Sarith's relationship, as Mini-Mini repeatedly muses about "[her] Misi Sarith."

FIGURE 2.1 Gaite Jansen as Sarith and Yootha Wong-Loi-Sing as Mini-Mini in *Hoe Duur Was de Suiker* (Entertainment One, 2013).

Hoe Duur Was de Suiker uses more intimate images of white and Black women than any text I have described so far. For instance, early in the film Mini-Mini bathes Sarith while both women stand topless before a mirror in Sarith's bedroom (figure 2.1). While the customs of slavery in rural Suriname explain Mini-Mini's exposed chest—Rachael is reprimanded when the family travels to a township because she should "cover [her] slaves"—the intimacy of the moment is not lost on twenty-first-century audiences who see the two women reflected in the mirror. Despite the connection between them hinted at in the film, Sarith very willingly assumes the role of enslaver that replicates her mother's attitudes. She speaks harshly to Mini-Mini when she suggests that Sarith wear a different dress than she intended: "Are you so dumb?" Although Sarith in the film treats Mini-Mini with little outright violence—whereas in the novel she is constantly giving Mini-Mini a "thick ear" for minor irritations—Sarith still performs her role as enslaver.

As the narrative shifts to focus on Sarith's unhappy pursuit of marriage, the film muddles Mini-Mini's story and shows her enthusiastic attentions toward "her misi." Later, after Elza marries a Dutch newcomer to Suriname, and when Sarith realizes that her physical beauty will not easily grant her a marriage that she wants, Mini-Mini holds a large leaf over Sarith's head to protect her from the rain as Sarith sulks. Sarith openly cries on Mini-Mini's shoulder while she laments that everyone is marrying and leaving her alone. Then, when Sarith takes Mini-Mini with her into town to visit the newly married Elza and her Dutch husband, Rutger, Sarith gives Mini-Mini some perfume to charm Mini-Mini's love interest, Hendrick, an enslaved man. Yet, when Mini-Mini attempts to woo Hendrik, he tells her that he has been sold into the Dutch army that is in pursuit of Maroons in the jungles, and he levels an insult at her, "You stink of your misi." Hendrik's comment further highlights how this plantation regime transforms enslaved people into extensions of their enslavers, recalling Colin Dayan's discussion of enslavement as "a conceit or counterfeit of intimacy" (189). Furthermore, at this point in the film, Mini-Mini appears to embrace her position. During their stay, for example, Mini-Mini stands up to the enslaved people of Elza's household—though Sarith has seduced Elza's husband. Even after Elza has finally kicked Sarith out of the house, Mini-Mini laments Sarith's position. When Sarith must return to Hébron Plantation, Mini-Mini's voiceover says, "There is no man here. There is no love here," while the camera shows images of Sarith moping throughout the rainy season. When Mini-Mini says, "There's just me here," the audience sees another image of intimacy between the enslaver and enslaved woman as they lie in bed together. However, as with previous scenes in which Sarith and Mini-Mini appear to have a more open, caring relationship than that of an enslaver and an enslaved woman, the audience should realize that Mini-Mini's enslavement has conditioned her to make herself available to Sarith always, so that she is Sarith's only advocate.

Moreover, the film overshadows montages of fleeting closeness between the women when Sarith exercises her racialized class privilege. She does this most blatantly when she orders the whipping of Ashana, an older enslaved woman. In the film, Sarith is the only white person left on the plantation while her family visits Elza's newborn. She (like Blanche in *Mandingo* and Claudine in *All Souls'*) uses her position accordingly to appropriate the absent white man's power: she selects an enslaved teenager to bring to her room for her own sexual pleasure. Clearly, Ashana does not approve, and she spits within Sarith's eyesight to convey her disgust. The next morning, Sarith confronts Ashana about her behavior, asserting her right to sleep with enslaved men (her reasoning: white men often sleep with enslaved women). Sarith grips Ashana's chin, forcing her to make eye contact, insults Ashana, and shoves Mini-Mini away when she attempts to interfere. Ashana, however, stands up to Sarith, asserting, "My name is Ashana." As her enslaver's most beloved, Ashana has held a privileged position in the house (although even this "privilege" entails that she must massage his back constantly). Still, Ashana's status as property is evident here, as Sarith demands that she be strung up and whipped.

In this whipping scene, the film allows Mini-Mini to connect Sarith's violence to the plantation system's greater violence. Departing from the novel's depiction of this scene, the film does not feature Sarith lashing out at Mini-Mini with the whip for attempting to interfere (McLeod 128). Instead, when Mini-Mini briefly tries to persuade Sarith to allow the enslaved man who is whipping Ashana to stop, Sarith merely threatens to hit Mini-Mini, at which point Mini-Mini backs away. When the enslaved man says, "Please, misi," Sarith loudly orders, "Whip her!" as she emphatically motions toward Ashana. When the enslaved man continues to whip Ashana, Mini-Mini's voiceover begins again, and the film intercuts images of Mini-Mini writing with the scene of torture. Mini-Mini says about Ashana, "I've learned to write her name," meaning that she will use her newfound literacy to record Ashana's life, and she continues to talk about Ashana's children who have also died due to the injustices of slavery. Mini-Mini speaks as the images of Ashana's children end and images of enslaved people working in a sugarcane field appear: "One day I shall write the names, of all the slaves. One day I'll write what the price of sugar was." At this moment, the film shows an enslaved man when a sugarcane press catches his hand. The machinery crushes his hand, and an overseer chops off his arm, while his spilt blood flows along with the sugary liquid (figure 2.2), a visual that invokes what Gert Oostindie and Alex Van Stipriaan call Suriname's "hydraulic slavery" (81). When Mini-Mini says, "One day I will write who paid the price of sugar," the camera cuts back to the whipping scene, focusing on blood-spotted leaves under Ashana's lifeless body. Mini-Mini articulates the film's titular "cost of sugar," the incalculable waste of the blood and lives of enslaved peoples, a trope repeated throughout this chapter. Yet, Mini-Mini can reflect in this scene because the film avoids having Sarith make her into a victim of her enslaver's—and the larger system's—sadistic violence. This scene, unlike the novel, privileges Mini-Mini's point of view because the film effectively spares her from victimization: *she* alone has the power to name Ashana and the countless others who have lost their lives to plantation slavery. She, after all, was distant enough from the violence inflicted on Ashana's body to reflect on its larger significance.

At this point, however, the film shifts back to Sarith's experiences to reveal that she suffers from her appropriation of white men's power. After this scene, Sarith—much like Blanche in *Mandingo*—has a sharp social downfall when her stepfather returns and orders her to leave his plantation. Though Sarith's stepfather does not know about her sexual license with his enslaved property—which was "regarded a heinous crime by the larger society," according to Aviva

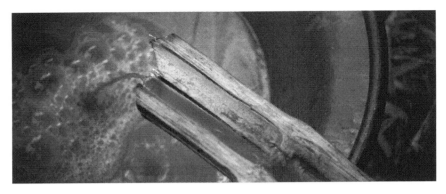

FIGURE 2.2 An enslaved man's blood runs into extracted sugar; Ashana's blood drops onto leaves below her body (Entertainment One, 2013).

Ben-Ur (156)—he banishes her for killing his beloved property, Ashana. While her mother insists that Sarith "has the right to punish a slave," and Sarith says she "demand[s] respect," her stepfather is still the most powerful person on the plantation. Indeed, he considers that she is "less than a Black mistress," meaning that she deserves fewer allowances than enslaved women who have sexual relationships with their enslavers. Sarith, realizing that she must marry to have any access to the upper-class lifestyle to which she is accustomed, marries the older enslaver Julius Robles Medina and continues to live extravagantly in town, away from his plantation. When Julius learns that Sarith's son Jethro was fathered by another man, he seeks solace in Mini-Mini, who has taken a backseat to Sarith's story. Counter to Mini-Mini's earlier reflections about Sarith's actions against Ashana, Mini-Mini still believes, "My misi is all there is." To this, Julius replies, "You're too good for your misi." With these words, Julius—an enslaver—begins a romance with Mini-Mini, and he teaches her to read and write Dutch, which confirms Sarith's social downfall.

Mini-Mini, accepting her role as Julius's lover with apparent enthusiasm, rejects Hendrik, now a member of a group of Maroon men who invade the Medina plantation. The film, therefore, shows Mini-Mini aligning herself with the enslaver class—even when she has the chance to join violent forces against them—because she identifies more with her enslavers. Additionally, the film portrays Hendrik as a self-emancipated man who has lost his way, pillaging and murdering enslavers but also attempting to rape young enslaved women. The film thereby casts aside Mini-Mini's potential for violent insurrection to then romanticize her relationship with an enslaver. When Sarith appears at the plantation after a prolonged absence and sees Mini-Mini wearing one of her blouses, she understands that Mini-Mini and Julius are now lovers. Sarith, though, still owns Mini-Mini and in a resulting chain of events has Mini-Mini kidnapped and sold in town. After Julius's frantic search for Mini-Mini, he purchases her for himself so they can continue their idealistic partnership.

In the film, Julius soon frees Mini-Mini, and the final scenes of the film reassert her voice while she writes in Dutch, "I am Mini-Mini." Having apparently achieved her desires through domesticity, Mini-Mini lives a quiet life with Julius and their children in a small house on the edge of a township that borders a sugarcane field.[10] Adopting a consolatory tone, Sarith appears at the house and says to Mini-Mini that Jethro "couldn't have had a better mother," and continues, "I couldn't have had a better friend. I'm sorry." The film significantly changes this scene, for the novel features a similar exchange between Sarith and her white stepsister, Elza, while the two women walk hand-in-hand (McLeod 290). Here, Mini-Mini (instead of Elza) tells Sarith the final lines of the film: "I can't forgive you. You will have to do that yourself." The conversation, however, only *seems* to empower Mini-Mini. This idealized ending—in which a formerly enslaved woman rejects a woman who enslaved her—merely withdraws from a systemic critique. Mini-Mini's freedom from plantation violence comes at a price not explicitly acknowledged in the film: Mini-Mini must live with her former enslaver in a house just on the edge of a sprawling cane field. The final shot of the film hints at the fact that Mini-Mini can escape Sarith but not the plantation, for Sarith returns to her carriage and rides off with another enslaved woman jogging beside her. While the camera shows the carriage moving into the distance, the neighboring cane field gradually takes up half of the screen.

The film *Hoe Duur Was de Suiker* provides a challenging narrative to consider in the context of circum-Caribbean plantation violence. The film characterizes a woman as an enslaver in a historically contextualized manner: she forgoes aligning herself with enslaved women to inflict violence on their bodies while she seeks power and pleasure on the plantation. The film also remarkably privileges the perspective of an enslaved woman. At the end of the film, Mini-Mini's declaration in writing, "I am Mini-Mini," in some ways echoes Lilith's assertion, "Me think me is Lilith," in *Night Women*. While Mini-Mini does not physically enact violence in the film, both women's narratives end with a sense of their developing "an agency," in Jenny Sharpe's terms, that is in opposition to the sadistic violence perpetuated by white women (xxv). Lilith and Mini-Mini, in other words, choose to live "beyond the sword," like the "machete woman" in Gayl Jones's poem (50). Still, despite *Hoe Duur Was de Suiker*'s focus on Mini-Mini's voice and implied agency gained through writing in Dutch, her emancipation entails that she must continue living with a former enslaver on the edge of a plantation.[11] While she eschews sadistic plantation violence, Mini-Mini cannot fully escape involvement in the racist, classist, and sexist norms of this society. Indeed, the only way that her former enslaver would be able to afford such a lifestyle is if he sold (and did not emancipate) his enslaved property. Although the film leaves open a space for audiences to consider Sarith's continued participation in the oppressive systems of enslavement, the film's ending undercuts Mini-Mini's sense of agency. While Mini-Mini can assert her voice—and thereby claim a sense of self—the film further entrenches her in her (former) enslaver's family.[12]

Hoe Duur Was de Suiker thereby features more scenes of (supposedly) mutual intimacies on plantation settings than any text I have discussed thus far, but the film's insistence that Mini-Mini avoid physical violence in order to align with enslavers forgoes the sense of revolutionary urgency in *All Souls' Rising* and *The Book of Night Women*. The film typifies the seductive appeal of narratives that depict (allegedly) mutual interracial intimacies inside the plantation household, for Mini-Mini seems content to live near other plantations with her former enslaver. *Hoe Duur Was de Suiker* disrupts the scripts of sadism evident in *All Souls' Rising* and *The Book of Night Women*, yet the film also falls into another pattern: the film is a romantic fantasy of interracial intimacy. As such, the film shows us more about present-day audience desire than the desires and aspirations of women who were enslaved. As chapter 3 will articulate, some texts subvert this narrative frame to show white women as sexual predators, as they inflict intimate violence on the bodies of Black women to claim agency on and beyond plantation settings.

CHAPTER THREE
Un-Silencing Sexual Violence

The silence answered for her.

—ANN ALLEN SHOCKLEY, *The Black and White of It*, 125

This chapter begins where it ends, with the final line of Ann Allen Shockley's story "Women in a Southern Time," because silence rings loudly in fictional representations of sexual assault between women here and in broader cultural discourses about sexual violence.[1] For instance, a person's silence during a sexual assault could be construed as the person's consent to the acts. In the eyes of the law in many societies, whether a person actively resisted the assault frequently determines their victimhood: Did they repeatedly say "no" with words? Did they say "no" but really mean "yes" with other words or gestures? And if the person said nothing verbally, does this silence not mean "yes" by default? Historically and in our contemporary moment, these questions resurface in sexual assault cases, their repetitions revictimizing survivors of violence to the extent that untold numbers of survivors do not speak out in the first place.[2] This is one reason why data about sexual violence provide an incomplete picture—the systems at work (perhaps especially *the law*) interrogate survivors of sexual violence with enough aggressive suspicion to silence them.[3] Furthermore, as anticolonial scholars and activists repeatedly bring to our attention, the discourse of *consent* is a colonizing form, and the practice of rape is a hallmark of colonial projects.[4] Some people's words thereby count more than others', as issues of race, nationality, gender, sexuality, skin tone, ability, and class combine to silence the testimonies of many survivors of sexual violence due to their social standing.

While the types of silencing I mention above happen to varying degrees when the perpetrator of sexual violence is a cis man and the victim is a cis woman, any other permutation of perpetrator and victim (cis man on cis man, cis man on trans woman, cis woman on cis man, cis woman on cis woman, etc.) is commonly dismissed to the point of silencing.[5] This is because reductionist thinking leads to assumptions about whose voices matter. This line of thinking holds that because the greatest number of survivors of sexual violence are cis women and the greatest number of perpetrators are cis men, then focusing on other permutations of sexual assault (at best) diffuses the conversation and allocation of resources or (at worst) falls into the politically conservative trap of believing that people who identify as LGBTQ+ are always already violent.[6] Wading into the discourse about sexual violence between cis women requires acknowledging all these ways survivors' voices are silenced, by perpetrators, by the law, and by social structures.

These cultural frames that silence survivors of sexual violence come to bear on the fictional texts in this chapter; each text employs some form of silencing to illustrate how white women attain and enact their power via sexual violence against Black women. By setting their narratives in antebellum U.S. contexts, the miniseries *Roots* (2016), novel *Property* (Valerie Martin 2003), and short story "The Mistress and the Slave Girl" (Ann Allen Shockley 1987) demonstrate how thoroughly corruptible the intersections of desire and power are when they intertwine with racialized sexual economies. Then, Shockley's story "Women in a Southern Time" (1987) reveals how the enduring legacies of slavery likewise affect women's same-sex desires in a post-emancipation Jim Crow setting. Just as chapter 1 traces a continuum from salacious to contextualized depictions of violence between women on plantation settings, so does this chapter make clear that representations of sexual violence between women appear on a continuum. Indeed, as chapter 1 argues, pulp novel cover artwork characterizes white women's violent actions as sexually deviant to lure readers—and certainly that would appear on the continuum. Here, I will examine how audiovisual and written texts depict sexual violence between women, ranging from suggestions of that violence to descriptions of violent acts.

Due to the level of contextualization necessary to discuss sexual violence between women on and beyond plantation settings, this chapter primarily focuses on cultural contexts in one nation, the United States. This is not to say that narratives depicting sexual violence between women in various plantation cultures do not exist. For example, the character Ursa in Gayl Jones's *Corregidora* (1975) knows about her Great Gram's experiences of sexual violence at the hands of a man and a woman who enslave her in Brazil: "I thought of the girl who had to sleep with her master and mistress. Her father, the master" (67). Moreover, as Jennifer L. Morgan shows in *Laboring Women*, "Women's work and women's bodies are inseparable from the landscape of colonial slavery" because "their reproductive lives were at the heart of the entire venture of racial slavery" (3, 4). Slavery was a system that regulated enslaved women's reproductive bodies; moreover, it was a system that granted both men and women power as enslavers *through* their control over women's bodies. For example, in dealing with the context of slavery in Bridgetown,

Barbados, Marisa J. Fuentes's *Dispossessed Lives* makes clear how "white women were intricately and intimately enmeshed within the sexual relations of slavery" because "the notion of honor, linked to white women's sexuality, was connected to both perceptions and expectations of their virtue and their ability to commodify another's sexuality" (69, 79). In Barbados, white women "accumulated sexual and racial power through the exchange of enslaved women's bodies and passed this power onto their relatives" (79). We should not be surprised, then, when narratives show women who enslave attempting to claim control of their own identities by inflicting sexual violence on enslaved women.

I thereby examine how each text (a television show, a novel, and two short stories) contextualizes the threat or act of violence at the intersection of race, gender, and sexuality on and beyond U.S. plantation settings. In doing so, this chapter shows how the texts filter sexual violence between women, from suggested taboo that is never acted upon (*Roots*) to action told through a first-person, enslaver-class lens (*Property*) and third-person narrative techniques that simultaneously convey and limit the perspectives of perpetrator and victim ("The Mistress and the Slave Girl"; "Women in a Southern Time"). The silences of these texts speak loudly here, for reading between the lines — decoding what is said and inferring what is not — urges us to address difficult questions about desire, gender, intimacy, and violence. While sexual touch could be understood as the most intimate of touches between women, the texts in this chapter reveal that white women are so embedded in their society that their (supposed) acts of social rebellion expressly rely on sexually abusing Black women. This chapter maintains that sexual violence between women on and beyond plantation settings is not outside the realm of possibility; in a context where sexual violence signals power, then women will use this violence to perform power, too.

That the 2016 remake of the miniseries *Roots* begins this chapter's analysis of women's experiences may be unexpected, given the masculinist narrative of Alex Haley's novel (1976) and the twelve-hour miniseries that set ratings records (1977).[7] Haley's novel and the original miniseries create a genealogy in which a family can trace its lineage from the United States back to their Mandinka warrior ancestor Kunta Kinte. This cultural legacy resonates in popular culture over forty years later, as Erica L. Ball and Kellie Carter Jackson explain: "According to the Rap Genius archive, the name Kunta Kinta [*sic*] has been mentioned over 277 times in the lyrics of hiphop music. From Missy Elliot's 'Work it' to Kendrick Lamar's 'King Kunta,' the name has come to represent a symbol of defiance, resistance, and exceptional black manhood. Even the Twitter world has taken to creating memes from some of the most prominent scenes in the original *Roots*" (45). The masculinist narrative of *Roots* has thereby found a life in U.S. popular culture beyond Haley's novel and the miniseries; indeed, even if people have not seen the miniseries or read the novel, the name Kunta Kinte probably invokes an image of manly bravery and determination.

The 2016 miniseries focuses on many of the same characters in Kunta Kinte's familial line and thereby mainly develops the narratives of men (Kunta, "Chicken" George, and Tom). However, the second and third parts of the remake (directed by Mario Van Peebles and Thomas Carter, respectively) devote more attention to Kunta's daughter, Kizzy (played by E'myri Crutchfield and Anika Noni Rose), than any previous iteration of the narrative. Even so, the 2016 *Roots* is hardly woman-centered. For example, a *Huffington Post* article anticipating the remake claims it "will tell the stories of all its most memorable characters, but viewers can also expect powerful black women to grace the screen, as well" (Gebreyes). The word "but" exposes the tensions in how contemporary audiences remember (and artists and marketers deploy) *Roots* as a narrative centered on men's experiences—the article, in other words, assures its reader that the new *Roots* will hold on to that tradition of showcasing "its most memorable characters" (who are men) "but" will also add another narrative layer, "powerful black women." The promotional material thereby adds Black women as a backdrop, which echoes how Black freedom movements are popularly remembered as masculinist enterprises, despite Black women's leadership and involvement on all levels.

The remake uses Kizzy's narrative to achieve this end, and the miniseries develops her character more than Haley's novel, in which the experiences of her son, Chicken George, quickly eclipse her story. Tim A. Ryan's analysis of the novel's pace speaks to how "cruelty . . . occasionally explode[s] into the narrative," especially in Kizzy's treatment at the hands of white men, "but the book swiftly neutralizes such horror in its depiction of the life of Kizzy's son" (121).[8] The 1977 miniseries follows suit, and the 2016 *Roots* tracks a similar trajectory: Kizzy is born to Kunta and Belle (an enslaved woman) in the late 1700s; she spends her childhood as a companion to her enslavers' child, Melissa "Missy" Kathryn (Genevieve Hannelius), who teaches Kizzy to read as a game and gifts her discarded clothing; then, when her enslavers discover Kizzy can read, they sell her away to another enslaver, Tom Lea, who routinely rapes her. Much can be said about the remake's representation of Kizzy's resolve and resilience in the face of such exploitation, as she repeatedly finds strength in remembering what her father told her about their Kinte lineage, but the series nevertheless truncates Kizzy's personal story to focus on her son.

Still, the 2016 retelling of *Roots* features a brief scene between Missy and Kizzy that underpins my argument about depictions of sexual violence between women. In 1798, when Kizzy is fifteen years old, Missy gives her a set of writing quills and paper for her birthday, and then the teenagers happen upon a human anatomy book in the study ("Part Two"). With Missy sitting on Kizzy's lap, they survey the section about puberty, and Kizzy giggles—"Have you lost your senses?"—when Missy turns to her and demands to see whether she has "hair down there," implying her crotch. Missy's insistence that it is her "right" to view Kizzy's body parts changes the scene's tone, and Kizzy nervously looks up to her young enslaver's face, speechless (figure 3.1). Earlier in the scene, Missy adjusted Kizzy's dress to show the teenager's cleavage, and while this could have been interpreted as Missy's wish that Kizzy wear her clothes in a fashionable manner, her styling of Kizzy's clothing retroactively takes on a sexual connotation. Though Missy began teaching Kizzy to read ten years earlier, and even chased another enslaver-class playmate with scissors when the girl said racist things about Kizzy, Missy has grown accustomed to calling Kizzy both "friend" and "mine." Therefore, by the time they are teenagers, Missy has so internalized the system of ownership in which enslavers control their properties' sexualities that she assumes Kizzy's body belongs to her.

It is jarring to view such a scene between two young women. While audiences probably come to expect a degree of sexual experimentation and/or play in productions that feature teenagers exploring their identities, they likely do not expect a young white woman to so boldly attempt to claim an enslaver's sexual prerogatives. Moreover, to my knowledge, the scene comes closer to acting out sexual violence between a white and Black woman on a plantation setting than any other studio-produced portrayal. Missy's insistence that she see Kizzy's body hints that she will, if given more time, break through those taboos of intimate violence (that a white woman would not touch another woman with forced sexual touch). Missy's tearful response when the elder enslavers discover Kizzy's literacy because she wrote a pass for a young man named Noah—she asks Kizzy, "How could you do this to me?"—thereby reinforces what the audience has already seen: Missy's one-sided desire for Kizzy. Because Kizzy chose Noah and refused Missy, the young enslaver understands Kizzy's infraction as a personal affront. Missy says she wanted to purchase Kizzy, and though Missy declares she "could have kept [Kizzy] safe," the young woman would have exploited Kizzy's body,

FIGURE 3.1 E'myri Crutchfield as Kizzy and Genevieve Hannelius as Missy in *Roots* (History Channel, 2016).

both her physical labor and sexuality, as was Missy's "right." Indeed, the miniseries repeatedly displays the sexual violence white men inflict on Black women because they can, and though the miniseries does not show sexual violence between women, Missy voices her desire to coerce Kizzy into sexual acts.

Though it should be no surprise that plantation settings "casually" conjure images of queer sexualities because, according to Michael P. Bibler, "the plantation has operated for so long as the ultimate symbol within the Unites States—and probably throughout the Americas—of how power works in tan-

dem with eroticism" (238), outright depictions of sexual relationships between women on plantation settings are rare.[9] Moreover, of the types of
violent touch I have discussed so far (mediated and skin-to-skin touch), portrayals of sexual violence between women who enslave and women who are
enslaved are (usually) less explicit. This is an issue of representation that extends back into nineteenth-century first-person narratives of women who
were enslaved. Recently, scholars have reexamined these narratives to un-
silence this form of violence. Sojourner Truth's narrative (1850), for instance,
explicitly vocalizes that some things she experienced under slavery should
not be recorded, because "were she to tell all that happened to her as a slave —
all that she knows is 'God's truth' — it would seem to others, especially the
uninitiated, so unaccountable, so unreasonable, and what is usually called
so unnatural, (though it may be questioned whether people do not always
act naturally,) they would not easily believe it" (82). Nell Irvin Painter focuses
on Truth's turn of phrase — that she calls some of her unutterable experiences
"so unnatural" — to surmise that Truth would have acknowledged a white
man's sexual abuse because it was a well-established trope in abolitionist writing; however, because of persisting assumptions about gender and sexuality, Truth would not have written about a white woman violating her body
when she was a child (16). Painter, then, draws the conclusion from Truth's
silences that "the sexual abuse came from her mistress Sally Dumont, and
Truth could tell about it only obliquely, in scattered pages" (16). While the
silences obscure any definite conclusions about the "unnatural" experiences
Truth endured, Painter explains how those silences create spaces for recog-
nizing white women's violence against enslaved people.[10]

Also using elusive imagery, Harriet Jacobs describes women who enslave
as "obscene birds" in her *Incidents in the Life of a Slave Girl* (1861) to offer an
image of white women "who ought to protect the helpless victim," but have
"no other feelings towards her but those of jealousy and rage" (81, 45). At
the hands of Mrs. Flint, Linda Brent (Jacobs) is doubly violated because
Mrs. Flint "does not blame her husband for his infidelity and rapacity but
projects her anger instead upon the unfortunate slave woman" (Ryan 155).
As Anne B. Dalton's psychoanalytic reading of Mrs. Flint indicates, she mirrors her husband's actions of violation: "As if she were a demon like her husband, Mrs. Flint molests the victim of her husband's 'vicious roving' while
she sleeps by reenacting his molestation of her. By portraying the mistress
as the defiling succubus, Jacobs reveals how the master's sexual abuses infect those around him" (45). In Dalton's summation, Mrs. Flint acts as her
husband's double to have some kind of power in the situation, and as

Hortense J. Spillers claims, Mrs. Flint *"embodies his* [Mr. Flint's] *madness that arises in the ecstasy of unchecked power"* (222, emphasis in original). Scholars have found that Jacobs's metaphoric language provides ways to see Mrs. Flint's participation in the grotesque sexual economies of slavery, because Jacobs's narrative "implies more direct and extreme forms of sexual abuse *by* the mistress" (Abdur-Rahman 44, emphasis in original). Despite the danger Mrs. Flint poses, Jacobs's narrative conveys a triumphant tone because she gains power over her former enslaver through putting her experiences into words (Gwin 65). As these analyses of Jacobs's narrative reveal, the text portrays an array of sexual violence through enslavers' lurking and invasive gazes. Both Truth's and Jacobs's narratives, to varying degrees, show how unsilencing enslaved women's lived experiences of sexual violence deeply implicate white women in their daily horrific bodily abuses.

Willa Cather's disjointed novel *Sapphira and the Slave Girl* (1940) also appears in this narrative genealogy of texts that indirectly depict white women's sexual violence. In Cather's novel, a woman who enslaves (Sapphira Colbert) is suspected by her daughter and Nancy (the titular "slave girl") of inviting a nephew for a prolonged visit to Virginia so he will seduce the virginal Nancy so that Sapphira's husband will no longer be interested in Nancy sexually. Sapphira's plan is not rational—Toni Morrison asks, "If Mr. Colbert is tempted by Nancy the chaste, is there anything in slavocracy to make him disdain Nancy the unchaste?" (*Playing in the Dark* 25). While Sapphira does not personally attempt to rape Nancy, she uses the nephew as a surrogate (Gwin 145). Because Sapphira has limited mobility and relies solely on enslaved people for her care (in addition to the fact that Sapphira is obsessed with Nancy's sexuality), Morrison asserts that "surrogate black bodies become her hands and feet, her fantasies of sexual ravish and intimacy with her husband, and, not inconsiderably, her sole source of love" (26). Furthermore, when Sapphira's daughter ruminates that her mother "was born that way, and had been brought up that way"—to be "entirely self-centered" and to "th[ink] of other people only in their relation to herself" (Cather 220)—the reader can connect Sapphira's conduct to her plantation society's grotesque obsessions with maintaining the status quo through sexual violence. Sapphira attempts to manipulate this power for her own purposes.

Morrison contends that *Sapphira and the Slave Girl* attempts to present Sapphira's story as one removed from conversations about race: "How can the story of a white mistress be severed from a consideration of race and the violence entailed in the story's premise?" (18). This is precisely where Valerie Martin's *Property* makes an imaginative intervention: the novel portrays the obsession of Manon Gaudet (a white enslaver-class woman in Louisiana) with Sarah (a mixed-race enslaved woman) in 1828. According to the way Martin's novel plays out, when the story of an enslaver is *not* split "from a consideration of race and . . . violence," then the story is able to depict—through an instance of sexual assault by Manon upon Sarah's body—the logical outcomes of a society that deems some people the property of others. In *Property*, Manon thereby appropriates an abusive mode of sexuality to claim an enslaver's power, the same illusory power that white women have chased throughout the previous chapters of *Grotesque Touch*. Moreover, the first-person narration limits audience access to Sarah's perspective—the very narrative structure virtually silences the abused woman.[11] Martin's novel, then, uses intimate violence between women and its silencing effects to highlight the grotesquery of plantation systems.

Going further than the brief scene between Missy and Kizzy in the 2016 *Roots* miniseries, Manon abruptly assaults Sarah's body. Like in *Roots*, the novel exposes the rampant sexual violence of antebellum Louisianan society throughout its pages. From the beginning of the novel, *Property* reveals through Manon's perspective a society kept in order through the employment of white men's sexual violence; ultimately, Manon wishes to embody the power this violence represents, and she does to some extent. However, at the start of her narration, Manon shows how her husband's uses of sexual violence prove how his actions ironically undercut his words. As Gaudet (her husband has no first name in Manon's narrative) forces young enslaved men to perform games that sexually arouse some of them, he claims their arousal shows they "have not the power of reason" (Martin 4). Manon's perspective reveals the irony of this situation: "The servant's tumescence subsides as quickly as the master's rises, and the latter will last until he gets to the quarter. If he can find the boy's mother, and she's pretty, she will pay dearly for rearing an unnatural child. This is only one of his games" (4). Here, the enslaver uses faulty logic to validate his rape of enslaved women—because his own sexual arousal comes from his sense of voyeuristic, sadistic control over the young men. Through such examples, the novel evinces the grotesque nature of this society, for even though Gaudet's actions are not met with verbal approval by anyone in the novel, he is at the top of social hierarchies, and his power to do what he pleases goes unchecked.

Although Manon enjoys privileges because of her race and class status, her position as a woman in this antebellum society is always constructed in terms of her relationship to men in the novel. In this way, Manon's circumstances mirror the white women in *Mandingo*, *All Souls' Rising*, *The*

Book of Night Women, and *Hoe Duur Was de Suiker* in chapters 1 and 2. Moreover, when Manon dwells on her feelings toward her husband—revulsion, shame, and disappointment—she tellingly depicts their sexual encounters as being violent assaults against her body: "Was there to be no trace of feeling for my helplessness, no tenderness in my marital bed? The answer to both these questions was no, none" (Martin 151). Even though Manon does not experience any satisfaction from sex other than her belief that her body is valuable to her husband, she "enter[s] the fray" of intercourse with him, until she finds out Gaudet has sexual encounters with Sarah (152). The shame Manon experiences leads her to take some control over her body through ingesting sleeping medicine before having sex with Gaudet; however, her husband's violent reaction to her condition overshadows her agency (through passivity): "he pulled me up roughly by my arms and slapped me hard across the face. I smiled and fell back on the pillow, tasting blood. I brought my fingers to my lips, smearing a little of the blood across my cheek" (56). Manon undercuts her husband's position, for although he can strike her and draw blood, she can still unsettle his sense of power through the ways she masochistically acts out. At the end of this scene, Manon tells Gaudet to leave her alone, and he never returns to her bed. While Manon employs some agency here, her husband thinks of her as his property through marriage. Though readers likely feel empathy for Manon's experiences, they must remember how, as Suzanne W. Jones indicates, in antebellum social mythology that was replicated even after slavery was abolished, "The white 'lady' was deprived of her full sexual and maternal identity, while the black woman was deprived of her equality and her humanity" (70). Whereas Manon's body is commodified (to an extent) in her marriage, reminiscent of Claudine's position in *All Souls' Rising,* Sarah is more explicitly configured as property, for she is at the mercy of both of her enslavers, Gaudet and Manon.

According to Manon's narration, several white men have beaten Sarah because of her unwillingness to have sex with them, including Manon's uncle who was "so enraged" by the fact that a man who wanted to buy Sarah was going to sue him that her uncle "had Sarah tied up in the kitchen and whipped her himself, in front of the cook" (Martin 19). This passing reference to the harshness of Sarah's experiences reinforces that this society normalizes such violence. For example, even the scant details Manon provides—that her uncle tied and whipped Sarah in the kitchen in front of another enslaved woman—confirm the routine nature of such violence in the household. No place is safe for Sarah in this house or society because she literally has no place, no position, other than to be what her enslavers want. Later, Manon describes the violence she witnesses her husband enact on Sarah when he discovers that she is pregnant with an enslaved man's child: he "commenced slapping and hitting her until she was flat on the floor, begging him to stop. It was not to be borne, he swore, that he should be treated in this fashion in his own house. When I spoke a word on her behalf, he pushed me out of the room and slammed the door in my face" (23). In this scene, Gaudet attempts to physically dominate Sarah so that he may regain prestige. Although Manon realizes her husband's desire to possess Sarah's body, Manon is true to her social position in the way she glosses over the violence enacted upon Sarah's body (he was "slapping and hitting [Sarah] until she was flat on the floor") so that Manon can tell how she suffers under her husband's rule ("he pushed me out of the room and slammed the door in my face"). In this plantation setting, separation between the classes of women is paramount. While Manon and Sarah could possibly connect because they both undergo a degree of sexual violence from Gaudet, this kind of bonding between the women is not possible, given the racist ideologies at work in their society.

Women's friendships, as Sharon Monteith summarizes, have long stirred up "patriarchal distrust and patriarchal disapproval" because such bonds have been thought of as "subversive, transgressive, and even political" (28), yet much recent fiction has sought to counter such hopeful depictions of women's interracial relationships during slavery. For example, Toni Morrison's novel *A Mercy* (2008) works in this vein as the women in the novel—who are from various ethnic and class backgrounds—make a temporary life together in an early Maryland settlement in the 1690s. However, the women's sense of safety and community quickly deteriorates, showing that idealizations of women's relationships are impossible given the United States' racialized social structure.[12] When placed in conversation with such texts, *Property* represents a novel in which a white author, Valerie Martin, is, to borrow Suzanne W. Jones's words, "rethink[ing feminists'] grand narratives about women's shared experiences, perceptions, and oppressions" (69).[13]

Regardless of their shared experiences at the hands of Gaudet, Manon and Sarah do not form a bond beyond that of enslaver and enslaved woman because Manon does not break free from her own social position, except to subjugate Sarah further. As Ryan claims, "Manon sees herself as a victim of patriarchy, but she is really an instrument and beneficiary of it. Thus she must continue to oppress Sarah as her husband did before her" (176). For instance, instead of reading Sarah's expression as one of a woman frightened and subdued by Gaudet, Manon interprets Sarah's look as one of wanton sexuality when the enslaved woman rushes from Gaudet's room after a fire breaks out in the sugar mill: "Her hair was all undone, her eyes bright, she was wearing a loose dressing gown I'd never seen before" (Martin 48). Manon does not care to contemplate what Sarah's looks might entail; instead, she implicitly longs for Sarah to share with her a degree of attention that Manon assumes Sarah must give her husband. Manon observes that Sarah wears "a very different look from the one [she had] seen in the night" when Sarah serves her coffee, and Manon experiences a feeling of anger when she realizes the difference (50). Passing references such as these highlight the complex emotions Manon feels toward Sarah, but the spark of jealousy Manon experiences does not foreshadow that the women will share a mutually fulfilling relationship. Instead, such reactions set the stage for Manon's claiming of Sarah's body in an act that mirrors her husband's abuse of Sarah.

Up to the point in the novel when Manon assaults Sarah, Manon has wanted to enjoy an enslaver's agency, but she feels limited by her society's expectations of her gender. Early in the novel, when Manon gazes through a spyglass to look at the enslaved people outdoors and believes one of the enslaved men sees her, she instantly moves away from the glass, and she wonders, "Why should I feel guilty?" (18). Here, Manon's internal questioning mirrors Mistress Epps in the film adaptation of *12 Years a Slave* when she spies on Patsey and then abruptly brushes off her hands. Though the audience does not hear Epps's thoughts, they can interpret from her actions that she feels sullied in some way because she intrudes upon the young enslaved woman's sense of independence. In *Property*, Manon takes this relationship between looking and power further: she finally appropriates the enslaver's power of voyeurism when she assaults Sarah by nursing at her breast just after Manon's mother succumbs to disease.

Although readers could initially connect Manon's nursing at Sarah's breast as a sign that Manon seeks a maternal connection, this reading would privilege Manon's selfish desires over Sarah's experiences (and would reiterate a shortsighted narrative of women's connections across racialized class lines). However, this scene clearly shows that Manon uses Sarah's body, much like her husband has used them both. When Manon sees a drop of milk hanging from Sarah's nipple while Sarah has been nursing, Manon wonders why Gaudet has let Sarah keep her child: "What had [Sarah] done to make him agree to it, what bargain had she struck, what promise given? . . . It was for his own pleasure, I thought" (75). Various texts present enslavers' assaults on enslaved women's bodies in this manner. For instance, the novel *Mandingo* (1957) portrays men who are enslavers sampling the enslaved woman Big Pearl's milk, the narration awash with sexual overtones as the men "stroke" and "savor" the enslaved woman's breasts (Onstott 537). Toni Morrison's novel *Beloved* (1987) offers a condemning depiction of white men stealing milk from Sethe (an enslaved woman) and her children. More recently, Alice Randall's *The Wind Done Gone* (2001), a reimagining of *Gone with the Wind*, features a telling moment when the mixed-race narrator Cynara sees her mother (called Mammy in Margaret Mitchell's narrative) breastfeeding the character based on Scarlett O'Hara (called Other): "I flushed in a rage of possession as those little white hands drew the nipple toward the little pink mouth, then clasped on" (13). By suckling at the Black woman's breast, the young Scarlett "get[s] her fill of pleasure, all raven-haired and unashamed of hunger," while her father (called Planter in this narrative) "only saw his daughter taking pleasure where he himself had done" (14). The pleasure enslavers experience as they steal Black women's milk evinces their mode of exerting power: they take because they believe— and they want to assert—that the enslaved women's bodies (and children's bodies) belong to them.

Manon's realization of her husband's pleasure at the expense of both Sarah and her child brings Manon to action as she drops to the floor, touches Sarah's wrists, then angles her body forward "to capture the drop" of Sarah's milk on her tongue (Martin 76). Manon's language in this scene is of discovery: "I could feel the smooth, round bones through the thin cloth of her sleeve"; "I raised my hand, cupping her breast, which was lighter than I would have thought" (76). She does not realize Sarah's humanity in this scene, though. Manon is discovering how to take pleasure from another's body: "This is what he does, I thought" (76). By mirroring her husband's actions, however briefly, Manon experiences a physical awakening that she then describes in her narration:

> A sensation of utter strangeness came over me, and I struggled not to swoon. I could see myself, kneeling there, and beyond me the room where my mother's body lay, yet it seemed to me she was not dead, that she bore horrified witness to my action. And beyond that I could see my husband in his office, lifting his head from his books with an uncomfortable suspicion that something important was not adding up. This vision made me smile. I closed my eyes, swallowing greedily. I was aware of a sound, a sigh, but I was not sure if it came from me or from Sarah. How wonderful I felt, how entirely free. My headache disappeared, my chest seemed to expand, there was a complimentary tingling in my own breasts. (76)

As I have argued elsewhere, Manon's awakening through her violation of Sarah's body causes her to relish her transgression of sexual boundaries while appropriating the male gaze as she imagines her mother's and husband's responses as witnesses ("Valerie Martin's *Property*" 224–25). Manon also goes a step further by confusing the sigh and "complimentary tingling" as evidence of Sarah sharing her pleasure, just as her husband undoubtedly thought Manon was experiencing a degree of pleasure from their sexual encounters (225). Instead of Manon connecting with Sarah through their experiences as women, Manon's actions and thoughts in this scene show her claiming an enslaver's sexual license. Before her aunt interrupts her, Manon opens her eyes to look at Sarah's face, at which point she realizes that Sarah is looking away from her: "She's afraid to look at me, I thought. And she's right to be. If she looked at me, I would slap her" (Martin 76–77). Manon's concluding thoughts solidify the true nature of the scene; though Sarah's posture might very well indicate the woman's rage (still, the reader cannot know exactly what Sarah's body language means because of her narrative silence), Manon reads her posture in a way that solidifies the enslaver's power. She does not wish to share an intimate moment with Sarah; she only wants to use Sarah for her own gain.

The language of Manon's thoughts in this scene configures her treatment of Sarah as an instance of sexual violence. Although Manon does not penetrate Sarah's body, the violation Sarah endures via Manon's actions undoubtedly adds to the traumas of enslavement and solidifies her social position as property to be used, even by a woman whose experiences might have created a bond of understanding between them. *Property*'s portrayal of sexual violence via unwanted touch between women creates an opportunity for the audience to think about the nature of power. Because Martin's novel shows a scene of sexual violence between women and narrates the scene through the perpetrator's perspective, the narrative enables the reader to see aspects of power that they might otherwise ignore. Although Manon may mistake Sarah's bodily responses as conveying shared pleasure, her violent touch does not connect the women; it separates them further. This shocking encounter exemplifies the grotesque nature of the plantation society. In this way, *Property* provides evidence for the pervasiveness of sexual violence in societies that grant a class of people absolute control over others.

Manon's violence against Sarah does not cause her a moment of contemplation after the act, which solidifies Manon's performance of an enslaver's power. Unlike Claudine Arnaud in *All Souls' Rising*, for example, Manon does not dwell on the violence she enacted on Sarah's body; instead, her attitude more closely mirrors Claudine's husband (Michel Arnaud) after he murdered an enslaved woman. Both Manon Gaudet and Michel Arnaud use enslaved women's bodies in a manner that does not cause them a moment of remorse after the fact. Through Manon's point of view as an enslaver who sexually violates an enslaved woman, *Property* thereby provides a rare example in literature of a woman who continues to benefit from claiming some of the privileges of a man who enslaves. The closest Manon comes to reflecting on the incident appears in her brief observation that Sarah has "kept out of [her] way since the night Mother died" (82). Instead, Manon continues to use Sarah for her own purposes, which is obvious when Manon believes she can trade Sarah to Gaudet to ensure Manon's freedom to live in her mother's house in New Orleans. Although Manon's "high card" (Sarah's body) almost sways Gaudet, he replies, "You are my wife" (103), which effectively undercuts Manon's illusions of possessing any real power in her situation at this time.

Even though Manon realizes her husband has the final say in the management of her inheritance — and, thus, the trajectory of her life — Manon continues to view Sarah's actions in terms of her own desires. The reality of Manon's selfishness is especially evident when self-emancipated men enter Gaudet's home and implicitly threaten the women. Manon understands that the men will most likely murder her (they kill Gaudet), yet she cannot understand Sarah's desire to escape the plantation as well. When Sarah bites and scratches Manon while they run toward Gaudet's abandoned horse, Manon can focus only on how Sarah's actions are aimed at her, personally: "'They will kill me,' I said, but she wasn't listening, or didn't hear. No, I thought. She heard me well enough. It was her hope that they would kill me" (117). Manon ignores the fact that one of the escaped men refers to Sarah as "Miss High Yellow," signaling that her place as Gaudet's prized sexual object puts her in danger at the hands of the men (110). Also, Manon cannot fathom why Sarah would escape once Gaudet is dead, as "it d[oes]n't make sense" to her (127). While Manon claims to long for freedom from her husband, she does not actually want to be free from the systems of power in which she lives. For example, she thinks after her husband's death, "I would hold fast to my independence as a man clings to a life raft in a hurricane. It was all that saved me from drowning in a sea of lies" (180). Although Manon can determine a "great lie" is "at the center of everything" in her society, she does nothing to break away from this society (179); instead, she makes every effort to have Sarah — her property — caught and returned to her.

The final pages of *Property* reveal that a connection will never be forged between Manon and Sarah beyond that of enslaver and enslaved woman.

Even so, Manon seems to make a tentative connection to enslaved women while she experiences a painful sensation when thinking about her husband: "My head was bursting. It felt as if an iron collar, such as I have seen used to discipline field women, were fastened about my skull" (182). Her momentary realization once again fails to bring her to empathize with these women, however. Manon predictably appropriates this vision of torture as her own pain, not the pain of countless enslaved women. Moreover, once Manon discovers that Sarah has been traveling in disguise as a white man to escape north, she reveals to her aunt her feeling of jealousy toward Sarah: "She has tasted a freedom you and I will never know. . . . She has traveled about the country as a free white man" (189). Sarah has consequently become property for Manon to desire at any cost, and she represents Manon's longing to appropriate power. By the end of the novel when a slave catcher returns Sarah, Manon has so used Sarah—in body and in thought—that Manon can no longer even guess at what Sarah is thinking. Manon continues operating via the worn assumptions perpetuated by enslavers—she tells Sarah, "No one ever holds you responsible for your actions. It's just assumed you have no moral sense" (191)—but at the same time, the audience has read episode after episode that prove Manon's own society is grotesquely absurd. When Manon hears Sarah describe having tea served by white people in a northern U.S. location, she believes Sarah has gone mad, and she concludes the novel with the thought, "It struck me as perfectly ridiculous. What on earth did they think they were doing?" (193). Readers by this point have already asked the same question of Manon and her fellow enslavers; their participation in the violence required to keep social hierarchies intact appears ridiculously grotesque at every turn.

While *Property* clearly depicts sexual violence between women—readers see ample evidence that Manon abuses Sarah—I turn now to a text that introduces overt audience titillation back into the matrices of representation. Ann Allen Shockley's collection of short stories *The Black and White of It* portrays white women—an antebellum enslaver and an employer in the 1940s—sexually violating Black women. This pairing effectively expands the themes in Valerie Martin's *Property* into a post-emancipation U.S. setting. Yet, while Martin's novel plainly depicts violence perpetrated by a woman, the representations of assault in Shockley's stories "The Mistress and the Slave Girl" and "Women in a Southern Time" are subtler. The reader must pay close attention to the narrators in both short stories to see how practices of enslavement have infiltrated—and established—the relationships between women in the nineteenth century and the twentieth century. To an even greater degree than previous texts in this chapter, the silences and ironies in Shockley's stories lead readers to this conclusion. Additionally, as with plantation pulp novels in chapter 1, the packaging of Shockley's collection of erotic short stories transformed throughout time, which furthers the collection's narrative ambiguity. Unlike other texts of plantation erotica, though, Shockley's two stories offer historical and social contextualization for her collection of short fiction.[14] The intertwining of both titillation and context ultimately calls into question the reader's own practices of desire.[15]

The subtleties of Shockley's fiction have led to widespread misreading of her work. First published by the lesbian-centered Naiad Press in 1980, *The Black and White of It* was initially criticized for being both too radical and not radical enough in its depictions of interracial same-sex relationships between women.[16] However, a handful of academics in the twenty-first century have reintroduced Shockley's work to the critical community through their refreshing takes on Shockley's novels and short fiction.[17] For example, L. H. Stallings argues that three short stories in the 1987 edition of *The Black and White of It* ("Holly Craft Isn't Gay," "A Meeting of the Sapphic Daughters," and "The Mistress and the Slave Girl") "work especially well together to create a continuous narrative regarding the impact of racialized sexuality on black females with same-sex desires" (68). As Stallings contends, the collection's "continuous narrative" shows "why black females with same-sex desires cannot rely on Western canons of sexuality" (69).[18] I extend Stallings's claim about continuity to the final story of the collection, "Women in a Southern Time," because *The Black and White of It* presents a unified message about how racist, sexist, classist structures of power have (mis)shaped Black women's formations of same-sex desire with white women.

Here, I look closely at the 1987 version of Shockley's collection that readers are more likely to revisit today. In the Naiad reprinting of *The Black and White of It*, Shockley added two stories to the end, "The Mistress and the Slave Girl" and "Women in a Southern Time." These additions, combined with an excerpt from "The Mistress and the Slave Girl" appearing in the book before the title page, encase the collection within a subtle message concerning the prevalence of inequalities in women's interracial relationships. By portraying an enslaver's desire for an enslaved woman ("The Mistress and the Slave Girl") and an employer's desire for a woman who works as her maid in the 1940s ("Women in a Southern Time"), Shockley provides readers with a final image of the ways white women seeking to fulfill their own desires have co-opted Black women's bodies and desires throughout time.

FIGURE 3.2 Front cover of the first edition of *The Black and White of It* (Naiad, 1980).

Because questions of audience desire are complex (Who is the audience? What do they expect? What appeals to them?), I begin with a material analysis of Naiad Press's 1980s editions of *The Black and White of It*. Julie R. Enszer's essay about Naiad Press's white editor, Barbara Grier, articulates how even the cover designs of *The Black and White of It* and two other books published by Black women with the press in the early 1980s (which feature pictures of Black women on the covers) "suggest African-American lesbians from a different historical time period, reinforcing the idea of both a history and a present for Black lesbians, an idea that was very important to Grier" (365). The first-edition paperback cover of *The Black and White of It* is so striking in its political move toward visibility and collectivity because it drastically departs from visual markers of objectification and voyeurism previously discussed in *Grotesque Touch* (figure 3.2). The woman on the cover of Shockley's collection "do[es] not look directly at the viewer—she looks off to the left, perhaps to an imagined utopia or perhaps to a current threat to her placidness" (365), which invites the reader to meditate on the woman's possible (contradictory) emotions.

That Naiad Press did not market Shockley's collection via a titillating image is even more noteworthy if we consider what Jennifer Gilley calls "the grandmother of all feminist publishing scandals," when Barbara Grier five years later promoted the Naiad book *Lesbian Nuns: Breaking Silence* (1985) via mass market means, including *Penthouse* (Gilley 3).[19] Grier's actions brought to the fore multiple issues in the politics of feminist publishing: "issues of exploitation (selling out to the pornography industry), audience (can an author ever have control over the audience their work reaches?), and marketing (the media blitz brought titillation and ire to the masses but also let closeted lesbian nuns and ex-nuns know they were not alone)" (3). Through this "commercial success at the cost of political purity" (9), Naiad Press could print (and reprint) less popular books, which brings us to the extended paperback edition of *The Black and White of It* that Naiad printed in 1987. This edition kept Shockley's original ten stories and added "The Mistress and the Slave Girl" and "Women in a Southern Time" to the end. The cover to this edition is less remarkable than the first; its black, white, and teal geometric design might more closely resemble a mathematics textbook cover than one belonging to a book of stories about people's relationships, much less a book that describes overt sexual acts (figure 3.3). At first, it seems that the press does not draw on titillation (or any form of corporeality) to entice readers—and yet, the curious shopper can pick up the book and read an excerpt from a seduction scene inside the paperback's front cover.

An epigraph describing a scene of seduction commonly appears in popular romance and erotica genres, and Shockley's 1987 edition strategically uses such an excerpt to enhance its overall themes. The epigraph of *The Black and White of It* is best read as a whole:

> Slowly Heather began to remove Delia's gown. "I want to see your beautiful body." Next, Heather took off her own garment. "Now! I can feel you better against me." Naked they embraced, body to body, warm flesh blending as one. Lightly Heather caressed Delia's breasts and round stomach. "You're so fragile, like a jewel. My precious jewel." She kissed her forehead, tasting the saltiness of her skin with the tip of her tongue. The trembling of the girl's body imparted the message she wanted to know. Fired with passion, Heather stroked the tapering tights inside and out.

This excerpt is obviously meant to entice readers to purchase the book; additionally, because the selection comes from the story "The Mistress and the Slave Girl," it invites the reader by using a part of the seduction scene between

Ann Allen Shockley

The Black and White of It

FIGURE 3.3 Front cover of the second edition of *The Black and White of It* (Naiad, 1987).

an enslaver and enslaved woman. It likely surprises readers when they see this excerpt reappear in "The Mistress and the Slave Girl," the collection's penultimate story. The narratives in *The Black and White of It* represent a range of Black and white women's relationships of same-sex desire, yet the title of Shockley's story — "The Mistress and the Slave Girl" — jolts readers, because the titles of her other stories have not been so blunt up to this point. For example, one story depicts a legislator who keeps her longtime partner a secret and will not use the word "lesbian" to describe herself, and the story's title — "Play It, But Don't Say It" — is more playful than the stark title "The Mistress and the Slave Girl." Readers discover that Heather and Delia from the collection's epigraph are the titular "mistress" and "slave girl," which acts as an invitation to consider another reading of the collection, one critical of prevalent means of classifying and experiencing desire.

Moreover, Shockley's story widens its critical lens to implicate women from northern U.S. cultures via their lustful gazing at enslaved women's distress and abuse. While Heather has been educated in the northern United States and has abolitionist inclinations, she also returns home to her family's plantation and immediately purchases Delia after seeing her body showcased on the selling block. "The Mistress and the Slave Girl" thereby adds to a narrative genealogy of people in the northern United States looking upon Black women's tortured bodies. This sense of violation by an "abolitionist" audience can be read in abolitionist tracts, such as H. Mattison's *Louisa Picquet, the Octoroon* (1861), in which the author (a minister) poses questions to a woman who was formerly enslaved and tarries on the details of punishment: "Well, how did he whip you?"; "How were you dressed—with thin clothes, or how?"; "Did he cut through your skin?" (12, 15). More recently, Dolen Perkins-Valdez's novel *Wench* (2010) employs such a voyeuristic scene to depict the brutal public beating and rape of a Louisianan enslaved woman named Mawu. Her enslaver Tip chooses to enact this violence before a crowd of people of various class and racial identities at a resort in Ohio in 1852: "Two white women sat on chairs fanning themselves and watching intently from a distance. . . . One of the white women uttered a high-pitched 'oh' and placed a handkerchief to her mouth. But neither of them stopped looking" (67, 68). Somehow even more disturbing, though, are descriptions of a licentious gaze employed by abolitionists, as Lorene Cary imagines in her novel *The Price of a Child* (1995) when the protagonist Mercer speaks to a crowd of women and feels their hungry gazes upon her: "They filled their eyes with her. They rubbed their clean, white fingers against each other impatiently, as men rubbed themselves, absently, when a woman walked by. . . . They wanted the knock-down-drag-out. That much she could tell. They wanted the horse whip and pony whip, the green sapling branch, the leather belt and bridle cord" (167). These narratives, going back to nineteenth-century abolitionist writings, incorporate representations of northern U.S. cultures into *Grotesque Touch*'s hemispheric conversation about sexualized violence and power. While these onlookers do not physically inflict pain on the bodies of enslaved women, they participate in a system that enacts violence beyond the geographical limits of the plantation.

Likewise, as the narration indicates in "The Mistress and the Slave Girl," Heather's gaze reveals her privileged position. According to L. H. Stallings, "Shockley's text acknowledges the position of power white women maintained over black females" because "Delia is the object and Heather the spectator" (71). Heather does not consider Delia an equal. Instead, all of Heather's ruminations about her contempt for the men selling and buying women at the slave market stop short of a critical look at the system she lives in—and profits from—while she desires Delia's body. According to the third-person narrator, "Something about the slave girl fascinated Heather as she took in the pink silk dress hugging the curves of her body. She knew that they dressed the goodlooking ones purposely like that. The sad haunting aura hallowing [the slave girl] only enhanced her beauty. Heather swallowed hard as she experienced a familiar sharp sensation piercing warmly through her" (Shockley 106). Shockley's story even more cleverly plays with the trope of the enslaver's gaze evident in 12 Years a Slave and Property, for Heather realizes that Delia's body is on display for her sexual qualities, and yet Delia's human reactions (her sadness) merely "enhance . . . her beauty" in Heather's eyes, sparking Heather's lust. Moreover, the narration's turn of phrase—that Heather's lust is "familiar" at this moment—creates an ambiguous space that could be read a couple of ways: more generally, that this warm feeling overcomes Heather when she is around women she finds attractive, and/or, more specifically, that Heather has developed a lustful affiliation with enslaved women. After she purchases Delia, Heather "feel[s] triumphant," as she always does "when outsmarting males at their own game," because "this was one slave girl who wouldn't be thrown to the wolves for a white master's breeder or concubine" (107). Although her thoughts show her awareness of this structure's violent mechanisms, Heather does not reflect on her own complicity within the system that keeps Delia as less-than-human property.

The narrative depicts Heather as an enslaver who—at every turn—profits from the plantation system. This ensures that Heather's actions reflect Manon Gaudet's in Property, even though Heather might think she has egalitarian motives. Stallings aptly observes that "Heather's actions mirror the dehumanizing efforts of white heterosexual men as slave owners," because Heather uses Delia for her own pleasure and identity formation (74). Despite Heather's supposed reluctance to enslave—"This was the first slave she had ever purchased, making her a firsthand slave owner. The idea did not cheer her" (Shockley 107)—the narration evinces her position in this system: she "look[s] out the window at the slaves leaving the fields in the twilight to go to their cabins" to "offset the unsettling stirrings" ignited by her desire for Delia's body (107). Heather is accustomed to the daily movements on the plantation, a process that (despite her protestations) comforts her.

The story's narration clarifies Heather's complicity within the slave system, for the reader never knows Delia's unfiltered thoughts. In this way, the narrative shows how Heather, as an enslaver, disregards Delia's views. Even though Heather reads "a hint of haughtiness . . . flashing [in Delia's] eyes" (108), Delia's thoughts are hidden from her, and Heather becomes obsessed with Delia's body, a fact reminiscent of Manon's obsession with Sarah: "The girl's skin was like velvet, soft, smooth, exciting, triggering want" (108). Furthermore, despite Heather's attention to Delia's body and statement of non-violence—"'I'll never strike you,' she said huskily. 'Ever'"—she does not consider Delia's physical needs (109). After cutting her hair short because, by her own admission, "It's much cooler this way," Heather orders Delia not to cut her own hair (109). In this example of privileging Heather's pleasure over Delia's comfort, the reader sees clearly Heather's desire to exact her own will over Delia's body.

While Heather privileges her own desires and feelings, she also considers Delia's enslavement in terms of paternal care—and this seems to increase Heather's pleasure. In a telling scene, "the girl's sobs subsided in the protective circle of her mistress's arms" (111). Much like the white women who want to claim white men's power in chapters 1 and 2, Heather attracts the suspicions of others belonging to the enslaver class; for example, her brother, Ralph, asks, "What role are you trying to play, dear sister?" (109). As in the stories of Blanche, Claudine, Isobel, Sarith, and Manon discussed previously in *Grotesque Touch*, Heather's society views her attempts to gain power (through claiming an enslaver's privileges) as suspect. Here, at least, Heather seems to be more empathetic to Delia's experiences. Nevertheless, even though Heather apparently "saved" Delia from sexual exploitation at the hands of men, the language of her thoughts reveals—especially as Heather seduces Delia—that she only grants Delia agency for her own pleasure. For example, as she waits for Delia's response when she asks Delia if she would like to have sex with her, Heather believes "she couldn't order, demand, for it wouldn't be the same" (111). Delia does not have much of a choice in this matter, though; even as Heather does not want to "order" or "demand" Delia to surrender her body, Delia knows Heather's position as enslaver grants her complete access to her body.

Delia breaks her silence when she vocalizes this reality to Heather while the enslaver attempts to project her own desire onto Delia. When Heather urges, "Delia, say my name," and Delia answers by calling Heather "Mistress," Heather replies, "half angrily," "No! I'm *not* your mistress. . . . I'm your lover. . . . And you are my love" (112, emphasis in original). This exchange between Heather and Delia confirms the relationship between them as that of enslaver and enslaved woman. Heather, after all, employs her power to demand that Delia act the part of a lover, and as far as the reader can infer, Delia complies to the extent that Heather interprets her acquiescence as mutual feeling. However, I want to avoid slipping into a discourse of "consent" here. Both *Property* and "The Mistress and the Slave Girl" offer glimpses into the minds of women as perpetrators of sexual violence; these narratives do not disclose enough of the enslaved women's thoughts to warrant *our* reading of their silences or compliance as their desires for sexual touch. As Saidiya V. Hartman makes clear, "the disavowal of rape" for enslaved women in nineteenth-century law "most obviously involves issues of consent, agency, and will that are ensnared in a larger dilemma concerning the construction of person and the calculation of black humanity in slave law" (80). Enslaved women could not legally consent to sex with their enslavers by law because "to consent" means that they would be on equal footing in terms of agency (thus, the power differential meant enslaved women did not fall under the protections of the law). However, this did not prevent a popularized pattern of thought about enslaved women: that they did enthusiastically participate in and consent to sexual relationships with enslavers. Hazel V. Carby's writing about rape is helpful here: "Sexual relations between black women and white men are often used as evidence of the existence of such complicity during the existence of the slave system. . . . Rape has always involved patriarchal notions of women being, at best, not entirely unwilling accomplices, if not outwardly inviting a sexual attack" (39). These injustices and ironies make up the backdrop to Shockley's story about an enslaver's so-called seduction of an enslaved woman, for the story's third-person narrator shows that Delia does not "outwardly invit[e]" Heather's actions, to use Carby's wording. The narration also features enough ambiguity (due to Delia's silences and selective vocalizations) to establish that she follows Heather's lead unwillingly. Throughout, the narrative thereby makes clear the power differential between Heather's and Delia's social standings.

Following the sex scene between the women, Shockley's story ends with Heather silencing Delia, which thereby hints at Heather's occlusion of Delia's humanity. The narrative abruptly ends with this short paragraph: "Months later, Heather freed the slaves and sold the plantation. . . . Heather moved to Boston, taking Delia with her. There they shared a house sheltered by love. No one knew they were lovers, only that the white and black women, who lived together, were terribly devoted to each other" (Shockley 113). Just as Heather uses Delia for her own ends, the narrative eclipses and discards Delia's desires in this take on the "Boston marriage" between women who have unequal social mobility. We can read between the lines here to understand that the story's sudden ending critiques Heather for essentially keeping Delia enslaved. For, even after the other enslaved people gain their freedom, Delia is still a captive whom Heather hides from society: "no one kn[ows] they [a]re lovers," just as no one knows Delia's actual desires (113).

This reading of "The Mistress and the Slave Girl" provides a new perspective concerning the excerpt from the story that appears as the epigraph in *The Black and White of It*. While the passage titillates, it also slyly provides an opportunity to reevaluate the other stories in Shockley's collection when the reader nears the end of the volume. As the epigraph (the scene of seduction) indicates, Delia is Heather's "jewel," although, readers now realize that in the scene Heather fully claims her property, Delia's body. Michael P. Bibler's cautiously optimistic reading of the seduction scene concedes the ambivalence of the narrative: "The lesbianism in the story partly allows Shockley to reclaim the interracial relationship as politically safe, but she still can't completely avoid invoking the historical legacy of slave domination. In short, the story captures the ambivalent tensions between sexual sameness and racial difference" (246). "The Mistress and the Slave Girl" may demonstrate narrative ambivalence; however, the collection's final story, "Women in a Southern Time," unambiguously highlights *The Black and White of It*'s message about how desire and power intersect. "Women in a Southern Time" shows how white women still use Black women's bodies with no regard for their desires—sexual and otherwise—well into the twentieth century, as issues of race, class, and sexuality intertwine in Shockley's stories across time.

In "Women in a Southern Time," readers see the thoughts of Eulah Mae, a young Black woman who works to earn enough money to attend nursing school. To do so, she is employed as a maid for Miss Tish, a wealthy white woman. While Miss Tish's husband is away during World War II, Miss Tish devotes most of her time to her friend (and rumored sexual partner) Miss Monti. Both her husband and Miss Monti die during the narrative, leaving Miss Tish alone with and dependent upon Eulah Mae. "Women in a Southern Time" functions as a companion piece to "The Mistress and the Slave Girl."[20] Furthermore, I argue, the story also responds to the collection's epigraph to more fully revise popular discourses about desire by revealing a continuum from plantation slavery to post-emancipation disparities manifest in U.S. domestic labor.[21]

As in "The Mistress and the Slave Girl," the story "Women in a Southern Time" depicts power imbalances between two women, a white employer and a Black domestic servant. The narrative evokes connections between the two stories several times. Most notably, the reader learns that "quietly Eulah Mae, too, grieved with her mistress" following Miss Monti's death (Shockley 122). The wording here—the narrator calls Miss Tish "mistress"—is essential to reading "The Mistress and the Slave Girl" along with "Women in a Southern

Time," as it adjusts the reader's expectations about the women's relationship. Once Miss Tish begins following Eulah Mae around the house after her husband dies, Miss Tish's behavior can accordingly be read alongside Manon's and Heather's: all three white women seek to claim Black women's bodies for their own purposes. The narrator describes Miss Tish's eyes as "devouring [Eulah Mae's] every movement" and "trap[ping] Eulah Mae's [eyes] in a vise," which connects Eulah Mae's and Delia's experiences (123). Both Black women, despite the distance of time between them, are objectified by white women to the point that they become bound inside the white women's desires.

According to the narrator, in the "monastic seclusion" of Miss Tish's home, the two women "bec[o]me imprisoned in a tangled web of need and giving" that leaves Eulah Mae unable to resign her position so that she may pursue a career in nursing (123–24). The narrator explains that Eulah Mae and Miss Tish are "bound together in an uncommon affinity of servant and mistress, black and white, whose roles ha[ve] become distorted in this southern time," and that Eulah Mae has "forgotten what she [i]s in their isolated milieu of oneness" (124). Despite this sense of "oneness," the narrative makes clear that her relationship with Miss Tish diminishes Eulah Mae's choices, so much so that she does not have the power to leave her employer. Once again mirroring the previous story, "Women in a Southern Time" portrays the seduction scene between women as one determined by social inequality. Just as Heather told Delia that she was beautiful and like a jewel, so does Miss Tish tell Eulah Mae that she is "very pretty"; yet, in this story, the "mistress" more obviously acts out of selfishness, and the narrator describes Miss Tish's eyes "like a cat's charming a bird" that "mesmerize" Eulah Mae (124, 125). Even though she does not have the actual mechanism of slavery at her disposal, Miss Tish uses her position of power to hold Eulah Mae captive inside her home. As with Heather and Delia, Miss Tish also ensures that Eulah Mae cannot improve her social position.

As stated earlier, the end of "The Mistress and the Slave Girl" skips over months of time to conclude the story with Delia's seemingly compliant subservience to Heather's wishes when they move to Boston. "Women in a Southern Time" ends, however, just as Miss Tish seduces Eulah Mae. The last lines of the story—and *The Black and White of It* as a whole—leave readers with an uneasy feeling that Eulah Mae will not be able to escape from Miss Tish and her role as a maid: "Eulah Mae felt smothered against the softness and warmth and flood of desire. Her answer was buried against the lips of Miss Tish. Trembling, she closed her eyes. She realized that she would never leave. She couldn't . . . now. The silence answered for her" (125). That this story, and Shockley's collection, ends with the silencing of a Black woman's voice is telling. Eulah Mae knows Miss Tish's "flood" of sexual desire will supplant her desires for a career. By paying close attention to women's abilities to articulate and act on their aspirations in these stories, readers gain a better understanding of the various ways that *The Black and White of It* calls dominant U.S. models of sexual desire into question. Shockley's stories show how—throughout time—the inequalities of race and class intersect with sexuality. Moreover, silences in both stories reveal the dangers of keeping quiet about the violence inherent in plantation slavery and post-emancipation domestic settings. Shockley's pairing of the stories, along with the erotic excerpt at the beginning of *The Black and White of It*, combine to implicate readers in this greater message about the social legacies of slavery and desire. What do we as readers desire when we seek out narratives that depict white and Black women participating in intimate relationships inside the white women's homes? Chapter 4 examines this question more closely in post-emancipation settings.

CHAPTER FOUR

Violent Denial in Post-Emancipation Households

> I go back to Mistress Sarah and her constant music, Donna
> Summer's music, to face the same shit, the same put-downs: you're
> talking nonsense. And she screams and howls when I read in the
> paper about the injustices they commit against blacks in South
> Africa. Not happy with the lynchings in Soweto and Johannesburg,
> they mutilated Steven Biko in a prison cell in Pretoria. Mistress
> Sarah grabs me by the hair, and she screams as hard as she can:
> you're talking nonsense, you're talking nonsense. And she drags me
> to the record player, and raises the volume as high as it will go. Now
> I can't even hear myself cry. And Donna Summer's voice, her black
> woman's voice, fills Mistress Sarah's house, jolting it with its
> rhythm.
>
> —AIDA CARTAGENA PORTALATÍN, "They Called Her Aurora
> (A Passion for Donna Summer)," 30

As shown in previous chapters, contemporary plantation fictions exist on a continuum of violence that features women participating in their larger societies' grotesque social norms. A notable number of these texts depict enslavers acting through violent skin-to-skin or mediated touch to exert power over other women per racist, sexist, and classist norms. How, then, do violent dynamics between an employer and an employee remain or change in texts that depict circum-Caribbean places after emancipation?

The epigraph, quoted from Aida Cartagena Portalatín's story "They Called Her Aurora (A Passion for Donna Summer)" (1986), begins to answer this question. The narrator is named Colita García by her mother and renamed Aurora by Mistress Sarah, which establishes the employer's power over her servant's labor and identity. In the scene referenced above, Aurora attempts to voice the atrocities in South Africa under apartheid, only to have her employer in the 1970s Dominican Republic deny this "nonsense," while she — ironically — drags her servant by the hair over to a record player booming Donna Summer's voice (30). Renamed, silenced, and assaulted by her employer, Aurora's first-person narrative is still powerful: her viewpoint cannot be silenced, despite her employer's violent efforts. Aurora's voicing of her experiences bursts through her employer's denial of structural violence. This is a fitting beginning for this chapter because many fictional texts deny the histories of violence between women as employers and employees; such fictions focus on women's "sameness" and "sisterhood" across racialized class borders in segregated societies. These romantic narratives, as this chapter will show, perpetuate a sentimental fiction about women in an age of decolonial struggles. However, the rarer examples that feature physical violence between employers and employees after emancipation, such as Portalatín's story, reveal continuities between plantation slavery and domestic labor.

I claim in this chapter that some texts reveal the persistence of racist, sexist, and classist violence from slavery well into the twentieth century, specifically through texts' strategic uses of silence. In such texts, violent outbursts between women belonging to different racialized class positions show how the grotesqueness of the plantation past persists into their present. As obvious as the trajectory of my claims might seem, this chapter counters two persistent lies: first, popular narratives that deny white women's violence against Black women in post-emancipation households; and second, popular narratives that often frame such violence (if it appears in a text) as *exceptional* to places and peoples via stereotypes (i.e., it only happens in "the South" or "the Caribbean"). Specifically, this chapter explores how Ellen Douglas's novella *Hold On* (1963), Toni Morrison's novel *Tar Baby* (1981), and the novel and filmic legacy of Jean Rhys's *Wide Sargasso Sea* (1966, 1991, 1993, and 2006) reveal or obfuscate social realities in the moments of violent touch between women. Moreover, my analyses of *Tar Baby* and adaptations of *Wide Sargasso Sea* go a step further to show how two-way altercations between women in the context of domestic labor create complex, sometimes contradictory, arguments about women's roles in colonial regimes. This chapter thereby charts a constellation of representations of women in texts ranging from popular romances of Black/white intimacies in U.S. settings to sensational portrayals of women's violence as exotic/erotic in Caribbean settings to countercultural depictions of contextualized violence. In other words, this chapter examines a wide variety of post-emancipation settings and contexts to determine how texts do or do not counter popular narratives about employers and domestic servants. As such, close readings of white women's violence in some texts expose how these women attempt to shape their identities through subjugating Other(ed) women, even well after emancipation.

At the end of chapter 3, I examined how both Delia (an enslaved woman) and Eulah Mae (a domestic servant) are silenced in deference to white women's desires in Ann Allen Shockley's *The Black and White of It* (1987). Ultimately, Shockley's stories reveal how white women coerce Black women in ways that reinforce the white women's sense of power in segregated societies; consequently, the Black women's narrative silence indicates their loss of choices. As Trudier Harris claims in her pivotal work *From Mammies to Militants*, the entire relationship between employer and domestic servant is one marked by silence in the United States: "The mistress, of course, never verbalizes . . . recognitions [of injustices] and neither does the maid. In fact, what is left unstated between them forms the basis of the ethical code that governs the relationships between Blacks and whites, especially in the South" (20). Shockley's stories act out this silence in its true form, as violence; for "in a world where language and naming are power," Adrienne Rich reminds us, "silence is oppression, is violence" ("Conditions for Work" 204). Although academic studies work to voice the lived experiences of women of color, popular fictional texts still enact the silencing of Black women.[1] First, this chapter shows how pervasive idealizations of women's *sisterhood* across racialized class lines contribute to this silencing.

Considering the wider context of debates and issues within twentieth-century feminist movements reveals a larger ideological current that attempts to silence Black women. In her essay "Disloyal to Civilization," Rich suggests, "The mutual history of black and white women in this country is a realm so painful, resonant, and forbidden that it has barely been touched by writers either of political 'science' or of imaginative literature. Yet until that history is known, that silence broken, we will all go on struggling in a state of deprivation and ignorance" (281). One such silence surrounds the issue of household labor. Women's domestic work has long been a clarion call for feminists; however, women's divisions of labor *inside white women's houses* remained a contentious issue throughout twentieth-century feminist movements.[2] As bell hooks asserts in her essay "Rethinking the Nature of Work," white feminists seemed to disregard the very silence they imposed on Black women who worked in domestic settings: "When these [white] women talked about work they were equating it with high paying careers; they were not referring to low paying jobs or so called 'menial' labor. They were so blinded by their own experiences that they ignored the fact that a vast majority of women were (even at the time *The Feminine Mystique* was published [1963]) already working outside the home, working in jobs that neither liberated them from dependence on men nor made them economically self-sufficient" (96). Along these lines, Bonnie Thornton Dill includes a criticism of mainstream feminism in the updated preface to *Across the Boundaries of Race and*

Class: "Despite . . . important first steps" scrutinizing the gender-based structures of household work, "feminism has failed to address the issues of unequal power and privilege among women inherent in any serious analysis of the structure and organization of private household work" (ix). At the time of her writing this preface in 1994, Thornton Dill acknowledges that "domestic work remains women's work and feminism has yet to confront the issues of exploitation and privilege that have resulted from the increased ability of professional women to hire working class women of color to do their housework" (x). Therefore, hooks and Thornton Dill draw attention to the fact that myopic feminist platforms did not incorporate paid domestic labor (historically performed by women of color) into their concerns during the twentieth century, which—among other issues central to decolonization—resulted in deep divisions between white and women-of-color feminist movements.[3] Winifred Breines looks back on feminism in the 1970s and summarizes that while "white and black feminists move[d] back toward one another, testing whether ground existed for trust and coalitions" in the latter part of the decade, "they never reconnected on the basis of idealism" (4). In other words, they could not cling to a sense of sisterhood that transcended race and class.

This *idealism* sets this chapter's concerns apart from previous chapters, for it seems that the bulk of texts written by white authors that feature domestic servants perpetuates a gendered idealism that occludes the violence between women so starkly evident in many novels written about slavery. I build this assertion on Sharon Monteith's claim in *Advancing Sisterhood?* that "the idioms white protagonists deploy are frequently . . . utopian and therapeutic—providing a soft-focus conciliatory perspective" (5). Writing in 2000, Monteith expands this thought to say that many twentieth-century representations of white employers and Black employees "endure beyond the historical point" of Jim Crow segregation, so that "black women characters have not yet been liberated from the kitchens of white women in contemporary fiction" (102–3). Monteith's claims are essential to *Grotesque Touch*, for previous chapters catalogue many texts that explicitly show plantation violence between women, but depictions of physical violence between women in post-emancipation U.S. households are rare (despite the proliferation of Jim Crow settings in contemporary texts).

Perhaps contemporary white authors feel the need to project gendered idealism onto the not-too-distant past of racial oppression during Jim Crow to rewrite white women's racist actions.[4] The best-selling-novel-turned-blockbuster-film *The Help* by Kathryn Stockett (2009) exemplifies this phenomenon. The novel's emphasis on a young white woman's (Skeeter's) enlightenment about the evils of her segregated society in early 1960s Jackson, Mississippi, creates the "soft-focus conciliatory perspective" Monteith describes. On the one hand, the narrative does not shy away from portraying white women as threatening cruel violence against Black women. However, on the other hand, the white women do not *physically* enact this violence, and neither is violence against Black women depicted *on stage*. Aibileen, one of the Black protagonists, says how—exactly—it comes to pass that white women do not lash out in violence against Black women in this novel:

> Womens, they ain't like men. A woman ain't gone beat you with a stick. Miss Hilly wouldn't pull no pistol on me. Miss Leefolt wouldn't come burn my house down. No, white womens like to keep they hands clean. They got a shiny little set a tools they use, sharp as witches' fingernails, tidy and laid out neat, like the picks on a dentist tray. They gone take they time with em. . . . It'll be a knock on the door, late at night. It won't be the white lady at the door. She don't do that kind a thing herself. But while the nightmare's happening, the burning or the cutting or the beating, you realize something you known all your life: the white lady don't *ever* forget. And she ain't gone stop till you dead. (Stockett 188, emphasis in original)

Here, Stockett's protagonist clears up for readers why they have not seen any woman-on-woman physical violence in the novel, *simply because white women do not commit physical violence*. The white women may be as murderous as their men, but they inherently (or so it seems) "keep their hands clean." Moreover, Tate Taylor's film adaptation of *The Help* (2011) does not even include Aibileen's reflection about white women's roles in violence; in this award-winning Hollywood-produced film, white women are entirely separated from depictions of violence on screen. *The Help* and other narratives by white authors portray white women as fundamentally incapable of performing physical violence, which sharply contrasts numerous narratives depicting plantation slavery.[5]

Though scholars such as Rebecca Sharpless, Jacqueline Jones, and Bridget Anderson have drawn explicit connections between white women's treatments of women of color during and after slavery, a persistent, popular lie that white women were not capable of such violence during Jim Crow remains.[6] Instead, throughout the latter half of the twentieth century and into our current moment, idealized texts focus on the personal-political enlightenment of a young white woman along with the *love* Black women have for her. This is what Rebecca Wanzo calls "white feelings" in "civil rights sentimental fiction" ("Civil Rights Sentimental Fiction"). Specifically, Wanzo states, these fictions depict individualized (not structural or political) "black freedom . . . made possible by white intimacy." Going a step further, I claim that these popular novels and films create myths of white women's feelings by avoiding white women's physical violence against Black women (like in *The Help*).[7] I suggest, then, that popular depictions of relationships between white and Black women set in the Jim Crow era create a curtain of silence and denial about the extent to which white women "dirty their hands" to uphold classist, racist hierarchies.

As chapter 3 reveals, a careful reading of Shockley's *The Black and White of It* exposes continuities between the ways white women exploit Black women under enslavement and Jim Crow. Likewise, the novella *Hold On*, written by the white Mississippi-born writer Ellen Douglas (Josephine Ayres Haxton), shows how physical violence is inherent to domestic employment in Mississippi in 1957. Douglas's narrative, I claim, works against the romance of "white feelings" by delving into the exploitation enacted on Estella Moseby, a Black woman who worked in a white woman's house. The story achieves this in a scene of violent touch during a boating accident that illustrates the social (and personal) separation between Estella and her former employer, Anna Glover, a white, middle-class woman. Through a startling display of actual and imagined grotesque violence in which Anna exploits Estella's body, the story shows how the women perform specifically racialized, classed, and gendered social positions in Anna's mind.

Hold On is a narrative engaged with the politics of memory, for what Anna remembers submerges the violence of what *actually* occurred between her and Estella during a boating accident. Anna's traumatic flashbacks in the first part of the story stop short of revealing her actions against Estella while they struggled in the water, "as if sight, touch, sound, turned for the moment inward and retraveled paths grooved nerve end to nerve end in her brain by the memory" (145). Because Anna denies the reality of what happened between them, details of the boating accident and the women's relationship take some time to surface. Early in the story, the narrator states that Anna's "telling and retelling and musing on the story began the day of the accident" (148), with her focus revealingly (and ironically) centered on her own survival during the event. Anna obsessively repeats, "[Estella] kept pulling me down, she kept pulling me down. . . . And the water . . . the water . . . I couldn't breathe . . . couldn't keep her up, she was too heavy. I couldn't keep her up" (148). When Anna's husband, Richard, attempts to soothe her manic repetitions, Anna knows she cannot stop revisiting the scene for fear that her actions against Estella will come through: "But I want to tell you about it. . . . I have to tell you about it" (148). The narration indicates that Anna is actually hiding something, as she "could create a romance about her actions, and could prick the balloon of her romance all at the same time" (150). At this point, Anna struggles to retain her sense of narrative control; though Anna realizes that her repetitions are not accurate, her experiences as an upper-middle-class white woman allow her to revise her actions to conform to a more palatable narrative. According to Jan Shoemaker, Anna initially constricts her story because it "is too real, too disturbing, too public, too racially ambiguous: not the kind of scene that a southern lady should become embroiled in. The main character, then, is silenced by her husband, by her race and by her culture. She can only 'try' to break the silence by narration, but time and space limit what is sayable" (86). However, when Anna meets with Carl Jensen, who rescued her from the lake, she realizes that he is also witness to her faulty memory, and "it str[ikes] her . . . that perhaps she [i]s not telling the truth" (Douglas 151).

Carl's memory of the scene—the women and Anna's children were struggling in the water—highlights what Anna has been trying to forget. According to Carl, he drew near the boat and was met with the vision of Anna holding a Black woman below the water: "I hadn't even realized you had hold of the colored woman. I hadn't seen her. She was underwater. You pulled on her belt and she came up. My God! You were holding her belt and she was floating underwater, out of sight" (151). That Estella's body was literally submerged mirrors how her experiences and perspectives are subordinate to Anna's memories and views. Anna's misremembered actions startle her at this point because she believed she had held Estella's hair in the water; Anna "had remembered the feel of stiff, greasy hair against her fingers," and now "she saw the implication of her mistake" (151–52). The "implication" here is twofold: Anna's mind attempts to reframe her actions in a manner that does not incriminate her as being racist; however, she also realizes that "everything she remembered or thought she remembered about 'it' [the incident] might be wrong. In the dark depths of herself she might be creating another story, a wholly false version of what had happened in the dark depths of the lake" (152). Indeed, if Anna could mistake the feel of a belt for the feel of Estella's hair, then she could be remembering other aspects of the wreck differently. Although Anna believes that she would have brought Estella's face up to the surface, Carl's story destroys her romanticized vision of heroics— Estella was thoroughly submerged by Anna's actions. The social implications of Anna's memory are difficult to ignore, as the narrative now reveals a bit more about Anna's unacknowledged racism and her participation in a system that harms Black women.

The story's next section uses a more detached narrator to describe the events leading up to the boating accident and the scene Carl Jensen remembers. The social dynamic of Anna and Estella's relationship thereby becomes clearer when the narrative shifts outside of Anna's mind. Each woman acts out "rituals of deference and maternalism" that Judith Rollins identifies in the employer/domestic employee relationship (157). The women's adherence to these roles—coupled with Anna's denial of her privileged position in this society that violently attempts to create and maintain social separation between white and Black—catalyzes the moment of violent touch between them. Anna's violence thereby signals the vast separation between them and the "silences not only between the women, but sometimes within them" (Shoemaker 84). At the beginning of their interaction, for example, Estella enthusiastically shouts out to Anna on the dock, calling her "Miss Anna" even though she has not worked for Anna since Estella's recent pregnancies (Douglas 167). Estella's deference is evident when her former employer invites her to join the fishing excursion on the boat. Despite Estella's obvious reluctance— she "hesitate[s]" and admits, "Boats make me nervous"—Anna assumes that she knows what is best: "Oh, come on, Estella. . . . You know you want to go" (167). Instead of listening to Estella's concerns, Anna shows that the women's relationship is predicated on her own preferences, and she treats Estella like one of the children.

Furthermore, Anna does not have a way to relate to Estella outside of their employer/employee relationship, which the story reveals during their conversation while fishing. In this scene, the two women appear to talk past each other: Anna wishes Estella would return to work for her, yet Estella's husband will not let her work because he believes she should take care of her own children; Estella admits that her nerves are frayed from watching her children, yet she knows that returning to work would not make fiscal sense (because she would have to pay someone to look after her youngest children); then, Anna suggests (not for the first time) that Estella should take preventive measures to avoid pregnancy, but Estella defers to her husband who believes these precautions are "against nature" (174–75). Next, as if to illustrate the point that their relationship will soon lead to outright violence, a venomous snake interrupts the women when it attacks their string of fish. This narrative break, much like a mass of writhing snakes that appears twenty-five years later in Douglas's *Can't Quit You, Baby* (1988), shows how the violence inherent to their relationship cannot be contained or denied. Douglas's later novel depicts the relationship between Cornelia, a white employer, and Tweet (Julia), her Black employee, as the truth of their social inequalities seethes (silently and precariously) just below the surface. Wondering about the politics of representing this relationship, the narrator asks, "What tangle of snakes have I been skiing over?" (131). This question connects Cornelia and a legendary water skier who met her end in a "writhing, tangled mass of water moccasins," because it is "always true that a tangle of water moccasins lies in wait for the skier. Always, always true" (131). Thus, Cornelia, the narrator, and the reader cannot escape the narrative without understanding some basic, painful truths about Cornelia's relationship to Tweet in terms of power.[8] Cornelia (and we as readers) cannot avoid the snaky tangle of power at the heart of their employer/employee relationship. Similarly, *Hold On* reveals that Anna's veneer of calm understanding dissolves when confronted by the relationship of power between her and Estella.

This dynamic is most apparent when Anna has an intense reaction to Estella's beliefs during their failed conversation. Estella, the narrative shows, comes from a community of strong cultural beliefs that Anna does not—and will not—understand. Although the narrative makes clear that Estella's deferment to her husband and community do not necessarily ensure her well-being—especially in terms of motherhood—Estella's thoughts outside of her dialogue are absent from the story, and readers can only infer her desires beyond her home (she is, after all, absenting herself from her family to fish alone). Instead of wishing to understand Estella's social position, Anna rejects her: "Her thoughts were in a tumult of exasperation, bafflement, and outrage. She tried unsuccessfully to deny, to block out the overriding sense of the difference between herself and Estella, borne in on her by this strange conversation, so foreign to their quiet, sensible friendship" (Douglas 182). Whereas Anna led herself to believe she could have a calm relationship of understanding with Estella inside her home, the truth of the women's relationship runs just below the surface of their interactions. The narrative uncovers Anna's naïve thinking that she could "wipe out, *at least in this one small area of her own personal life*, the universal guilt, the heritage that builds itself every day into a more complex and hate-filled present" (183, emphasis mine). Anna therefore believes she could selectively deny the violent power structures of her racist, classist, sexist society inside her home, though that is the very place where Estella's role as maid demands deference. Anna realizes here that a fragile sense of equality between her and her former employee crumbles when Estella's firmly held cultural beliefs differ from her own. In this moment, the reality of their social positions (i.e., the social hierarchies enforced by Anna's upbringing) confronts Anna with a sense of impending doom, for she thought that she and Estella lived outside of racist structures: "It was as if a chasm had opened between them from which there rose, like fog off the nightmare waters of a dream, the wisps and trails of misted feelings: hates she had thought exorcised, contempt she had believed rendered contemptible, the power that corrupts and the submission that envenoms" (183). Yet, Anna's feeling of horror is not enough to force her to examine her relationship to Estella; she never realizes what Lillian Smith articulates in *Killers of the Dream* (1949): her elders taught her "to believe in freedom, to glow when the word *democracy* was used, and to practice slavery from morning to night" (L. Smith 29, emphasis in original). Anna instead struggles to deny the hate, contempt, and power that her social position has conditioned her to accept. As with the enslaver Heather in Shockley's story "The Mistress and the Slave Girl," Anna does not acknowledge her compliance in systems of power that deem Estella subhuman. Anna obsessively focuses her thoughts on her feelings (her dismay) until her actions during the boating accident force her to see her own position of power via violent touch.

Anna's feeble feelings of liberalism do not withstand the physical violence she exerts on Estella's body, and what happens below the lake's surface makes apparent Anna's internalization of the women's social positions. Only when a rogue wave starts to tip their boat does Anna realize "one paralyzing thought: She can't swim. My God, Estella can't swim" (Douglas 189). Instead of ensuring Estella's safety, Anna's sense of maternalism (she believes she knows what is best for Estella) therefore puts both women in danger because Anna insisted that her former employee join her on the boat. The language of this scene while both women struggle in the water reflects Anna's failed maternal relationship with Estella: "Then both women came up and Anna got hold of Estella's arm again. 'Come *on*,' she gasped"; "She won't do *anything*, Anna thought. I can't make her help herself" (192, emphasis in original). In this primal scene of survival, Anna's thoughts reflect her racist attitudes toward Estella in general, as her society—and Anna—regard Estella as "this reasonless two hundred pounds of flesh with which she had to deal" (193). As the women's bodies struggle for air, Estella relies on Anna to save her: "She kept her arms gently, trustingly around Anna's neck, and pulled her down" (194). This language suggests that Anna ultimately regards Estella as a thing that hinders her. While any person's physical reaction to drowning would spur them to selfish action, the narration of this scene—filtered through Anna's perspective—evinces that Anna believes Estella is childlike because of her trusting embrace.

Thus, Anna is much like other fair-weather white moderates in her society, those whom Martin Luther King Jr. said were "more devoted to 'order' than to justice" (366). Anna believes underwater that she can do nothing more for Estella because their struggle is bringing her down as well. Therefore, to survive, Anna decides to act: *"She's going to drown me. I've got to let her drown, or she will drown me"* (194–95, emphasis in original). The narration depicts Anna's violent actions in startling detail that serve as a metaphor for their positions in this grotesquely unequal society: "[Anna] drew her knee up under her chin, planted her foot in the soft belly, still swollen from pregnancy, and shoved as hard as she could, pushing herself up and back, and Estella down and away. It was easy to push her away. The big arms slid off Anna's shoulders, the limp hands making no attempt to clutch or hold. They had been together, close as lovers in the darkness or as twins in the womb of the lake, and now they were apart" (195). This description of the women conjures several cultural images. First, Anna kicking Estella's maternal body, "the soft belly," suggests Black women's forced role as "mammy" to white women's children during slavery and after emancipation. Although Estella seems to have avoided this role by staying with her own children, this brief scene of violence below water connects a much wider history of Black and white women to this point in the mid-twentieth century. Kimberly Wallace-Sanders's *Mammy* provides essential background for the mammy figure Douglas's work draws on; Anna forcefully pushes away the "maternity" of the mammy (Wallace-Sanders 5), represented by Estella's soft stomach.[9] Also apparent in this scene is how easily Anna inflicts this violent touch and how quickly Estella slips away. Although the women have been closely intimate—like the generations of white and Black women who lived in compulsory proximity inside the plantation house before them—the personal familiarity cultivated by Anna is illusory. Shoemaker asserts that this scene "suggests an almost erotic attraction/repulsion to the 'other' that reinforces Anna's ambivalent feelings about her responsibility to Estella's race and casts doubt on the authenticity of their friendship" (85); yet, my reading sees even less hope here. This underwater scene repeatedly shows how Anna dehumanizes Estella, as Estella becomes a series of body parts ("the belly," "the arms," and "the hands"). Confronting this truth would mean Anna's admission of racist thoughts, and Anna's mind performs elaborate maneuvers to avoid this reality.

Despite her evasion, Anna knows she purposefully kicked Estella's stomach to break them apart, and this action (coupled with her holding Estella's motionless body underwater) weighs heavily on her mind. Remarkably,

Estella survives the ordeal to bear further witness to Anna's actions. After Estella regains consciousness in the hospital, Anna visits her and begins to mentally break away from her actions. When Estella says that her entire body feels sore, Anna replies, "I reckon that's from the artificial respiration. . . . I had never seen anyone do it that way before. They pick you up under the stomach and then put you down and lift your arms. And then, too, I kicked you. And we must have banged you up some getting you into the boat. Lord! The more I think about it, the worse it gets" (Douglas 220). Anna uses the vague word "it" to connote the fear of near-drowning, but "it" could also represent Anna's evasion when she glances at the grotesque horror of violence that runs barely beneath the surface of her segregated society. Her words also downplay the violence she inflicted on Estella's body, and yet, Estella immediately asks in confusion, "You kicked me?" (221). Still employing a maternal role, Anna tells Estella her misremembered story that the kick was "lucky" because it made Estella pass out so that Anna could hold her hair while rescuers came to their aid. The narrator interjects, "So [Anna] told it at the time, and the kick was only an insignificant part of the story" (221); however, the kick *is* the story. Their relationship as employer and domestic servant repeats patterns of violence to uphold social order.

Although the women could begin to bridge the socially sanctioned separation between them with honesty, the story ends ambiguously. As the narrative jumps forward to Anna's conversation with Carl, she at least admits to herself that her memories (that she has tried to contain) represent "a nightmare of failure, of cowardice" (222). Anna tries to imagine other ways she could have acted (perhaps she could have knocked Estella out with a paddle), but she denies her willingness to treat Estella like a thing: "But I would never have done that. *Never*" (222, emphasis in original). Anna does finally concede, "It's nothing but an accident that [Estella] didn't die" after she "kicked Estella away" (223, 231). Yet, what will Anna *do* with this realization? The answer remains unclear: Anna still seems to lack the ability to scrutinize her position in this society that deems Estella a thing, much like the women who enslave other women in chapters 1, 2, and 3. Douglas's novella instead ends with a vaguely uplifting scene when Anna and Carl see Estella fishing off a walkway. Anna "call[s] through the dusk, across the distance between them . . . 'Come on down and join us'" (232). The last words of the story imply connection despite their differences, but Anna—once again—adopts a maternal role when she believes she and Carl "can give [Estella] a ride home" (232). Perhaps her actions underwater have indeed changed Anna; maybe she will no longer abuse Estella. Nonetheless, the story ends with the probability that Anna does not fully understand her privilege and power, nor the violence fundamental to her social position.

Although Ellen Douglas's protagonist Anna tries to deny the realities and implications of her actions and attitudes (and therefore stands in as a symbol of the all-too-common silence concerning violence between employers and domestic servants in the United States), women of color have long spoken out against this violence. Their accounts give voice to women of color who have labored in other women's homes as employees throughout the nation, while at the same time these narratives bring to light the potential risks of talking back. Such countercultural depictions of violence originate in the nineteenth century; for example, Harriet E. Wilson's novel *Our Nig* (1859) shows the continuities of white women's treatments of Black women throughout the nation just before the Civil War. To drive this point home, Wilson states in the preface, "My mistress was wholly imbued with *southern* principles" (3, emphasis in original). The preface connects Wilson's novel to the depictions of enslavers and enslaved women in *Grotesque Touch*'s previous chapters, for Frado, a Black domestic worker (assumingly based on Wilson's own experiences in a northern U.S. city), constantly experiences grotesque physical violence at the hands of her employer Mrs. Bellmont and her employer's daughter Mary. Together and on their own, Mrs. Bellmont and Mary show how generations of U.S. citizens thrive on inflicting pain on Black women. The novel depicts the women "spicing [Frado's] toil with 'words that burn,' and frequent blows on her head" (30), "applying a rawhide," "propping her mouth open with a piece of wood" (35), "kick[ing] her so forcibly as to throw her upon the floor" (43–44), and even throwing a large knife at her (64). Much like Mrs. Flint in Harriet Jacobs's autobiography, Mrs. Bellmont is an ever-present "right she-devil" who thoroughly enjoys abusing Frado (17, 66).

If Mrs. Bellmont's character is consistent with "southern principles" in a northern U.S. place, then the book gestures toward the realities of racism, classism, and sexism throughout the nation. The novel depicts Mrs. Bellmont as "self-willed, haughty, undisciplined, arbitrary and severe" (25), and she repeatedly calls Frado a "nigger" and the shortened slur "Nig" without any resistance from other white people in her northern U.S. society. Ultimately, no white person can make lasting change for Frado's work conditions. As Cynthia J. Davis argues, "Wilson vividly represents Frado as raced and vehemently condemns the racism that induces whites to abuse black bodies" (392). This is especially evident in Mrs. Bellmont's own words about the beatings: "I'll take the skin from her body" (Wilson 46); "She shall learn her place" (47); "I'll beat the money out of her" (90). Even as the Bellmonts' son James "assure[s] her that [his] mother's views [a]re by no means general" (75), his weak attempt to console Frado actually shows the ineffectiveness of denying structural harm. The novel's descriptions of Mrs. Bellmont's "arbitrary" violence against Frado and the inaction of witnesses critique national systems, as Frado's racialized and gendered class position places her at the bottom of structures of power in the United States.

Still, later in the narrative, Mrs. Bellmont is momentarily struck with a sense of the accumulation of her violence against Frado. She wonders what "experience" Frado related to members of the church she attends, "as if she expected to hear the number of times she had whipped Frado, and the number of lashes set forth in plain Arabic numbers" (103). DoVeanna S. Fulton connects Frado's experiences to enslavement here, for Wilson "employs the language of slave law" by indicating a certain number of lashes (47). Before this instance, Mrs. Bellmont and Mary both threaten Frado with death and permanent silence if she dares to tell anyone about their exploits (Wilson 65, 72). Although they have been able to treat Frado in any way they wish, the white women fear Frado's articulation of her experiences. Consequently, when Frado finally speaks out against her employer—"'Stop!' shouted Frado, 'strike me, and I'll never work a mite more for you'" (105)—she learns the power of her voice. Although the Bellmont women and U.S. society's structures at large still beat and abuse her, Frado's speaking out means that she "learn[s] how to conquer," to a degree (108). Speaking out essentially allows her to think in terms of insurrection: "She contemplated administering poison to her mistress, to rid herself and the house of so detestable a plague" (108). In a limited way, then, Frado embodies the emergent militant maid of Trudier Harris's theoretical framework, as one who is willing to speak against the status quo (16). "By documenting, by testifying again and again to her pain," Cynthia J. Davis argues, "Wilson effectively takes control of that pain, wresting power from her torturer and appropriating it for herself" (399). In writing this narrative, then, "Wilson's[/Frado's] speech act takes the contents and discourse of the domestic sphere, . . . and publicizes them, thereby, subjecting her mistress to public censure" (Fulton 49). Unlike Anna's silencing of Estella in *Hold On*, Wilson's narrative thereby offers an early example of a Black woman speaking up and speaking back to the people and systems that seek to silence her.

Frado illustrates militant tendencies in literature about domestic servants who speak out in the face of physical violence, a theme that persists. Alice Childress's *Like One of the Family* (1956), for example, is a fictional epistolary narrative about a Black domestic worker's thoughts concerning her day-to-day life working for white people in mid-twentieth-century New York City. This narrative takes another step, as the protagonist Mildred constantly writes about her own speaking out to her employers. For instance, Mildred clearly speaks back to her employer's "white feelings" (to use Rebecca Wanzo's term) in an early letter: "In the first place, you do not *love* me; you may be fond of me, but that is all. . . . In the second place, I am *not* just like one of the family at all!" (Childress 2, emphasis in original). More recently, the novel *The True Nanny Diaries* (2009) by Nandi focuses on the psychological breakdown of Valdi, a Trinidadian woman who comes to New York City for graduate study at Columbia University but instead ends up working for decades as a nanny to wealthy families (when her scholarship is revoked due to political reasons outside of her control). Amplifying the trope of speaking back in Wilson's and Childress's narratives, Valdi's voice finds power through sharply critiquing her social position as "just a stroller-pusher bent on preserving the image of the American Mammy, as little white dreams rooted and blossomed out of [her] black, fucking nightmare" (52). Valdi's experiences as a migrant domestic servant in the United States connect to this chapter's larger themes by voicing her self in the face of stereotypes that work alongside a colonizing culture's denials of oppression. In Valdi's narrative that takes place during the early days of the twenty-first century, readers see social divisions that U.S. employers amplify by abusing migrants' tenuous socioeconomic positions.[10]

Valdi's story calls attention to the myriad ways employers can exert control over the bodies of their employees. Moreover, domestic servants who speak out against the status quo are likely to sacrifice their physical well-being due to violent retribution from white people who are unwilling to hear Black employees assert themselves. One example of this struggle occurs in Alice Walker's *The Color Purple* (1982), set in early twentieth-century rural Georgia. When Sofia replies "Hell no" to Miss Millie, the white mayor's spouse, when asked if she "would . . . like to work for [her], be [Miss Millie's] maid," Sofia and the mayor exchange blows (86). He then locks her away for years of hard toil, only to be released from prison to work for Miss Millie. Sofia's punishment for voicing her self, then, is to be sentenced to the very domestic labor she wanted to avoid, and as Monteith observes, "Walker finds little to distinguish between the severity of the two forms of sentence" (104).[11] Yet, the narrator, Celie, marvels at Sofia's persistence: "Three years after she beat she out of the wash house, got her color and her weight back, look like her old self, just all time think bout killing somebody" (Walker 98). Although Sofia does not commit direct violence against her white employers—the same family who imprisoned her and continue to separate her from her own children—her presence is a constant reminder of violence, and this frightens Miss Millie (99).[12]

As Wilson's, Childress's, Nandi's, and Walker's novels demonstrate, narratives can employ a variety of strategies to show women speaking out and speaking back to oppressive structures in domestic labor. Like in chapter 2's discussion of reciprocal violence, some narratives also depict domestic workers' direct, physical violence. Here, we can consider the small selection of militantly violent servants in literature; as Trudier Harris describes, they are those who "wear southern masks [of mammyism] only to bring about violence or never wear them—instead confronting exploitation directly" (23). Some employees, says Harris, "wear masks, like Brer Rabbit at his most militant, only to cover violent, destructive intentions: they are without mercy and without guilt" (34). As Monteith adds, such "fictions by black writers that depict house slaves, black maids, or domestics are often so infused with black militancy, particularly following the civil rights activism of the 1950s and 1960s, that the image of the benign, longsuffering family retainer is turned around" (103). These violent employees—like the enslaved woman Lilith in chapter 2—embody what Rollins calls *"ressentiment,"* which is "more than hostility"; it is "a long-term, seething, deep-rooted negative feeling toward those whom one feels unjustly have power or an advantage over one's life" (227, emphasis in original). In his commentary on violent servants in fiction, Albert Memmi states that he is "convinced that the key to the excessive violence of the domestic servant is found in this extremely intimate relationship between servant and master; because their lives are so interwoven in such an intimate manner, the servant will attack all the more angrily. The oppression of the domestic becomes more profound and more unbearable the more it is padded and in some ways accepted" (178). Therefore, if the intimacies between enslavers and enslaved women are violent, then it follows that employer and domestic employee relationships after emancipation can carry residual violence from plantation slavery. As with depictions of enslaved women, violence enacted by domestic servants has the potential to deeply unsettle social norms and the narratives that perpetuate them (including sentimental narratives about employers and employees). Authors of color repeatedly bring these possibilities into focus.[13]

As a part of this narrative genealogy, the two-way violence between a Black employee and her white employer in Toni Morrison's novel *Tar Baby* explodes from *ressentiment*, to apply Rollins's term, due to the corrupt intimacies prevalent in their relationship. Furthermore, *Tar Baby* exports the women's relationship to a Caribbean setting (they were born in the United States, and the novel is primarily set on a fictional island). There, the violence inherent to their social dynamic breaks through a veneer of civility. In the novel, Isle des Chevaliers, which is near the island Dominique (loosely based on Haiti), functions as a microcosm of neo-imperial realities in the region; the island predictably offers the wealthy, white U.S. citizen Valerian Street a vacation home during his retirement from candy production. As Stelamaris Coser argues in *Bridging the Americas*, Valerian's house and island "become the stage for the continuing conflicts between dominant interests and values and a resisting black culture" (109). The Streets' house serves as a privileged space amid disadvantaged Caribbean peoples, evinced in the fact that the Streets keep Caribbean-born servants nameless and then easily replace them (110–11). Both Valerian's business (candy production) and the anonymity of his servants are reminiscent of the ways enslaved people were made expendable in sugar production, as I examine in chapter 2's discussions of *All Souls' Rising* and *Hoe Duur Was de Suiker*.

In this fraught setting, where Valerian and his wife Margaret enjoy leisure made possible through inexpensive, tireless, yet also expendable labor reliant on Caribbean people of color, the relationship between Margaret and her longtime servant Ondine Childs, an African American woman, comes to a head. Morrison's novel thereby creates a Caribbean space for the characters Margaret and Ondine, both born in the United States, to act out their roles as employer and employee, a performance that exposes the violence inherent in household, national, and hemispheric systems of labor. To illustrate, the Streets believe Ondine occupies a stable space inside the home as their head servant; however, her involvement with the family's domestic lives in the United States and now on Isle des Chevaliers means that (on top of the unending physical labor she must perform for the Streets) she must act as the untiring receptacle for Margaret's secrets and fears. Ondine's experiences as a domestic servant mirror Rollins's claims that exploitation "grows out of the precise element that makes it unique: the personal relationship between employer and employee. What might appear to be the basis of a more humane, less alienating work arrangement allows for a level of psychological exploitation unknown in other occupations. The typical employer extracts more than labor" (156). Likewise, Mahnaz Kousha finds that domestic labor has always "included a hidden 'emotional labor' wherein workers were compelled to respond to their employers' emotional needs," and she writes about employees' methods of coping with "this emotionally intimate yet socially distant relationship with their employers" (78, 79). As Patricia Hill Collins indicates, this intimacy (through an employer's questioning, gifting, and confiding) is another method that they use "to structure domestic work's power relationship and solicit the deference they so desire" (56, 57). Margaret and Ondine's relationship operates inside such exploitative forms of intimacy, which exposes the lies of women's "sisterhood" perpetuated by sentimental fiction set in the civil rights era.

The emotional labor Margaret extracts from Ondine thereby stretches the women's relationship beyond what Ondine can continue to provide. Indeed, Ondine's unacknowledged and exploited labor catalyzes the violence between the women during a dinner scene, when their families were supposed to enjoy an elaborate meal together. As Ondine asserts her opinions to Valerian Street, because he fired her Caribbean kitchen helper, she levels a verbal jab at Margaret that claims the domestic space as her own: "Yes my kitchen and yes my help. If not mine, whose? . . . The first time in her life she [Margaret] tries to boil water and I get slapped in the face. Keep that bitch out of my kitchen. She's not fit to enter it. She's no cook and she's no mother" (207). Ondine juxtaposes her place in the domestic sphere—she provides the family's physical necessities and emotional comforts—and Margaret's nonplace as outsider because she does not deliver any of the domestic labor as *cook* or *mother*. Furthermore, by asserting her position as woman of the house, Ondine claims what class status should grant Margaret: Ondine says that the "kitchen" and "the help" are hers.

Margaret, upon hearing Ondine (who should be *her* "help") articulate how she has no place inside the household, now springs into action. Margaret throws a glass of Evian at Ondine, which weaponizes a luxury good that Margaret routinely takes for granted. In this moment, the women's physical responses to each other actualize the implicit violence of their relationship, and as retribution, Ondine rushes around the table, "at the target of all her anger," and slaps Margaret's face (208). The violence continues when Margaret grabs Ondine's braids and attempts to knock her head against the table, yet Ondine's retaliatory blows prevent further injury. This violent scene between employer and employee peaks when Ondine shouts that Margaret is a "white freak" because Margaret injured her son Michael for her sadistic pleasure, and Margaret yells, "Shut up! Shut up! You nigger! You nigger bitch! Shut your big mouth, I'll kill you!" (208). In this heated exchange, the women throw verbal jabs that reiterate their society's gendered racial norms, for Ondine calls into question Margaret's white womanhood via her failed motherhood, while Margaret has at her disposal language that attempts to debase Ondine as a Black woman. In response to Margaret's racist, sexist speech,

Ondine insists more emphatically that Margaret is not a fit white woman, and she stresses her claim to the family's domestic spaces: "Yes my kitchen. Yes my kitchen. I am the woman in this house. None other. As God is my witness there is none other. Not in this house" (209). Despite Ondine's speech in which she asserts her power over the house, Margaret falls back on the assurance of her race and class. Margaret, appearing "serene and lovely," ends the scene by saying, "I have always loved my son. . . . I am not one of those women in the *National Enquirer*" (209). Although Ondine confronts Margaret with her failures as a white woman, Margaret can have the last word in the matter due to her social position as a wealthy white woman on this Caribbean island.

By forgoing narrative silence to feature a scene of two-way physical violence between white and Black women from the United States, *Tar Baby* exposes the exploitation rooted in domestic labor. In this moment, masks of propriety fall from Ondine and Margaret's relationship, and as Ondine weaponizes her intimate knowledge of the Streets (from the preparation of their daily meals, to Margaret's inattention, to Margaret's child abuse), Margaret's reaction tears away any illusions of their closeness. When physical violence is not enough, Margaret hurls racist speech at Ondine to attempt to silence her, and the scene makes clear how easily these words, and her violent actions, rise to the surface. Morrison's novel shows how Margaret's feelings dictate the terms of their relationship: as such, the novel makes clear how "sentimental fiction" that privileges white women's feelings, to recall Rebecca Wanzo's terminology, enables the continuing exploitation of domestic servants' physical and emotional labor. In this way, *Tar Baby* counters popular narratives about employers and their domestic servants in a U.S. context via a scene of violence that reveals ongoing systems of racialized, forced labor extraction. That Margaret does not "keep her hands clean" of physical violence merely shows readers what was already evident in the inequalities of her relationship with Ondine. However, Ondine's retaliatory violence also shows her acting and speaking out against a regime that would have her suffer silently for the sake of preserving a grand fiction about white women's goodness and Black women's selflessness. Here, despite Margaret's assertion of her privilege at the end of the scene (in which she attempts to silence Ondine), the narrative itself carves a space for Ondine's response to the systems that entrap her, a narrative space not granted to Estella in Ellen Douglas's *Hold On*. Moreover, *Tar Baby* plays out the tensions between a U.S.-born employer and a U.S.-born employee in a Caribbean location to connect these representations to a much larger context of neo-colonialism, including migration and tourism. The two-way violence between Margaret and Ondine thereby illustrates the violence of the entire enterprise of silencing the experiences of women who work in other women's houses, both domestically and abroad.

Similar to the long-running narrative silences about African American women's experiences as domestic workers, Caribbean women's experiences in transnational movements and power structures were ignored for far too long. As Janet Henshall Momsen states, for example, the Caribbean women who migrated to take domestic labor positions in the United States, Canada, and Great Britain after World War II "until recently, . . . were statistically invisible in migration data and . . . remained largely unrecorded in censuses, and often out of reach of labour unions and non-governmental organizations" (1).[14] Likewise, A. Lynn Bolles emphasizes how Caribbean tourism industries have always depended on expendable, invisible labor, as resorts rely on local and migrant women forced into low-paying labor, including sex work, without opportunities for promotion (228–30). And while employees' labor might be *invisible* to a tourist's eye, long-running stereotypes about the allures of Caribbean people's bodies also make them *available* for exploitation and violence (in the eyes of colonizers). The narratives produced and replicated via tourism industries about Caribbean people (i.e., their sexual availability) reach back into the nineteenth century, when, as Mimi Sheller claims, colonizers "reconstituted power relations of bodily proximity and domination" in post-emancipation colonies through tourism (156).[15] The remaining portion of this chapter will interrogate these seemingly competing narratives about Caribbean domestic workers (for example, their invisibility *and* their availability). To do this, I will examine how filmic adaptations of *Wide Sargasso Sea* either perpetuate or counter such narrative traps. Moreover, as we will see, colonizing narratives tend to rely on a set of stereotypes that "other" *all* Caribbean characters.

Jean Rhys's novel *Wide Sargasso Sea* (1966), now a staple of post-colonial literary studies, is one of many novels that show colonial power structures at work inside Caribbean households. Indeed, from the twentieth century to today, Caribbean literary productions have tended to expose the fraught relationships between workers' positions as colonial, national, and neo-colonial subjects. As Supriya M. Nair summarizes, "Current [creative and analytic] work now locates the female domestic worker in circuits of global capital, disrupting any singular notion of the domestic as immobile . . . and highlighting the role of Caribbean women in transnational domestic work, as we see in the fiction of Paule Marshall, [Jamaica] Kincaid, and Edwidge

Danticat, and in a host of Latin American and Caribbean sociological studies" (53–54). Unlike in popular narratives that frame Black domestic servants in the United States as being *like members of the family* who are isolated inside the homes of their white employers, "In Caribbean literature of any ethnic background, the private space of the home is never too disconnected from the history of slavery, servitude, violence, and exile" (Nair 49). Homes "do not function as cozy settings of bourgeois domesticity" and instead reflect the traumas of cultures in contact throughout time, as Caribbean literatures create "intense dystopia in [their] visions of domesticity" (49). For example, the collection *Green Cane and Juicy Flotsam* (1986), from which I quote in this chapter's epigraph, gives voice to those people silenced throughout the Caribbean because of their race, ethnicity, class, gender, nationality, sexuality, ability, and skin tone. Many of the stories in the collection feature characters who are victimized domestic servants; furthermore, the collection creates connections between peoples throughout the world via their anticolonial mindsets and struggles.

Closely reading scenes of violence between women in Rhys's novel adds another dimension to this chapter's discussion of narrative silence and structural violence because the novel implies how colonial norms connect post-emancipation Jamaica in the nineteenth century to Jamaica in the mid-twentieth century. The novel, as I will detail, depicts complex two-way altercations between white and Black women, which show how they are attempting to claim some agency in a colonial context. These scenes exhibit the violence of colonization to a readership in the twentieth century, similar to *Tar Baby*'s scene of violence between Margaret and Ondine. This chapter does not stop with Rhys's novel, however. Just as chapter 1 shows how iconography and narratives exist and morph beyond the pages of a single novel (take *Mandingo*'s filmic, visual, and pornographic legacies, for instance), so do filmic adaptations of *Wide Sargasso Sea* offer examples of how colonizing cultural narratives drive studio-produced depictions of Caribbean places, peoples, and cultures. In ending with a close examination of three adaptations of *Wide Sargasso Sea*, this chapter articulates a troubling trajectory about violence in narratives, for a film that shows violence between women in a Caribbean household is not necessarily progressive. Indeed, such a film must carefully contextualize such violence to avoid exoticizing or eroticizing the women.

Published in 1966, when independence was newly won in Jamaica and was on the horizon for Dominica, the novel *Wide Sargasso Sea* can be read in multiple ways. We can certainly read the novel as a post-colonial text talking back to an English "mother-text," Charlotte Brontë's 1847 *Jane Eyre* (Rody 133). Also, because it moves *Jane Eyre's* setting to the 1830s (from an earlier period), *Wide Sargasso Sea* depicts domestic upheaval during the years following the Emancipation Act of 1833. Within this context, the novel can also be read as a twentieth-century Dominican expat's portrayal of the complexities the British colonial system posed for a white Creole elite class in Jamaica. The novel's plot hinges on Antoinette Cosway's (the white Creole protagonist's) interactions with Black Jamaican women who are domestic servants. These interactions between women are fraught with the residual violence of slavery, both in Rhys's novel and in historiographies of gendered labor in Jamaica. The historian Michele A. Johnson, for example, asserts that domestic labor in Jamaica during the mid-twentieth century "is primarily a study in women's labour" due to "the belief that domestic service was 'women's work'" (402). Johnson continues to connect gendered disparity to colonial history, as women's social places in Jamaica were marked by exploitation and ambivalence (403). Just as recent studies of domestic labor in the United States have focused on the complex—and often volatile—intimate nature of employment, so does Johnson find this relationship intimate in Jamaica, especially in terms of punishment, which "was often of a very personal nature" (404).

Similarly, these violent relationships extend beyond Rhys's novel to many novels set in Jamaica. For example, the earliest Caribbean novel to focus on a Black Caribbean protagonist, *Jane's Career* by Herbert G. de Lisser (1913), shows the everyday violence and manipulation of the young Jane at the hands of her Jamaican employer.[16] As a girl from the countryside, Jane must adapt to city life in Kingston, where she is abused by Mrs. Mason, who is called a "lady" because she belongs to the middle class and has a lighter skin tone than her servants.[17] One of Mrs. Mason's house servants connects her employers' attitudes to those of enslavers who lived generations earlier: "Mose of de people I work wid is de same like dis one. Dem all t'ink you is a slave an' a t'ief" (34). Mrs. Mason proves this point when she strikes Jane repeatedly; in one scene, she demands that the girl stop making sounds, but "she yet want[s] her to give outward and visible sign and vocal expression of suffering" (54–55). Given such a mixture of contradictory orders throughout her employment, Jane finally stands up for herself—"I do me work, an' I don't do noten for anybody to beat me for" (73)—and sets off to find factory work. *Jane's Career* ends with the possibility of class mobility in colonial Jamaica, as Jane ultimately becomes the head of her own lower-middle-class home: "It is Jane, who now herself employs a schoolgirl, who submissively calls her

Miss Jane, and obeys her slightest command" (196). This context concerning domestic servants in twentieth-century Jamaican society and literature is essential to foreground the roles that Black women play in Jean Rhys's *Wide Sargasso Sea*. As Johnson's study shows, violence was still very much a means of controlling domestic workers generations after emancipation, a reality central to de Lisser's fictional representation of a Black woman who worked her way into a higher class. Given this context, *Wide Sargasso Sea* acts out racialized class struggles after emancipation to reflect similar anxieties in Rhys's twentieth-century present.

While *Wide Sargasso Sea* employs a writing style that submerges the violence inherent in Jamaica's and Dominica's histories of colonial exploitation in the 1830s and beyond, this narrative cannot maintain the denial of the past for long. Like Douglas's *Hold On* and Morrison's *Tar Baby*, *Wide Sargasso Sea* features key scenes of violence between women that are central to understanding how the novel confronts colonizers' denials of their violence in Jamaica and Dominica. Moreover, the novel goes a step further than *Hold On* to feature a complex two-way altercation between women from different racialized classes, similar to *Tar Baby*. In this way, Rhys's novel counters sentimentalized fictions of domestic labor. This section will examine depictions of violence in three scenes: the Coulibri house fire scene in which Tia (a Black child) strikes Antoinette Cosway (a white Creole child) with a stone; the fight scene between Amélie (a mixed-race servant) and Antoinette as an adult; and then the concluding scene in which Antoinette dreams of Tia's encouragement to jump from the roof of the English manor house. These scenes reveal that, despite Antoinette's longing for sisterhood between her and women belonging to the domestic servant class, the novel consistently indicates how the cultural context of slavery and colonization foreground any interaction. Thus, the violence that suddenly wells up between Antoinette and Tia, then Antoinette and Amélie, is expected, as this violence was always just below the surface.

Because Antoinette belongs to the recently defunct enslaver class, her childhood at the former plantation Coulibri in Jamaica is lonely; her family's newly impoverished state post-emancipation leaves her separated from other white Creole families who have fared better or left the island. Antoinette's loneliness connects to Marlon James's depiction of white Creoles in *The Book of Night Women* in chapter 2, as the name of the Jamaican plantation Coulibre in James's text invites comparison. *Night Women* reimagines *Wide Sargasso Sea* through the perspectives of Black women before emancipation; read as such, James's novel evinces *Wide Sargasso Sea*'s narrative lapses concerning

Black women's experiences of social norms that remain intact after emancipation. There are also numerous narrative parallels between Isobel (in James's text) and Antoinette (in Rhys's text). Yet, in *Wide Sargasso Sea*, Antoinette does not mirror Isobel's vehement racism. Young Antoinette in part 1 of the novel, for example, welcomes the companionship of the cook's daughter, Tia, whom Antoinette believes is "soon . . . [her] friend" (Rhys 469). Still, the deep inequalities in their social conditioning (and Antoinette's learned racism) are apparent when Antoinette and Tia play at the bathing pool and Antoinette loses a bet that she can turn somersaults underwater. Antoinette initially thinks, "I hadn't done [the somersault] good and besides pennies didn't buy much. Why did I look at her like that?" (470). Antoinette then confirms her social position by calling Tia a "cheating nigger" (470), and she, in Sandra Drake's words, thereby "rejects Tia before Tia rejects her" (109). Tia's response complicates this scene further when her words trigger Antoinette to dwell on the social ostracism of being poor: "Real white people, they got gold money. They didn't look at us, nobody see them come near us. Old time white people nothing but white nigger now, and black nigger better than white nigger" (Rhys 470). As a social ghost to wealthy white Creoles, Antoinette is only visible to formerly enslaved people who deride her family's once-powerful position. However, Antoinette has also been conditioned to believe herself above people of color, which her thoughts about Tia confirm when the girl runs off with Antoinette's pristine dress and leaves her servant's dress: "I put it on at last and walked home in the blazing sun feeling sick, hating her" (470). While the narrative concisely records Antoinette's thoughts, it also points to a much deeper history of violence. Underneath the surface conflict between two young girls lie the ongoing inequalities between their class positions, which are dependent on skin tone.

Later, Antoinette approaches understanding her unstable place in this society when Tia throws a stone at her while servants burn Coulibri. Tia asserts through a violent action that she is above Antoinette in post-emancipation Jamaica, and in this scene Antoinette could be learning the cost of social hierarchies based on race and class. Though she and Tia have "eaten the same food, slept side by side, bathed in the same river" (483), they do not belong to the same racialized class position, and Tia's violence physically reinstates their social separation. Antoinette sees herself mirrored in Tia (blood trickles down Antoinette's face and tears run down Tia's), perhaps signaling Antoinette's persistent view of their connection despite racial difference (Rody 142).[18] However, I wish to focus specifically on the language of the scene. Years after emancipated people burned Coulibri, Antoinette still cannot fathom Tia's violent actions. Because Antoinette "did not see her throw it" and "did not feel it either" (Rhys 483), Antoinette can (in her memories) attempt to deny "it," the fact that the stone's impact solidifies their social separation. Much like Anna Glover in Douglas's *Hold On*, Antoinette's narrative stifles the truths of social inequalities. Moreover, this scene of violence (that physically separates two girls of different racial and class backgrounds) essentially foregrounds Antoinette's subsequent relationships with Black women in the text. The moments of physical violence between Antoinette and Tia—then Antoinette and Amélie—reinforce that, though she does not want to admit it, Antoinette's identity in colonial Jamaican and Dominican societies hinges on her ability to be legible as white to English colonizers. Her class position depends on her ability to separate herself from Black women.[19]

After Antoinette marries the unnamed-but-implied English character Edward Rochester from *Jane Eyre*, her interactions with the house servant Amélie in the cottage Granbois in Dominica draw on Antoinette's experiences with Tia. These interactions ultimately show that the histories between the women's social positions are always about to explode into the present. Still, Antoinette seems detached from the action when Tia throws a stone at her face because Antoinette is reflecting on a painful moment of separation; likewise, the narrative also seems detached from the sudden scene of violence between Antoinette and Amélie because Rochester narrates the scene in part 2. Rochester observes the women when Amélie taunts Antoinette with the news that her longtime servant Christophine is leaving and that "Christophine don't like this sweet honeymoon house" (517). Amélie sees Rochester and continues to goad Antoinette with, "Your husban' he outside the door and he look like he see zombi. Must be he tired of the sweet honeymoon too," knowing that the white Creole woman will react to the implications of her unsteady marriage and resulting social ostracism (517). The actual exchange of violent touch between the women is sparsely narrated through Rochester's perspective:

> Antoinette jumped out of bed and slapped her face.
> "I hit you back white cockroach, I hit you back," said Amélie. And she did.
> Antoinette gripped her hair. Amélie, whose teeth were bared, seemed to be trying to bite. (518)

Because Rochester describes this scene, Antoinette's earlier interactions with Tia help make sense of the violence; otherwise, it can seem random, animalistic, or—as in the filmic adaptations—exceptional to Caribbean women as a group. The scene, however, is not exceptional. Because of the novel's careful framing of Antoinette's relationship with Tia, Antoinette's relationship with Amélie demonstrates the white Creole woman's failures to connect with Black women. Antoinette acts superior to the servants because she has been conditioned to, yet Amélie knows that Rochester questions Antoinette's legitimacy as a white woman (the novel configures her Creole lineage as *not quite white*, and Rochester also expects that she will inherit her mother's *madness*). In *Reclaiming Difference*, Carine M. Mardorossian adds to this analysis that "although Edward [Rochester] uses clichés to establish commonalities between his wife and the black subaltern, . . . the African Creoles resist this excision of the cultural, class, and historical contexts that are constitutive of their identity" (84). The eruption of violence between Antoinette and Amélie is yet another reminder of the violent histories existing between the women's racialized class statuses that Rochester (and, to an extent, Antoinette) deny. In this way, the women's scene of two-way violence connects to Margaret and Ondine's relationship in *Tar Baby*. Furthermore, the scene is also about the shifting currents of power after emancipation in this colonial state, and the implicit shifts of power after independence in the twentieth century. Tia and Amélie can lash out against Antoinette because they do not fear retribution. Because of Antoinette's disempowerment as a white Creole woman without any monetary power of her own, no system works to her benefit. She cannot claim English colonial power, and (as the novel repeatedly implies) neither can she claim a sense of cultural rootedness that Antoinette believes Black Jamaicans possess.

Instead, readers could interpret that Antoinette longs for the kind of power that Christophine possesses because she has some influence over Black Jamaicans and Dominicans. For example, Antoinette sees Christophine's power to control Amélie when the rumored Obeah woman uses fear of violence to assert herself after Antoinette and Amélie fight: "Smile like that once more, just once more, and I mash your face like I mash plantain. You hear me? Answer me, girl" (Rhys 519). After Christophine implicitly threatens to use Obeah against her, Amélie "look[s] frightened" and "cre[eps] out of the room," showing that Christophine's influence could possibly help Antoinette maintain a sense of power through illusion (519). However, Christophine leaves the cottage after Rochester threatens her with imprisonment, and then Rochester has sex with Amélie in the room adjoining Antoinette's. In the matrices of power defined at the intersections of nationality, race, class, ethnicity, skin tone, sexuality, ability, and gender, neither Antoinette nor

Christophine has the agency to change what Rochester—as a colonizing figure—wishes to do.

The final scene of the novel is vital to consider when determining what Antoinette's relationships with Tia and Amélie reveal about denied (silenced) histories. At the end of the novel, after Rochester has taken Antoinette to England (where she is totally subordinated by her colonized position), she dreams of an alternate ending to her story. Here, she imagines that her plunge from the top of Thornfield Hall could possibly reconnect her with Tia at the end of her life: "It might bear me up, I thought, if I jumped to those hard stones. But when I looked over the edge I saw the pool at Coulibri. Tia was there. She beckoned to me and when I hesitated, she laughed. I heard her say, You frightened?" (574). The text upholds an interpretation of this dream as one speaking to Antoinette's past ambivalence about her position as a white Creole woman. The dream also shows how she—at the end of her life—literally burns down an image of British colonialism (the manor house) and jumps toward her Caribbean past, embodied in Tia: "Someone screamed and I thought, *Why did I scream?* I called 'Tia!' and jumped and woke" (574, emphasis in original). This scene, on the one hand, reverses Antoinette and Tia's divisive encounters earlier in the novel (Drake 109). It also reveals, on the other hand, "the deep structure of Rhys's revision and of the model she bequeaths to Caribbean (and many other) women writers: 'horizontal' identification with and yet against a beloved female other" (Rody 148).[20] As this reading of Rhys's novel implies, excising Antoinette's interactions with Tia from the plot would decontextualize her skirmish with Amélie and would uproot what Rody calls the narrative's "deep structure of Rhys's revision."

One of this chapter's main interests is how misrepresentation enacts (and repeats) the violent silencing of women's experiences within a context of domestic labor. Viewing the filmic adaptations of Rhys's novel with this lens exposes how studio-produced films about Caribbean places, peoples, and cultures still violently distort women's relationships. Specifically, here I will examine transformations of the scenes I analyzed from Rhys's novel (or comment on the absence of them) in the three filmic adaptations of the novel: Brendan Maher's *Wide Sargasso Sea* (2006), John Duigan's *Wide Sargasso Sea* (1993), and Michael Gilkes's *Sargasso! A Caribbean Love Story* (1991). The first two films fall back on stereotypical depictions of violence between women, which dramatically misrepresent the intersecting issues of race, gender, ethnicity, sexuality, ability, nationality, skin tone, and class. Furthermore, these two most widely available adaptations of *Wide Sargasso Sea* notably alter the implications of Antoinette's identity formation through her occasional violent interactions with Black women from the servant class. First, Brendan Maher's *Wide Sargasso Sea* (2006), produced by BBC Wales and distributed by BBC (Great Britain) and Acorn Media Group (United States), does not show scenes from Antoinette's past in Jamaica; rather, the film is more simply an account of Antoinette's relationship with Rochester. Second, John Duigan's *Wide Sargasso Sea* (1993), produced by Laughing Kookaburra Productions and distributed in the United States by New Line Cinema, follows more closely the narrative arc of the novel (beginning with Antoinette's childhood in Jamaica); yet, the film merely lumps Antoinette's interactions with Tia in with other short encounters with servants and does not focus on them in a significant way. Both versions elide Antoinette's past with Tia and thereby decontextualize her confrontation with Amélie. In doing so, both productions display Antoinette's explosive physical violence against Amélie in a sensationalized manner that triangulates Rochester, Antoinette, and Amélie. These narrative changes effectively silence any structural critiques of the colonizing effects of imperial gender, sexuality, race, ethnicity, class, ability, skin tone, and nationality implicit in Rhys's novel. While Maher's and Duigan's films show two-way altercations between women, we need not celebrate them as such: instead, focusing on the lack of cultural and personal context for such violence exposes the two films' colonizing perspective that distances audiences from the Caribbean characters on the screen. By dehumanizing these characters, both adaptations create narrative violence with serious cultural implications.

Maher's *Wide Sargasso Sea* most plainly narrows the focus to Antoinette and Rochester's relationship at the cost of decontextualizing their conflict. The film is a frame story that begins when a disheveled Antoinette (Rebecca Hall) escapes from her attic cell at Thornfield Hall and experiences a series of flashbacks when she finds Rochester (Rafe Spall) sleeping in a chair. When Antoinette discovers Rochester after an implied long absence from him in the attic, she leans in to inspect his face and smell his neck, which triggers momentary flashbacks to their scenes of sexual encounters years earlier. This jolts her into action: she starts a fire with her stolen candle; then, the camera tilts up her body and zooms into a medium close-up of her face while she stares at a brightly colored painting of a Caribbean island. While the camera tilts, the audience hears various lines from Rochester in the past, especially, "I'll keep you safe." The bulk of the story is a flashback that starts when Antoinette sees this painting on the study wall.

The beginning of Antoinette's flashback seems to be related via Rochester's perspective from part 2, and this limits the film's ability to show Antoinette's experiences and the context from which the servants are acting. Instead of going back to Antoinette's story in part 1 of the novel, the film focuses on Rochester's first interactions with Antoinette leading up to their wedding in Jamaica. Because viewers do not see scenes from Antoinette's childhood, the fleeting glances from Black servants seem more menacing toward Rochester alone. Amélie and Christophine's constant and abrupt appearances in doorways (which startle and unnerve Rochester) mark the couple's arrival at their honeymoon cottage.

Without context, Antoinette's violent interaction with Amélie thereby seems individuated (and exceptional) in a manner that forecloses structural critique. In this film, Christophine and Amélie have their confrontation in which Christophine threatens violence *before* Antoinette and Amélie fight. Thus, Christophine is already absent from the house when Rochester sits drunkenly in a chair outside of Antoinette's room while Amélie enters with water and begins antagonizing her. Antoinette, still in her nightclothes, lies in bed facing away from Amélie as she orders, "Leave me alone." Amélie quickly replies, "Creole woman like you—you're always alone," to which Antoinette turns and yells, "Get out!" Then, Amélie stops short of the door, turns around defiantly, and approaches Antoinette's bed with her verbal jab (like it appears in the novel): "Your husband outside there. . . ." The film frames Antoinette's and Amélie's faces with medium close-ups while the servant adds, "Too much sweet make a person sick in the stomach—sick in the head sometimes too." This additional line prompts Antoinette's physical violence; she casts off her bed covering and shouts, "Don't you speak to me like that, you hear me?" She then throws Amélie against the wall. At this point, Amélie asserts herself with "White cockroach!" and both women end up on the bed, with Antoinette pinning Amélie. The scene shows the action of the women—up to this point—through the camera's third-person perspective (unlike its counterpart in the novel that Rochester narrates), but the film invites the audience to consider what Rochester sees when he enters the scene at this moment: his wife is straddling a woman in bed. The implications are difficult to ignore because Antoinette struggles with Amélie in the messy sheets of her marriage bed that Rochester now avoids. This imagery sexualizes the women's struggle as they fight over Rochester.

Through this adaptation's deletions and insertions, the scene loses its ties to Antoinette's childhood experiences, and her violence seems random until she replies to Rochester's startled questions. As he rushes into the room, Rochester questions, "Antoinette, what are you doing?" He then hurriedly pulls her away from Amélie and orders the servant, "Go away, girl!" Antoinette replies, "Girl? Why, she is as old as the devil himself!" while Amélie leaves the room and casts a knowing look and smile toward the couple. Because Christophine is already absent from the house in this adaptation of the novel, Amélie's subversive look stands. When Antoinette asks Rochester, "What's happened to you?" he recoils in horror and dismay and asks, "To me? What about the way you just attacked that girl?" Here, Rochester calling Amélie "girl" connotes his social standing above her—as well as Antoinette's apparent overstepping of social bounds—but his terminology has changed from the novel. In Rhys's text, Rochester calls Amélie "child" (518). This alteration reinforces my claim that the film purposefully uses Amélie to triangulate Antoinette's relationship with Rochester so that the women seem to struggle for his attentions. When he claims he "side[s] with no one" in the matter but "judge[s] for [him]self," Antoinette replies with an increasingly impassioned plea, "Judge who? She called me a white cockroach. That's what they call me. . . . Or . . . or . . . or . . . white nigger. 'Cause I'm Creole. I'm not like them, but I'm not English like you. Between the two of you, I sometimes wonder who I am myself!" As she nears the end of this speech, Antoinette's eyes widen, her voice increases in volume, and her hair falls over one eye, giving her the appearance of the "madwoman" Rochester already expects to find lurking inside her (figure 4.1). He gazes on her with a look of thinly veiled disgust. Although the audience has witnessed Amélie taunting Antoinette, the film ultimately makes Rochester's character more sympathetic here, as he and the audience know only what they have seen. Antoinette may proclaim her displacement in this society, but without the context of her childhood struggles with Tia and other servants, the film leaves narrative gaps about Antoinette's motives for attacking Amélie. This is one way the film uproots Rhys's novel's careful attention to context; the film adaptation focuses on Antoinette as an individual acting out of jealousy. The film thereby *silences* structural critique of colonial Jamaican society to favor a simplistic narrative about an emotionally unstable Caribbean woman.

Likewise, when Rochester (and the audience) finally hear Antoinette's story about her past, it provides too little information too late in the narrative of Maher's film. Although Antoinette's speech includes exact wording from part 1 of the novel—"They say when trouble comes close ranks, and so the white people did" (465)—she does not say anything about Tia, only that her family was "driven out" of Coulibri. Rochester replies dryly, "Very dramatic." The audience is likely to side with Rochester, for the film has built up Antoinette and all Caribbean people and landscapes to be "dramatic" and exceptional: the film's soundscapes and disorienting shots ensure "that the

FIGURE 4.1 Rebecca Hall as Antoinette in *Wide Sargasso Sea* (Acorn Media, 2006).

place and people remain strange to the viewer as well" (Heffelfinger and Wright 109–10). Despite the film's brief inclusion of Antoinette's past through her dialogue, the narrative once again emphasizes that this place and its people are beyond understanding. According to this logic, Amélie and Antoinette are both exoticized and eroticized rivals for Rochester. After their last sexual encounter in which Antoinette uses an Obeah potion, a disoriented and angry Rochester has rough sex with Amélie against the door that connects his room to Antoinette's. The film plainly depicts this scene as the tipping point for Antoinette's mental decline because she sits with her back leaning against the door as the couple's movements jar it.

After she poisons Rochester and he has sex with Amélie, Antoinette is trapped in a catatonic state that continues while she is imprisoned in the English manor. Her attitude changes at the end of the film when she looks at the Caribbean painting in Thornfield Hall and thinks, "But I know now why I'm here." She proceeds to set the manor house ablaze and goes to the roof where a medium close-up shows her face (while a red light shines behind her and wind blows her loose hair). Her voiceover says, "I know what I must do." A wide shot shows Antoinette standing on the edge of Thornfield's dark roof in a white nightdress, and when the camera moves to a medium shot of her face, Antoinette smiles before she jumps. The film ends here, not with the sense that Antoinette finally embraces Tia and her Caribbean heritage at large, but with the sense that her memories of Rochester finally spark her to find some justice. When Antoinette leaps off the roof, Maher's narrative forecloses any metaphorical connection with Antoinette's Caribbean past; Antoinette has no symbolic flight back to her Caribbean identity, because the audience witnesses Antoinette's actual leap into death.

Maher's production of *Wide Sargasso Sea* leaves out scenes of Antoinette's past experiences to the detriment of fully developing Antoinette's character as a woman torn between several identities. Given these narrative silences, then, John Duigan's version (which had a U.S. release with an NC-17 rating in 1993) seems remarkable in the fact that it *does* begin with Antoinette's childhood in part 1 of the novel. Yet, while the film attempts to contextualize Antoinette's actions as an adult by showing her life at Coulibri, the film still falls short of integrating Tia into the plot in a meaningful way. The film instead builds up Amélie's role to the extent that—again—she is clearly a rival for Rochester's affections. Here, as in Maher's adaptation, Antoinette's rivalry with Amélie solidifies her difference as a Caribbean woman—oversexualized, used, and silenced.

Unlike Maher's version, Duigan's *Wide Sargasso Sea* begins with Antoinette's voiceover about her childhood; however, Tia is barely present in this narrative. The only interaction between Antoinette and the young servant who must be Tia (although she is unnamed in the dialogue and is not credited) happens when the girls are playacting as a pirate and slave. The girl asks Antoinette, "Why not you be the slave?" to which Antoinette replies, "Because pirates are white, silly." Then, the girls' playtime is cut short when they stumble upon the corpse of Antoinette's mother's slain horse. Although the scene does divulge Antoinette's learned social ranking based on skin tone, the scene is too brief to show Tia as a person essential to Antoinette's development. Tia is merely a part of the backdrop upon which the young Antoinette can show her believed superiority. In fact, all servants are like scenery to Antoinette, who—after her English stepfather's wealth clothes her in frilly white dresses—walks by a servant holding a basket of flowers, looks up at the woman's face with a haughty expression, and then takes a flower while the woman looks down at Antoinette with contempt. In this version of the story, the young Antoinette does not seem to have *any* connection to Black Jamaicans beyond their service to her. Furthermore, in this film Antoinette is afraid of Christophine's use of Obeah (she sees a bled chicken in Christophine's room, while the novel leaves Christophine's actual use of Obeah practices unclear). Later, Antoinette looks from her mother to the Coulibri house engulfed in flames instead of seeking solace in her friend. Even though the Tia character can be spotted in the crowd of people while she holds a torch and chants along with them, there is no final conflict between Tia and Antoinette because Tia is merely a part of a mob.

Because of Antoinette's reluctance to see servants as individuals when she is a child, her knowledge about the servants as an adult is perplexing. In Duigan's version, Antoinette knows Amélie from Coulibri, and she admits Amélie was "born at Coulibri like [her]" but was not there long because she was sent to work in the summer house. Because Amélie's skin is lighter than other servants', the audience could assume that—perhaps—she is somehow related to Antoinette, which is merely one of Rochester's ponderings in the novel. This strengthens the film's setup that Amélie is Antoinette's darker double who is also vying for Rochester's attention. While Rochester's perspective in Rhys's novel does group Amélie and Antoinette together—they are both from and personify "this place" to him (495)—Duigan's film explicitly pairs the two women's bodies together. For instance, the camera focuses closely on Amélie's glistening body while she and another servant, Hilda, dance aggressively to drumbeats outside of the house during one of Antoinette and Rochester's intense sexual encounters. This scene features a series of quick cuts from Antoinette, Rochester, Amélie, and a drummer—showing close-ups of Amélie's deep cleavage and the drummer's bared chest, alongside Antoinette and Rochester's faces—in a way that mixes up the pairings of couples to the extent that they are all entwined (figure 4.2). Therefore, during their (frequent) sexual interactions, the film configures Antoinette and Rochester's union alongside (and in conflict with) Amélie. This rivalry extends to other scenes added to this adaptation. During a daytime scene, for instance, Antoinette approaches a group of dancing servants, and when they reluctantly allow her inside their circle, Amélie aggressively dances up to her. However, Antoinette's facial expression shows that she is delighted because the servants include her in the dance; only after Amélie casts out her arms in a threatening fashion does Antoinette's facial expression appear serious, but her overall attitude seems to be one of playfulness. Up to this point, Antoinette does not display any worries about her position as Rochester's wife and lover. Rochester, though, sees this scene just as he returns upon reading Daniel Cosway's letter (which raises doubts in his mind about Antoinette's sanity). Viewing Antoinette dancing among Black servants must signal to Rochester that his wife's racial background is suspect as well (Heffelfinger and Wright 109), and seeing her and Amélie dancing together likely brings them together more firmly in his mind. Much like in "jungle melodramas and exploitative travelogue[s]" (109), the drums connote an unrestrained sexuality that has long been used in colonizing descriptions of Caribbean landscapes and peoples.

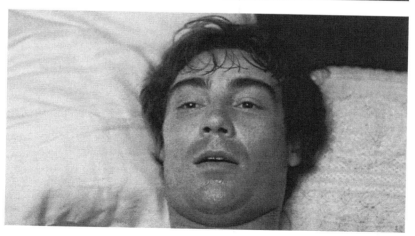

FIGURE 4.2 Rowena King as Amélie, Karina Lombard as Antoinette, and Nathaniel Parker as Edward Rochester in *Wide Sargasso Sea* (New Line, 1993).

The film's reliance on stereotypes about Caribbean women's sexualities, then, predictably results in Rochester raping Antoinette. In Duigan's film's logic, Rochester rapes Antoinette soon after this dance to assert a colonizing order. Heffelfinger and Wright connect this added scene to the film's casting of Karina Lombard for the role of Antoinette: according to the authors, Lombard's brown skin tone "invigorates racial difference as a sign of sexual promiscuity," so that the film "investigates a set of racial and sexual dynamics that alter the politics of the novel" (110). Here, the film even more explicitly sets Antoinette up to represent the allures of Caribbean peoples—which (as per racist, sexist colonizing beliefs) lead Rochester astray. Thus, just after he rapes Antoinette, Rochester prepares to leave the rural house to seek the civilizing effects of a city. During Rochester's departure scene, the film reiterates how Amélie is Antoinette's darker-skinned double when Amélie appears nude in the doorway of her shack. As Antoinette's double in this film, Amélie represents the untamed sexuality that Rochester sees in Antoinette; this is what Amélie's fully nude body connotes as Rochester leaves to visit Spanish Town in hopes to clear his mind.

That Duigan's film then does not play up sensuality in the fight between Amélie and Antoinette is puzzling; however, the film has already solidified Amélie and Antoinette as clear sexual competitors for Rochester. As in Rhys's novel, Rochester views the skirmish while outside the doorway; in this adaptation, though, he has just arrived from his trip to Spanish Town and is in good spirits because, the film implies, he is willing to give Antoinette another chance (to act like a proper Englishwoman). "By permitting Edward to recognize the hypocrisy that buttresses the racial and class hierarchies perpetrated by Spanish Town elites," Heffelfinger and Wright assert, "Duigan encourages us to sympathize with the more liberal husband who returns to the summer home to make amends with his wife" (111). However, when he views the violence between Antoinette and Amélie—and then quickly breaks up the fight—Rochester understands that his optimism is unfounded. Antoinette is too much like Amélie to be a viable partner for an Englishman. Although this scene more closely follows the novel's depiction than Maher's adaptation (here, Amélie pretends to cry and then sings the song comparing Antoinette to the white cockroach), Antoinette does not articulate that her identity is split between how Black servants regard her and what Rochester expects of her. Unlike the novel, the fight scene appears outside the context of Antoinette's childhood; it confirms to Rochester—and the audience—that Amélie is Antoinette's slightly darker double.

As a result, the end of Duigan's film is perhaps even more perplexing than Maher's. In Duigan's adaptation, Antoinette sits in front of the fireplace in her attic room while the English servants discuss Rochester's upcoming marriage to Jane Eyre. While she gazes into the fireplace, Antoinette sees Coulibri ablaze, and she says in a voiceover, "Now I know what I must do. . . . I will dream the end of my dream." She takes her guard's keys and a lamp when night falls, sets fire to curtains, and proceeds to dance on the rooftop amid smoke. The audience could infer from this scene that she is attempting to prevent Rochester's happiness with another woman. In the purple and yellow lighting on the rooftop, Antoinette apparently dances with joy: in silhouette, she holds her red dress from Jamaica while non-diegetic flutes and drums play. While the film does provide some connection between Antoinette's past in Jamaica and her actions—she sits in front of the fire holding her red dress and sees her mother running into the burning Coulibri house—the ending does not establish thematic continuity: Why does a memory of her mother running into their burning home make her think she must burn Thornfield? The ending of Duigan's film (while it attempts to make connections between Antoinette's final actions and her Jamaican past) features a confusing array of images that seem arbitrary compared with the novel's careful pairing of Tia and Antoinette. Through a narrative that privileges Rochester's viewpoint (even after he rapes Antoinette), Duigan's adaptation of *Wide Sargasso Sea* "others" Antoinette's position as a Caribbean woman. Once again, the narrative leaves narrative gaps that prevent audiences from contextualizing Antoinette's actions.

By comparing the treatment of Antoinette's past in these two filmic adaptations of the novel, I do not mean to conclude that there is only one "mother-text" with an infallible depiction of Antoinette's experiences. The wealth of scholarship available obviously signals that Rhys's novel does not lend itself to one interpretation. Still, when compared with Duigan's and Maher's studio-made adaptations, the novel connects Antoinette's conflict with Amélie to her overall struggles with her identity that we see in her memories of Tia. How, then, could the novel be adapted to film differently, in a way that represents how Antoinette's past with Tia shapes her sense of identity in a racist, sexist, classist colonial society? One answer to this question lies in independent filmmaking, which can more fully break away from colonizing discourses and representations of Caribbean peoples and places. Now, I turn my attention to a third filmic adaptation of *Wide Sargasso Sea* that makes important thematic connections between Tia and Amélie in Antoinette's story. The 1991 short film *Sargasso! A Caribbean Love Story*, directed and produced by Michael Gilkes for the University of the West Indies, is an independent film venture, yet—even with its minimal budget and focus on educating the audience—the film more successfully relates how Antoinette's childhood experiences with Tia influence her interactions with Amélie and the end of her story.[21]

Sargasso! adapts scenes from Rhys's novel into vignettes that, when considered together, provide a sense of the narrative's whole. The film appears on its DVD after a brief overview of Jean Rhys's life, works, and themes in an informational short called "The Writer's World." Then, shot on location in Dominica, *Sargasso!* transitions to a scene in which Rochester writes to his father about his arrival to Jamaica in part 2 of the novel. The film subsequently shows Rochester and Antoinette landing in Dominica for their honeymoon. In fact, this is the only filmic version of *Wide Sargasso Sea* to show that Antoinette and Rochester honeymoon in Dominica, not Jamaica, which demonstrates the filmmakers' careful attention to context. In the arrival scene, a group of servants meets the couple at the dock, and Antoinette introduces them to Rochester. Amélie makes an appearance—foreshadowing her role—while she speaks her greeting to Rochester about the "sweet honeymoon house" in a Creole language. Soon after, Rochester's voiceover dictates, "English she is not," while Antoinette's face fills the shot. The image of adult Antoinette fades into Antoinette's face as a child, and the next scene depicts Antoinette and Tia's quarrel in the bathing pool. Gilkes's film thereby reshuffles scenes to provide a sense that Antoinette's insecurities come from her troubled relationships with Black women.

In Gilkes's adaptation, Tia is even more assertive than she is in the novel, for she asks Antoinette outright, "Why you look at me like that?" instead of Antoinette asking herself this question. Tia also voices the section in Antoinette's thoughts about "white niggers" when she leaves Antoinette shivering alone in the bathing pool with her castoff dress. In this adaptation, Tia even inserts herself into the dining room scene in which Antoinette's adult family members debate the threats that Black Jamaicans pose to white Creoles and people from England. Here, Tia tries to peek around the adults to see Antoinette. By adding and changing some dialogue and actions, this adaptation of *Wide Sargasso Sea* makes clear that Antoinette and Tia have a complicated bond, and their interactions anticipate the next scene in which the house burns. This is notably the only adaptation of the novel to include Tia and Antoinette's confrontation on the Coulibri lawn. The scene is shot simply, moving between shots of Tia looking at Antoinette, to Antoinette smiling,

FIGURE 4.3 Caroline Wilkins as Antoinette and Esther Henry as Tia in *Sargasso!*
A Caribbean Love Story (Banyan Productions, 1991).

to Tia throwing a rock, to Antoinette frowning with a bloodied face, to Tia's
face mirroring the blood with a tear (figure 4.3). The dark background
clouded with smoke makes the girls' faces the focus and connotes the importance of their exchange. The film's simplicity works in its favor to make
clear what Duigan's and Maher's versions avoid: Antoinette's relationships
with Black women are dependent upon her early experiences with Tia.

Gilkes's film thereby contextualizes Antoinette's actions when she fights
Amélie in the honeymoon cottage. In this film, Amélie is near Antoinette

when she insults her with dialogue taken directly from the novel, and then Amélie is on top as the women fall onto the bed in their struggle. Antoinette gains the upper hand in the fight just before Rochester enters the room (she flips on top of Amélie), but then the scene progresses just as the novel outlines, with Amélie singing the song about a "white cockroach" and Christophine threatening Amélie. Although the scene is still sensationalized because Amélie and Antoinette fight on the bed, as in Maher's production, the film adequately contextualizes Antoinette's reaction to Amélie. The film's emphasis on Tia earlier signals that Antoinette might be striking out at Amélie because the woman reminds her of her failed childhood relationship as well as her failed sense of identity.

Sargasso! is the only film adaptation of *Wide Sargasso Sea* to frame the narrative in two essential ways: it solidifies and maintains the importance of Tia in Antoinette's relationships with Black women, especially Amélie; and the film ends by reiterating how Antoinette's relationship with Tia catalyzes her actions. In the manor house, Antoinette holds a candle up to her red dress as she says in a voiceover, "It reminded me of something I must do. . . . I will remember, I thought," while the faces of her and Tia as children are superimposed onto the flame. Then, the film shows flames shooting up from stone, a shot from the Coulibri fire that foreshadows what Antoinette will do to Thornfield Hall. Ultimately, Gilkes's film counters popular, colonizing narratives about employers and domestic employees. Mainstream narratives about the relationships between employers and servants are mired in stereotypes that either sensationalize these relationships of violence (as in Maher's and Duigan's adaptations of *Wide Sargasso Sea*) or refuse to acknowledge the fact that violence can—and does—occur between women. Understanding cultural context about women's relationships as employers and employees in U.S. and Caribbean settings helps identify continuities and differences between systems of exploitation after emancipation. Moreover, careful attention to cultural context in depictions of two-way violence between women is necessary to avoid sensationalizing women's actions. Merely showing violence between women in a domestic space is not radical or revolutionary— context is essential to show the unexceptional nature of violence; it is intrinsic to colonizing labor practices.

As this chapter shows, acknowledging the contexts of women's labor— including women who work inside other women's homes—is a step toward decolonizing depictions of women of color. The scholarship and imaginative fiction I cite in this chapter make clear that we must acknowledge the violence white women have enacted and continue to enact against women made vulnerable due to their racialized class positions and nationalities. As my analysis of the filmic adaptations of *Wide Sargasso Sea* show, we must also speak out against the narratives that incessantly tell us that women's violence (and women's experiences of such violence) do not matter because they are "exceptional." Silence *is* violence, and writers like Ellen Douglas, Toni Morrison, and Jean Rhys depict how silence enables and perpetuates violent social structures. Through these texts, scenes of women violently touching other women expose the inner workings of racist, classist, sexist, and ableist norms that persist because of the grotesque social divisions in "emancipated" societies. In chapter 5, these monstrous norms surface in contemporary settings as abject scenes of horror.

CHAPTER FIVE

The Horror of Intimate Violence

> They snapped their teeth like dogs, and when it was possible sunk
> their nails deep into each other's skin. The crowd shrieked with
> hysteria. . . . [It] must have seemed like hell itself.
> —GEORGE LAMMING, *In the Castle of My Skin*, 106

George Lamming's novel *In the Castle of My Skin* (1970) describes violence be-tween women on the streets of a Caribbean village in a predictable way: one woman (Sheila) remarks that another (Baby Parker) is "two months behind the times," a challenge to her social standing (104). Baby Parker then raises the tension of the scene to suggest Sheila's uncleanliness—"You's a nasty woman"—in a "confidential" tone as spectators tighten their circle (105). Consequently, the women exchange "murderous glances" for a "murderous embrace" when they "fall . . . to the ground and . . . bit[e] fiercely at each other's limbs" while rocks tear their clothes and white marl cakes their ex-posed skin (106). The constable then imposes order when he enters the scene with a condemning question, "Why all you can't live like the people in Belle-ville?" (106). He implies a question that comes from colonial conditioning: Why can't the people of color in the village behave like white people in the more affluent neighborhood? Although the narrator states that "the day in spite of its turbulent dawn was coming to life quietly, correctly," this is—ironically—only because the constable takes advantage of the women's social positions (106). Instead of jailing them, the constable will force Sheila and Baby Parker to pay for their transgression with their bodies; he will rape them. While an outsider would regard the scene as "hell itself," an elderly member of the village community comments, "It is the way we live" (106, 108).

In addition to its condemnation of colonial violence perpetuated by all strata of a Caribbean island's society, this scene from *In the Castle of My Skin* depicts the women's rivalry for social prestige. Moreover, the scene of vio-lence between Sheila and Baby Parker describes the public aspect of their violence: the violence entertains the community, but the narrator also ac-knowledges that the scene is hellish. The spectacle of women fighting each other entices and repels the viewer; the women's violence is grotesque and abject. This scene encapsulates the abject nature of women's violence in this chapter, as *Grotesque Touch* considers depictions of rivals as monstrous women in a popular television show, *American Horror Story* ("Coven" 2013–14). Then, the chapter demonstrates how the contemporary novels *Unburnable* by Marie-Elena John (2006) and *Memory Mambo* by Achy Obejas (1996) use the vocabularies of abjection to exhibit how such violence is symptomatic of colonial, post-colonial, and neo-colonial societies at large.[1] By enacting grotesque violence against others, these monstrous women attempt to gain or retain a level of social prestige, which reflects how intimate skin-to-skin violence operates as a means to oppress and control in the wake of slavery.

The trope of a rivalry threatening social stability is not new; both autobiographical and fictional representations often depict enslavers and enslaved women as sexual rivals, and their resulting violence also threatens to upset the women's social positions. The danger of unstable social divisions can be theorized as *abjection* in the context of Julia Kristeva's *Powers of Horror*, which describes the abject as repulsions from (and strange attractions to) the body's wastes and decay. Kristeva argues "it is . . . not lack of cleanliness or health that causes abjection but what disturbs identity, system, order," as abjection comes from "what does not respect border, positions, rules"; it is "the in-between, the ambiguous, the composite" (4). Responding to Kristeva's work, Barbara Creed's now-canonical essay "Horror and the Monstrous-Feminine" neatly connects abjection to the horror film genre, not only via the bodily wastes that run aplenty, but also through the audience's ability to maintain borders while watching such films (40).[2] Creed claims that horror films maintain these borders by ousting the "monstrous-feminine": "the horror film brings about a confrontation with the abject (the corpse, bodily wastes, the monstrous-feminine) in order, finally, to eject the abject and redraw the boundaries between the human and nonhuman. As a form of modern defilement rite, the horror film works to separate out the symbolic order from all that threatens its stability, particularly the mother and all that her universe signifies" (46). This chapter thereby mobilizes Kristeva's and Creed's theorizing of abjection and horror to reframe the grotesque nature of U.S. and Caribbean societies through various imaginings of monstrous women as rivals and lovers.

American Horror Story is a logical starting point in this discussion, most obviously because the title of the show connects "America" with "horror" narratives. Since its premiere in 2011, Ryan Murphy's serialized FX show terrorizes its characters (most usually women) with the horrors of U.S. cultural norms. Along these lines, the third season of *American Horror Story* ("Coven"

2013–14), which concluded with the show's highest ratings at the time of its airing (O'Connell), delves into the violent past of the United States by intertwining two story lines: slavery in New Orleans, Louisiana, which literally haunts the present via flashbacks to the 1830s; and the rivalry between white witches and Black voodoo practitioners from the 1600s to the present. In both narrative strands, women violently combat other women (usually with mediation of some kind), and the rivalries themselves reveal the undying legacies of the country's violent past. Here I will focus on the narrative of Madame Delphine LaLaurie (Kathy Bates) in both 1830s and 2010s New Orleans, because her violent actions in the past constantly resurface and "haunt" the present-day setting. *American Horror Story* uses the monstrously grotesque LaLaurie—and her monstrous whiteness—to entertain via reversals of racist exploitation cinema and horror tropes, such as the white woman turned bad by "Black influence" and the ethnic outsider as vampiric monster. These reversals are especially evident through LaLaurie's often-violent interactions with the immortal voodoo practitioner Marie Laveau (Angela Bassett) and the young Black witch Queenie (Gabourey Sidibe), as white monstrosity infects these women's relationships with each other. The show reveals that Laveau has been made into, and Queenie is at the risk of becoming, a monstrous woman because of their experiences with LaLaurie's cruelty. Furthermore, the contentious relationships between voodoo practitioners and witches are brought to bear on Queenie's body, which serves as a literal voodoo doll. The show's imagery of Queenie as an agent of destruction and self-destruction— all while being stuck in the middle of currents of racism, classism, sexism, and ableism (her weight is repeatedly the butt of others' jokes)—most clearly unites all the strands of abjection that the season depicts. While *American Horror Story* could be lauded for its willingness to display the nation's past of racist, sexist, classist violence, the show depicts LaLaurie's monstrous brutality (against enslaved people, her daughters, and present-day people of color) as exceptional. Even with trope reversals that counter some racist narratives, *American Horror Story* revels in the familiar, misogynistic horror trope of the monstrous-feminine as it magnifies women's exceptionality as monsters that can then be removed completely. In the end, Queenie restores order in her society by murdering LaLaurie, the abject figure of racism.

Whereas the previous two seasons of *American Horror Story* were set in a haunted house and an asylum, "Coven" widens the net to depict the violently racist past of the United States via a monstrous-feminine whiteness that haunts the show's past and present. This season extemporizes on the historical Madame Delphine LaLaurie of nineteenth-century New Orleans, whose torture of enslaved people in the attic of her townhouse made her a figure of folklore. Indeed, speculation and fictionalization of LaLaurie's deeds has remained a cottage industry, as local "haunted" tours and publications highlight her monstrosity.[3] The show magnifies the lore surrounding LaLaurie to draw on a familiar horror type, the monstrous-feminine, as this monstrous woman of the past physically haunts the show's present in 2010s New Orleans. Segments of LaLaurie's past appear in six of the season's thirteen episodes. On the one hand, these segments disrupt the present-day scenes, but, on the other hand, they provide context for the various rivalries that run throughout the season's plot. Read in this way, the opening scene of the first episode ("Coven: Bitchcraft") is essential to examining the season, as it begins with Delphine LaLaurie's past in 1834.

From the start, the show demonstrates LaLaurie's sadistic pleasure derived from torturing enslaved people as well as her daughters, and the narrative significantly shows her violence in conjunction with her high-class standing.[4] The first scene opens to a party at the LaLaurie townhouse, where the matriarch showcases her three daughters to potential suitors, only to have her youngest daughter, Pauline, assert her sexuality when LaLaurie says that she is not sure what Pauline's greatest talent is: "Perhaps my talent is in the *boudoir*, Mother Dear." As the camera frames Pauline's face with an iris, the shot reverses to show Bastien, an enslaved man, also framed in an iris while he views her from another room. The light atmosphere of the party scene—indicated by tinkling piano music—immediately ends, though, when the next scene begins with a close-up shot of LaLaurie's face. Here, the camera acts as her vanity mirror in her bedroom while she stares straight into the mirror/camera. To the non-diegetic sound of the show's trademark dissonant and jarring electronic music, LaLaurie opens a dish of blood and proceeds to smear a bloodied brush on her temple, down her cheek, and down her neck (figure 5.1). She punctuates her movement with a slight twitch of her lips before she does the same to the other side of her face. Then, she smears the bloodied brush down her forehead, continuing to her nose. LaLaurie's husband, upon entering the room during her beauty regimen, is not affected by the sight of his wife's bloody face; in fact, neither of them shows qualms about her appearance when she tells him, "When the blood dries, my skin is supposed to be tight as a drum. Look at this wattle." She jabs at her lower chin with the bloody blush and remarks, "This blood's not fresh." Then, Monsieur LaLaurie reveals his intention for interrupting his wife's regimen: their daughter Pauline was found with Bastien. The true "horror" to them is miscegenation, not the obvious blood smeared on LaLaurie's face.

FIGURE 5.1 Kathy Bates as Madame Delphine LaLaurie in *American Horror Story* (FX, 2013).

This scene, contrasting yet also complementing the previous scene of high-society mingling, makes Delphine LaLaurie into the image of a vampiric white monster, a reversal of the ethnic-outsider-as-vampire trope popularized in Bram Stoker's 1897 novel *Dracula*. This scene sets up a narrative that, like Jewelle Gomez's novel *The Gilda Stories* (1991), "invert[s] the script of European enlightenment narratives of progress by positioning white people as atavistic vampires" (M. Richardson 30). In Gomez's narrative, a young enslaved woman running toward freedom (initially called "The Girl") in the 1850s recalls her mother's warnings about white people because they "suck up the world, don't taste it" (Gomez 11). The white French-American Delphine LaLaurie sucks up the world, in finery and blood, like the enslaver class in Gomez's *The Gilda Stories*. Because LaLaurie's nightly beauty treatment uses the blood of enslaved people, her routine reveals the ironic nature of her society that deems Black bodies disposable but also highly necessary to the beautification of white bodies and, moreover, the continuation of the national economy.

This opening segment for the third season of *American Horror Story* continues to expose LaLaurie's monstrosity by showing her chamber of horrors in the attic of her New Orleans townhouse. Here, Black people appear in a variety of disfigurement (all are chained and caged); the camera lingers on the face of a woman whose skin has been peeled away and another whose eyes and mouth have been sewn shut. LaLaurie lightly reacts to these gruesome sights while carrying a candle and white flower (to mask the odor): "*Bonsoir*, my pets"; "Oh, *merde*, now we're gonna have flies up here"; "Hush up, or I'll rip your lips open and stuff more shit in there." LaLaurie literalizes the abjection of enslaved people, placing bodily wastes where they do not belong to actualize her power over them. In other words, through her means of torturing enslaved people, LaLaurie literalizes the fact that white supremacy relies on the abjection of Black people.[5] Therefore, when a caged man asks pitifully, "Why? Why are you doing this to us?" she matter-of-factly replies with a slight smile, "Because I can." Her attitude signals power over the bodies of enslaved people; yet, the show also indicates the inherent instability of this society's logic. When LaLaurie's sadism culminates in this scene as she orders a child to place a hollowed-out bull's head over Bastien's, her ironic statement — "Bastien, you wanna rut like a beast? Then we're gonna treat you like one" — strikes the viewer as ludicrous. While Delphine LaLaurie and her husband (who approvingly dotes on his wife's actions) treat enslaved people as things, these high-class enslavers are the bestial monsters.

In this and other scenes, *American Horror Story* diverges from a sanitized version of "haunting" that it mocks later in the first episode when Nan (a clairvoyant witch) in the 2010s leads the witches from Miss Robichaux's Academy for Exceptional Young Ladies to the LaLaurie townhouse. They meet a guide giving a typical haunted home tour, and she refers to the house as a "center of New Orleans high society," but "also a place of abject horror," where the Code Noir was replaced by LaLaurie's "code of terror." The docent's simplistic understanding of the Code Noir is at odds with my exploration of the code in chapter 2 as a legal mechanism for enslavers to inflict grotesque, sadistic violence on enslaved people. The guide's narrative thereby sets up LaLaurie to be exceptional to her time and place, as, according to her, LaLaurie's actions "spawn[ed] 179 years of hauntings." In this scene, a sudden flashback to the 1830s connects the past to the present while LaLaurie explains why she uses the bloody mixture to keep her looking young: she tells her daughter Borquita to blame her father and his "fresh-faced whore" for their nightly ritual. When the tour enters what the guide calls "the infamous chamber of horrors," the guide says, "No flash photography, please," and the scene alternates between shots of enslaved people's bleeding body parts and shots of the present-day women walking in the attic. The cuts effectively blur temporal lines between past and present. Nan, however, was not drawn to the townhouse by what lures tourists (the torture and murder of Black people); she was attracted by the very presence of Delphine LaLaurie, who is physically preserved under a courtyard because she was enchanted to live forever and then buried by Marie Laveau. The show does not support the conventional ghost tour narrative (i.e., that murdered enslaved people haunt the house); instead, LaLaurie's past actions intrude upon the present-day setting.[6] Throughout the season, the audience witnesses LaLaurie commit increasingly brutal and sadistic acts on the bodies of enslaved people: she oversees her daughter Borquita gouging out an enslaved man's pancreas to make her beauty mixture ("Coven: Bitchcraft"); she laughs with glee as she harvests eyeballs and intestines from her caged "pets" in order to use them as entertainment in her Halloween party ("Coven: Burn, Witch. Burn!"); and Delphine LaLaurie amuses herself by telling her handmaiden Sally that she killed Sally's infant son (Monsieur LaLaurie's child) to make a batch of her beauty mixture ("Coven: The Dead"). As demonstrated in the first episode, these acts—displayed, not just implied—interrupt the season's narrative flow and, thus, haunt the present-day setting and characters.

From the beginning of the season, LaLaurie's physical presence in the modern-day New Orleans setting connects past and present atrocities and attitudes. As a physical marker of the grotesque norms of enslavement, LaLaurie's appearance in the 2010s signals that racist, classist, and sexist norms of the past are very much alive and relevant in the show's present. After LaLaurie is let loose in the academy, she very quickly commands to a Black witch, Queenie, "Out of my way, slave." When Queenie (an attitude-wielding young woman from Detroit) abruptly replies, "Who are you calling slave, bitch," LaLaurie hits her over the head with a candlestick. Unsurprisingly, LaLaurie commits her first violent action in the 2010s on the body of a young Black woman. Throughout most of the season, LaLaurie's rage in the present day (she laments the presidency of Barack Obama in the next episode ["Coven: The Replacements"] and continuously uses racist speech) is no match for the season's integration of scenes of torture from the 1830s. Scattered throughout the season, the violence LaLaurie committed on the bodies of enslaved people actively interrupts the flow of the 2010s narrative, consequently giving immediacy to the past violence and a context to the violence of characters in the present day. Furthermore, LaLaurie's torturing of Black people does not remain in flashbacks; she later gleefully mutilates a man in present-day New Orleans ("Coven: Protect the Coven"). Showing how the racism of the past does not disappear with time, the horrific abjection of the past embodied in LaLaurie invades the present-day coven at Miss Robichaux's Academy.

However, Delphine LaLaurie's presence in the 2010s is not the only marker of a haunting, monstrous past; this is also evident in Marie Laveau's resurrection of zombies to attack the coven ("Coven: Burn, Witch. Burn!"). Because the academy houses LaLaurie, Laveau literally brings back the past to punish LaLaurie and the white witches via the corpses of the LaLaurie daughters and other reanimated figures. Interestingly, each member of Laveau's zombie army appears to be white (a flapper, frontiersman, and Confederate soldier among them), as the narrative once again proves that divisions between life/death and past/present are not firm. The show does not do the predictable, which would be to use Black bodies to haunt and harm whites. This is a trope carried well into the twentieth century in productions such as Paul Maslansky's Blaxploitation film *Sugar Hill* (1974), in which Diana "Sugar" Langston recruits the help of the spirit Baron Samedi to exhume an army of corpses belonging to formerly enslaved people (complete with shackles).[7] Sugar reanimates the dead to exact revenge on the gangster Morgan's (mostly white) posse after he arranges the murder of her husband so he can take their club (aptly named Club Haiti). Sugar then pays Baron Samedi with Morgan's white girlfriend, the foul-mouthed racist Celeste, who earlier physically fights with Sugar because Sugar will not give the club up and is, in Celeste's words, acting "uppity." The film heavily implies—as Baron Samedi carries a screaming Celeste away—that Samedi will rape her and that she will eternally be his sex slave. More recently, this trope of a "dangerous Blackness" appears in Iain Softley's film *The Skeleton Key* (2005), in which a young white woman is "sacrificed" to the hoodoo practitioners Mama Cecile and Papa Justify so that they can use her body as a vessel for eternal life. Indeed, both films use Blackness to signify monstrosity, which in itself merely conforms to racist thought. Instead of recycling these stereotypical tropes of a "dangerous Blackness" that haunts whites, *American Horror Story* draws on a different imagery—an imagery of white monstrosity—to show white supremacy's abjection. The past always bleeds into the present, and this season of *American Horror Story* never romanticizes the past. Indeed, the past always threatens the present with its white supremacist violence.

It bears repeating that *American Horror Story* also invests in a *female* white monstrosity, which is in line with Creed's theorizing of the horror genre. When adding race to its matrices of power, *American Horror Story* draws on yet another cultural narrative, that of the "white witch," a white woman turned bad by "Black influence." Herbert G. de Lisser's popular novel *The White Witch of Rosehall* (1929) concisely plays out this trope. The narrative predictably focuses on the experiences of a British-born gentleman, Robert Rutherford, as he deals with the "white witch," Jamaica's Annie Palmer, to give readers a "civilized" point of view. In 1831 Jamaica, which is on the cusp of emancipation, Robert vacillates between contempt for Annie's methods of control as an enslaver and his attraction to her; early on he thinks, "Only a devil would willingly watch the agony of others as she had done" (32). Much like the British and American filmic adaptations of *Wide Sargasso Sea*, de Lisser's novel clearly sets up a Caribbean/European, witchcraft/Enlightenment, female/male, insane/sane dichotomy typical of popular representations of Caribbean cultures.

The White Witch of Rosehall conveniently plays out its stereotypical, dichotomist moral tale by encapsulating it in a narrative of rivalry between Annie, the white enslaver, and Millicent (Millie), a free woman of color, as both compete for Robert's fickle affections. Annie's "conjuring" of dreaded Caribbean duppies in the novel (spirits such as the female vampire Old Higue/Hige) comes specifically from her sense of being threatened by Millie's rivalry, which signals Annie's tenuous social position (de Lisser 223). To increase her own power through "witchcraft mummery," Annie uses what she considers to be "inferior" people's firmly held beliefs about Obeah (159). The novel thereby portrays Annie as an unnatural product of her place; white European men living in Jamaica (who get to speculate at length on her background) believe her girlhood in Haiti most likely corrupted her (240). Although the novel merely suggests this as one possibility for Annie's depravity, elements of class, ethnicity, race, gender, sexuality, and nationality come to bear on her contamination, according to the white men in the narrative.[8] Because the narrative cannot further support her unnaturalness, Annie Palmer (unsurprisingly) dies at the hands of an Obeah man. She is abject, and as a figure that lives on in folklore, much like Madame Delphine LaLaurie, Annie Palmer embodies female white monstrosity.[9] However, unlike this popular narrative set in Jamaica, *American Horror Story* does not imply LaLaurie's contamination by Black cultural beliefs and practices. Instead, white supremacist thinking in the United States influences her actions. *American Horror Story* thereby uses viewers' preconceived notions about female monsters to show—through Delphine LaLaurie and other characters—that white supremacy's monstrosities infect women's relationships with each other.

Generally, the season's portrayal of witches as women (with the exception of one gay man who also sits on the witches' council, a role played by Leslie Jordan), juxtaposed with the show's depiction of witch hunters as (implied) heterosexual men, goes along with Creed's thesis that horror films routinely expel the monstrous-feminine to regain social balance. Yet, *American Horror Story* also illustrates Creed's concluding thoughts that "the feminine is not a monstrous sign per se; rather, it is constructed as such within a patriarchal discourse that reveals a great deal about male desires and fears but tells us nothing about feminine desire in relation to the horrific" (63). In light of Creed's theories, the season's very obvious equating of women (both white and Black) with magic underscores popular fears about women's power that, if united, women could undo social structures.[10] Additionally, the fact that powerful Black and white women are caught in a vicious rivalry with each other reiterates what I mention in chapter 4: Black feminists have long claimed that white women's reluctance to address their own collusions with white supremacy makes attempts at "sisterhood" impossible.

Taking this a step further, *American Horror Story* shows how white women are at least complicit in—and sometimes active participants in—the systemic oppressions of women who are marginalized. *American Horror Story* displays LaLaurie's racist prerogatives when she literalizes the disposability of Black bodies, and we observe that white women's sense of power in the show's present-day setting often echoes their supposed superiority. For example, this is blatantly obvious in the interactions between the coven's leader Fiona Goode (Jessica Lange) and Marie Laveau. On the one hand, Goode treats Delphine LaLaurie as a second-class citizen when she forces LaLaurie to be the coven's maid and later Queenie's "personal slave" because, in Goode's words, "There's nothing [she] hate[s] more than a racist" ("Coven: The Replacements"). On the other hand, Goode has already revealed her obviously racist and classist attitudes toward Laveau in the previous episode: "Your kind and my kind have been going after each other for centuries, though it is kind of like a hammer going after a nail" ("Coven: Boy Parts"). Although Laveau has been alive and practicing communal magic for centuries, her store of cultural memory and power is not enough to combat Goode's learned sense of superiority, as Goode shows when she mocks Tituba, the enslaved woman of color who was one of the first to be accused of witchcraft in Salem, Massachusetts, in 1692: "Tituba, voodoo slave girl, who graced us with her black magic. She couldn't tell a love potion from a recipe for chocolate chip cookies if she had to read it" ("Coven: Boy Parts"). Laveau insists that the white witches of Salem learned everything from Tituba: "Everything you got, you got from us. . . . *You* made [Tituba] a slave. Before that, she came from a great tribe. The Arawak. She learned the secrets of the other side from a 2,000-year-old line of shamans. Necromancy. She gave it to your girls of Salem. A gift repaid with betrayal." Still, Goode makes light of Tituba's illiteracy and the socioeconomic status of current voodoo practitioners to show that they are inferior to whites. Laveau's place of business is in New Orleans's Ninth Ward, close to the people she serves and represents, but Goode readily ridicules this location: "Maybe in another century, you could have two shithole salons." Goode, though, is losing her own youth and vigor, much like Delphine LaLaurie two centuries ago. She came to Laveau's place of business specifically to demand Laveau's secret for prolonged life and youth. And, like LaLaurie, Goode is willing—and deems it her right—to exploit Black people to get what she wants.

All these contentious relationships are brought to bear on the body of Queenie, one of the coven's members. Curiously, Queenie's magical power is her ability to use her body as a voodoo doll; thus, she can inflict great pain or death on others by stabbing, burning, cutting, and shooting herself. In the show's depiction of Queenie's power, issues of race, class, gender, sexuality, and ability converge and intertwine. As early as the season's first episode, Queenie proclaims her status when she says, "I'm a human voodoo doll," which a young white witch, Madison, meets with the wry observation, "Well, that was disturbing" ("Coven: Bitchcraft"). Indeed, the season's embracing of Queenie's literalized abjection is the most disturbing aspect of her character; her embodiment of disposability echoes long-standing controlling images.[11] Later, Queenie sacrifices her body to preserve Laveau, whose actions in the present come from her hatred of LaLaurie ("Coven: Head"). When Queenie resurrects herself via her "voodoo doll" powers, *American Horror Story* structures Queenie's story as one of rebirth through her bodily sacrifice. Whereas Queenie previously seeks a community of women, she is more assertive after she reemerges in the eleventh episode. When Queenie reappears, she leads LaLaurie by a leash, which at once makes Queenie's transformation apparent but also reaffirms the show's theme that Black women are constantly fixated on LaLaurie's monstrosity ("Coven: Protect the Coven").

The season's imagery reinforces the conclusion that Delphine LaLaurie's white monstrosity has led Black women to commit their own monstrous acts. Via this logic, *American Horror Story* shows in the seventh episode that Queenie gives up LaLaurie to Laveau only after LaLaurie has told Queenie about the worst atrocity she committed, which was using Sally's baby in her poultice. Because LaLaurie refuses to accept Black Americans as her equals, Queenie is willing to mutilate LaLaurie's flesh ("Coven: The Dead"). Taking the knife from Laveau's hand, Queenie moves toward the caged LaLaurie while commenting, "I'd love to." Although the scene ends here (and therefore does not show whether Queenie mutilated her own body or LaLaurie's body directly), the camera implies, because it cuts away, that Queenie applies the knife directly to LaLaurie. The season suggests that this level of re-

FIGURE 5.2 Angela Bassett as Marie Laveau in *American Horror Story* (FX, 2013).

venge does not need magical mediation. Instead, blood meets flesh, again, as Laveau mirrors LaLaurie's monstrous acts at the beginning of the season: Laveau smears LaLaurie's blood on her face (figure 5.2). Reversing the movement of Delphine LaLaurie's application, Laveau starts at her neck and moves up her face. She completes the ritual while snarling at the camera/mirror before she says, "Beautiful." The season overall implies that Laveau has been made into, and Queenie risks becoming, a monstrous woman because of her experiences with Delphine LaLaurie, who enacts racist violence in the nineteenth and twenty-first centuries.

However threatening Delphine LaLaurie might be, her departure from the plot occurs abruptly in a manner that proves her monstrously abject role in the narrative. In the end, Queenie makes a deal with Marie Laveau's "voodoo master," Papa Legba, to allow Laveau and, therefore, LaLaurie to lose their immortality ("Coven: Go to Hell"). Once Queenie ensures LaLaurie's mortality, she stabs her in the heart, just after LaLaurie gloats about her superiority to the current world, one in which people are "a pack of sniveling hypocrites." She has spent the past few days acting as a tour guide in her former townhouse, trying to convince curious sightseers that she was "a woman ahead of her time." She tells Queenie that she "wept for the state of this world[, a] world of lies" that incorrectly tells people of different races that they are equal. At this moment, Queenie realizes that LaLaurie will not change, and she sends her "straight to hell" when she stabs LaLaurie. In this way, Queenie "redraws boundaries," according to Creed's terminology (46), by directly stabbing Delphine LaLaurie on screen (instead of using her "voodoo doll" powers)—an act that removes LaLaurie's horror from the present. In doing so, Queenie restores order in her society by ousting LaLaurie, the abject figure of racism. The audience later discovers that LaLaurie and Laveau are together in a hell of their own making, one in which Laveau must repeatedly torture LaLaurie and her daughters. According to the show's conclusion, both women suffer because of their "sins," which include the fact that Laveau allowed her hatred of LaLaurie to consume her.

Once Marie Laveau and Delphine LaLaurie have died, their departure from the plot signals a utopic beginning for the new coven. In the final episode, the plot arc to find the next leader of the coven takes over, as LaLaurie and Laveau no longer threaten the coven's unity ("Coven: The Seven Wonders"). The concerns that have driven the characters up to this point—the dangers of racist, sexist, and power-hungry villains—immediately disappear, and the coven comes "out of the closet," so to speak, when the new leader Cordelia, a white woman, invites all young women who have magical powers to join the coven so that they will all "thrive," not just "survive." The final scene of the season features Cordelia standing on the coven's staircase (with Queenie and the young white witch Zoe at her side) as they face a long line of eager, multiracial young women who wish to join the coven. While Queenie does find a place in the coven's new hierarchy during the season's denouement, her place is still subordinate to the white witches. Because Queenie's actions bring about this utopic ending, her character ultimately conforms to what Kinitra D. Brooks identifies as a common characterization of Black women in horror genres; a Black woman's "body is often surrendered to the privileging of complicating non-black and/or non-female characters" (12). Although Queenie sacrificed her body numerous times and drove out Madame Delphine LaLaurie's horror, the show, according to Amanda Kay LeBlanc, "ultimately (re)arranges whiteness at the center of its universe," creating a "colorblind" vision of the present that ignores and enables systemic racism at the heart of U.S. culture (274).

In the end, Madame LaLaurie was a remnant that could easily be expelled. She and her racism were truly abject in the sense of Creed's theories of horror. While *American Horror Story*'s "Coven" plays on and transforms various iterations of monstrosity, the season's focus on literalizing the horrors of racism and classism through LaLaurie's monstrous-feminine character inherently limits its scope and repeats sexist tropes often seen in the horror genre. Moreover, although the show reverses some common racist tropes to depict white supremacy's violence, it also privileges a shortsighted ending in which the "haunting whiteness" of the past has been ousted to bring about a post-racial utopia. In doing so, it mirrors present-day cultural amnesia that readily forgets the horrors of history.

Similar to *American Horror Story*'s representations of women's monstrosity, Marie-Elena John's novel *Unburnable* depicts violence between social rivals that follows a grammar of horror. Yet, the narrative does not expel the monstrous-feminine; instead, grotesque violence merely ensures that racist, classist, and sexist social structures continue from colonial Dominica into the nation's post-colonial/neo-colonial present after independence in 1978. In *Unburnable*, readers see "the baroque character of the postcolony," as Achille Mbembe articulates in his chapter "The Aesthetics of Vulgarity" (115). Because post-colonial Dominican society perpetuates classist, racist, and sexist harm on its citizens, the novel shows the post-colonial society's "unusual and grotesque art of representation, its taste for the theatrical, and its violent pursuit of wrongdoing to the point of shamelessness" (115). Specifically, the novel ties sexual violence between women to the culture's grotesque patriarchal codes by depicting a gruesome rape inflicted on a "deviant" dark-skinned woman (Iris) by her rival's light-skinned Creole mother (Mrs. Richard), who belongs to a higher class. Through this instance of violence that an older woman inflicts on a younger woman, John's novel calls attention to the systemic violence inherent to a colonial society that controls women's bodies through a complex class system that each generation of women inflicts upon the next.[12] The novel depicts women policing other women's bodies and identities in mid-twentieth-century Dominica through abject sexual violence that consequently traumatizes generations of women into the post-colonial/neo-colonial present.

The scene of sexual violence between women in *Unburnable* differs from my examples in chapter 3 because of its explicitness: here, a woman's violent touch disfigures another woman's sexual organs. As such, *Unburnable* represents what Carine M. Mardorossian sees in fiction written by Caribbean women, as they create startling and complex representations of rape that "take . . . the blurring of the victim/perpetrator boundary to its extreme by turning rape's most likely victims—women—into its most sadistic perpetrators" ("Rape by Proxy" 28). Mardorossian claims that these "extraordinary" instances of rape enacted by women expose gender and racial hierarchies (31). Occurrences of woman-on-woman rape in contemporary Caribbean narratives are thereby not necessarily sensational plot devices; such examples of rape may instead emphasize that sexual violence between women is common to patriarchal, colonial structures. Moreover, novels often contextualize sexual violence between women with generational memories and experiences of social structures, such as Edwidge Danticat's *Breath, Eyes, Memory* (1994) in a Haitian-American context and Gayl Jones's *Corregidora* (1975) in Brazilian and U.S. contexts. In such texts, generations relive and reenact sexual violence.

Likewise, *Unburnable*'s depiction of woman-on-woman rape appears in a narrative that focuses on generations of women in Dominica whose bodies are routinely used to maintain the colonial project in the wake of slavery. Then, these women are left to bear their traumas in isolation. In this way, *Unburnable* echoes Donette A. Francis's reading of how Danticat's *Breath, Eyes, Memory* "underscores the difficulty of communicating black women's histories of sexual violations, which while contained within their bodies have no medium or language for expression" (85). John's novel takes great care to depict the trauma of slavery's legacies in Dominica by intertwining the narratives of Lillian Baptiste, her grandmother Matilda, and her mother, Iris. As the stories about these women's pasts gradually come to light throughout the novel, readers learn about Lillian's traumatic childhood in which her mother and grandmother were kept a secret from her. By focusing on Lillian's attempts to find the truths about her family embedded in folklore, hearsay, and songs, *Unburnable* "lays bare the hierarchies, problematics and ambiguities inherent in oral stories, even as it demonstrates their abundant and empowering possibilities" (Bailey 33). According to the infamous, and grossly oversimplified, tales and songs about these women, Iris was an insatiable sex worker in the city Roseau and Matilda was a rural Maroon Obeah woman hanged for murder. People's relentless repetitions of these narratives lead Lillian's adopted mother, Icilma, to shield Lillian from her family's past by withholding information, and Lillian is sent away to the United States after she attempts suicide as a young teen. In light of these plot points, the scholar Lorna Down focuses on Lillian's need to reconcile her maternal heritage, as "lack of communication with others is replaced by Lillian's highly charged sexuality, where sex becomes a 'clawing' for connection with the other" (239). What Lillian needs—a complete understanding of her heritage—comes from what Down calls a reconnection with her motherland, Noir, a Maroon village that was established by women, existed outside of colonizing hierarchies, and was where Matilda worked as a healer and magistrate (235). Although Down concludes that Matilda, Iris, and Lillian's "relations to nature, in particular the spiritual dimension of nature, allow [them] . . . to 'fly inna massa face,' that is, effectively challenge dominant (colonialist) power structures" (233), I claim that a fuller reading of the novel considers how Mrs. Richard's actions have so traumatized Lillian that she cannot reconcile her maternal heritage. Lillian's trip back to Dominica as an adult to reclaim the story of her maternal family members ends—as the narrative implies—with her impending suicide. As Lillian contemplates jumping from the heights of Noir to join the Maroons who did so to evade capture decades earlier, the novel implicitly criticizes colonization's legacies, which have made it impossible for Lillian to reclaim her sense of belonging through knowing the women in her family.

From the beginning of the novel, the race and class of the women in Lillian's family determine what people remember and tell about them. To highlight this, the tone of the third-person narrator creates a bitter sense of irony concerning Iris's fate in the colonial setting of Dominica. The narrator thereby understates the story's action to underline the corrupt nature of colonial social hierarchies adopted by all classes. For instance, the narrator claims that Dominican men knew Iris for her voracious sexual appetite before her death in 1971: "Men, though, would . . . say it was the quality of the sex Iris offered that was the thing, for her mother had taught her a number of tactics for keeping her vagina in pristine condition, despite the damage that had been done to it many years before by a broken Coca-Cola bottle" (John 1). The evasive language, "done to it," signals the men's reluctance to voice the violence that another woman committed via rape with the broken bottle when Iris was a teenager. They also assume that Iris's mother Matilda instructed her daughter to keep her vagina "pristine" for men's pleasure. No one realizes that as an adult Iris takes out her anger and resentment on the men's bodies. Furthermore, the narrator creates irony through calling the villagers "sophisticated" in their acceptance of Iris's role as a sex worker, as she did not have this role until Mrs. Richard raped and disfigured her. This was the only social position left for a woman of her class, color, and notoriety. From the start of the novel, the narrative style effectively conveys Iris's devalued position in this hierarchical society, one that does not allow her to have her own voice.

Iris's society considers her to belong to a lower class, one that would allow her to bear the illegitimate children of a wealthy man, but not to marry into an upper class. At first, however, class does not factor into Iris's conception of her self, although she—turning fourteen in 1945—encounters "a society that [i]s still too near the time when one group of people owned another," a description of Dominican society that ties a past of slavery to the colonial present (68). Patrick L. Baker's study *Centring the Periphery* illuminates some historical context for the hierarchical society depicted in John's novel. *Unburnable* sketches a society consistent with the village communities in which marriage, then pregnancy, "transformed a woman into a *gwah fem*, or 'big woman'" (Baker 115). Still, marriage between people of appropriate class status was essential, because "a single woman could lower her status by marrying below herself" (115). This system therefore fostered great competition among women belonging to the same class, which in theory created such social pressure to prevent a lower-class woman from marrying into a drastically higher class. The novel includes an example of what happens when a "beautiful dark-skinned woman" marries "too rich for her color": the poor people of Roseau "despise" her (John 69). The dark-skinned upper-class woman is the constant object of derision for her "unfamiliar American haute couture standards of *Vogue*," and the lower-class women regularly line up to boisterously make fun of her clothing choices to quell their feelings of injustice (69). The narrative implies that only a wealthy woman "from a big island" could possibly be "popular in her circle" in Dominica, thus making Iris's ascension to the upper class impossible (69). Considering this context, Iris's naiveté concerning class stratification counts as a serious transgression. Nevertheless, Iris—who is half-Black, half-Carib Indian—believes she can marry a light-skinned upper-class Creole man, John Baptiste. This same man saw the fourteen-year-old Iris and believed she was a "bold little slut who had openly propositioned him" and "would get what she was asking for" (73). Through Baptiste's thoughts, readers realize early in Iris's story how the girl's society will put her in her place, and the violent rhetoric confirms that Iris will suffer bodily for her impudence, for wanting to marry above her station. However, Iris learns her lesson about color and class status at the hands of a woman who profits from empire, John Baptiste's mother-in-law, Mrs. Richard.

The incident that spurs Mrs. Richard to action is Iris's public display of sexuality during Masquerade, the predecessor to Carnival. At this Masquerade, Iris "gyrated up to" her light-skinned, upper-class rival Cecile Richard Baptiste (who had just given birth) and "had shown Cecile what she did with her husband, demonstrated to her the act of fornication," before tearing off Cecile's mask, pajamas, and underwear and thereby exposing her "swollen, milk-dripping breasts" (115, 116). Although some (especially Mrs. Richard) read Iris's actions as insurrection, most onlookers see the scene in terms of its abject qualities. The scene of the naked women struggling on the ground brings the crowd out of their stunned silence because, according to the narrator, "there is no sight more arousing to a man than that of two women together. Whether they are making love or doing battle against each other is of no consequence, since to an observer, in the absence of the context, there is no visible difference between the two" (116). The narrative shades this interjection with a degree of humor; nonetheless, it also reaffirms the women's positions as objects in their society—positions defined by a male gaze that sees women's bodies (and especially maternal bodies) as objects of grotesqueness, lust, and entertainment. For example, years later, Cecile's own son (and Lillian's father) Winston Baptiste sings along to the song associated with the Masquerade outburst, "Naked as They Born," with his friends while he is on his way to visit Iris for sex the night before his wedding. By this time, the song has embellished the narrative so much that it says the two women "had tried to twist off each other's breasts" and refers to Cecile "as a cow on account of the amount of milk that had wet down Iris by the end of the fight" (170). Even though Cecile belongs to an upper class, her society repeatedly—even years after the fact—assigns to her maternal body grotesque qualities that reveal how a patriarchal society does not actually value women (of any class) above what they can physically produce. However, regardless of the constraints imposed on her as a married upper-class woman, Cecile's class status still acts as a buffer between her and the harsh realities of being a lower-class woman in Dominica. People in this society continuously train their violent gaze upon Iris's body, and as is apparent in the first pages of the novel, Dominicans misinterpret and fetishize Iris's actions—her use of her body as protest—as cultural and sexual oddities.

As Iris's public spectacle of sexuality gets appropriated by Dominicans of all classes, her use of Masquerade as a public space to protest her social marginalization reinforces her subordinate position. The implications of Iris's employment of the Masquerade setting to enact her humiliation of Cecile are twofold; not only does Iris publicly shame her upper-class rival, she does so during an event that supposedly subdues the lower classes so they will not go above their stations to enact such violence. As the novel reveals later, women of the same (lower) class are expected to seek each other out and publicly assert their rivalry—with cursing, tearing of clothes, and even slicing of the skin with a cutlass (191–92)—but this practice should be unavailable to Iris to use against Cecile, or vice versa. Their relationship is supposedly built on the separateness of their class, color, and sexuality, and Iris's actions (that threaten to overturn social systems) bring about her silencing.

Mrs. Richard's violence against Iris does not alienate the older woman from her class in the eyes of other Dominicans; instead, the sexual violence she enacts upon Iris's body further solidifies her role as a guardian of colonizing structures. What Mrs. Richard, with the help of her two servants, does to Iris's body totally revises Iris's conceptions of her place in society, and her fellow Dominicans—even those women from her class—allow Mrs. Richard to inflict this lesson on her. As she approaches Iris's apartment, Mrs. Richard knows neither the police nor Iris's neighbors will intervene because "they would understand that a limit had been reached, a boundary crossed: there had been an abomination, after all" (117). Even Iris is "waiting for them" as she expects retaliation (118). Furthermore, Mrs. Richard does not have to ask her two servants (who share the same great-grandfather as their "mistress-cousin") to assist her in this act of retribution (117–18). As Mardorossian claims, the novel consequently uproots the connections supposedly forged between women (through having similar circumstances) to reveal a class structure that prevents women from aiding each other ("Rape by Proxy" 30).

The actions and thoughts of the washerwomen—those who physically assist Mrs. Richard in the beating and rape of Iris and those who hear Iris's screams but do nothing to interrupt the assault—all reinforce what their social class deems appropriate. They may outnumber Mrs. Richard (and the light-skinned, upper-class Creoles in general), but the washerwomen have internalized their social place to the extent that they consider Iris to be "a bona fide lunatic" for "what she did to Cecile Richard Baptiste" during her public spectacle of agency (John 113). The washerwomen, however, are not opposed to Iris's relationship with John Baptiste; instead, they have encouraged her relationship with Baptiste from the beginning. For example, they feed Iris special meals to help sustain her during long sexual encounters with him (90). The washerwomen essentially "mother" Iris in this way to help her conceive, for—as their thoughts imply—the best option for a woman of her station is to bear an upper-class man's progeny so that her children would have a better life. The fact that Iris has not borne a child before Baptiste's marriage to Cecile constitutes an emergency, for Iris must conceive a child before he marries in order that the child might receive economic and social benefits (91). The washerwomen therefore attempt to instruct Iris as to the proper way to conceive, advice devoid of her pleasure—"she would have to take it on her back"—which, once again, evinces a stark gender hierarchy (91). Repeatedly, the novel shows that this society has conditioned the women to believe there are no other possible avenues; so, in the case of Iris, the washerwomen "we[ep] for the poor mad girl" who believes she can marry above her station, and then they deem Mrs. Richard's physical violence unavoidable, to restore social harmony (95).

To counter these social perspectives, the novel's representation of violence between women takes on the language of horror and abjection, as the reader becomes spectator to the violation and disfigurement of Iris's reproductive body. The narrator indicates a shift in the scene, from the beating by the washerwomen to the cold, calculated rape by Mrs. Richard. Iris's silence as she "took her beating as she had intended, like a Carib" (119), is replaced by Iris's sounds during sex—according to the washerwomen listening outside—when she realizes that the beating is about to change to rape. When the violence turns blatantly sexual, "Iris . . . sound[s] exactly like she did when she and John were fucking" (120). Here, readers can rethink the washerwomen's earlier assumptions that Iris made such sounds out of pleasure while having sex with John Baptiste, for Baptiste likely abused the fourteen-year-old girl during violent sexual intercourse. While there is room for some ambiguity, especially because readers never know Iris's unfiltered viewpoint about the matter, the understated description of the horrific act perpetrated by Mrs. Richard and her servants leaves readers with a sense of the injustice of Iris's entire situation. In the scene, Mrs. Richard "move[s] away from the wall, where she had stayed quietly watching the beating," in order to become an actor as she swings a Coca-Cola bottle to create a jagged glass instrument of torture (120). The fact that Mrs. Richard uses a Coca-Cola bottle to inflict this violence reaffirms Iris's position as *colonial subject* and calls to mind the blood spilled to harvest and process sugar, from slavery to the novel's present. At this point in the scene, Mrs. Richard's movements "stopped being graceful as [she] planted the jagged end of the [broken Coca-Cola] bottle as far up into Iris as her hand would go. And then again, and then again. Until finally her hand came out empty, covered with blood midway to her elbow" (121). The description of this sexual violence notably focuses on the bodily actions of the perpetrator (as torturer) and the victim's bodily response, as Iris's body is once again reduced to its "monstrously feminine" parts—here, a bleeding vagina. The image sums up Iris's position in this society as nothing more than a reproductive body that the upper class may exploit.

This scene does not merely serve as an account of horrific torture, however. The narrator immediately frames what Iris undergoes by mentioning the washerwomen, specifically the advice they had given to help her conceive: "They left Iris on her bed in the position her well-intentioned neighbors had once counseled her to assume. Advice she had never taken. She was flat on her back with her legs wide open, and as her neighbors had also advised, she was not moving at all" (121). The narrator's ironic delivery of this description reinforces the reality that the washerwomen actually had no meaningful advice for Iris in the first place. Even in the most ideal situation, according to the washerwomen's outlook, Iris would always be an impoverished lower-class woman with so few options that she would have to give up her body to men in hopes of bearing children. The washerwomen's kind of "mothering" (their guidance to help Iris conceive) is ultimately of no use to her, for their absence during her time of need—their complacency during her rape—shows that they merely accept the violent social and racial hierarchies already in place.

The absence of Iris's inner thoughts during the narration reveals how trauma after sexual violence "unvoices the victim," to borrow Carole Sweeney's phrasing (58). In this way, *Unburnable* mirrors the narrative silencing of Black women who experience sexual violence during slavery and after emancipation in chapter 3. Moreover, the use of a third-person narrative voice throughout the novel also symbolizes Iris's marginalized status as a poor woman of color. The closest the novel comes to providing Iris's own thoughts—instead of other people's interpretations of her thoughts or actions—appears in a section set apart from the rest of the narration after the neighborly washerwomen attempt to make her see the sense in having Baptiste's child before he marries: "She did not understand the meaning of her poverty, nor her resulting place on the bottom rung of the social ladder. Later on, when she finally understood, she was still never able to determine which one of the three—color, class, or poverty—was responsible for the inescapability of her destiny. To her mind, when she still had it, each was an equal part of the same whole" (John 95). The reader sees Iris's ability to articulate, with stark clarity, what feminist scholars have described: the interconnectedness of race and class. However, Iris does not have the critical skills to identify how her gender is also integral to her social standing; she has internalized her society's misogyny.

Playing on Creed's definition of the monstrous-feminine, the true "monster" in this narrative is thereby Mrs. Richard, who spilled Iris's blood to feed her society's ideals of power and social place. In the novel, Mrs. Richard confirms through her actions and thoughts her participation within a violent patriarchal system, one that rewards her initiative for protecting class—and color—lines (Mardorossian 31). One scene that best showcases Mrs. Richard's attitude occurs during the Masquerade celebration a year after Iris disgraced Cecile and Mrs. Richard raped Iris. In this Masquerade, John Baptiste belongs to the most feared performance troop solely because of Iris's and Mrs. Richard's actions. The violence inflicted upon other women—first Iris upon Cecile, then Mrs. Richard upon Iris—proves Baptiste's masculinity in this society (even though he fainted at the sight of the women fighting). The women implicitly evince his supposed power via their actions. Yet, the narration goes on to state that "the real hero" to the crowds is "his mother-in-law" because she enforced the hierarchies of class, color, and gender by "put[ting] the servant" Iris "in her place" (John 131). In this cultural context, Mrs. Richard was not exhibiting a masculine sexuality when she raped Iris; instead, she was enforcing what her society deems suitable for men and women according to their class. Her "sacrifice"—the mutilation of Iris's sexual organs— operates as "some kind of purification to placate the gods of social order and the gods of class distinction and the gods that allowed a man to have as many women as he so pleased" (117). Because Mrs. Richard at the top of society will commit rape upon another woman's body to enforce social hierarchies, so do women below her police these same expectations.

Mrs. Richard is monstrous—not because she is an outlier in her society, but because she *embodies* the logical outcomes of that society's strictly policed social norms. As Lillian's grandmother Matilda believed, those in power in Dominica are "the modern-day slave masters" that she and the other Maroons remained hidden from after emancipation (John 270). Living as a lower-class woman in both colonial and post-colonial Dominican societies, as *Unburnable* suggests, means having no control over your own story. Thus, the fallout from Mrs. Richard's sexual violence is traceable in *Unburnable*'s narrative not only because Iris's body bears the damage Mrs. Richard inflicts but also because Iris's trauma extends to her daughter, Lillian, in the narration. According to Lillian's adoptive mother, Icilma, Lillian's "whole life was the trauma," because Lillian inherited "madness" (198, 199). Indeed, Lillian's line of "madness" appears to come directly from Iris's rape at the hands of Mrs. Richard: it sets into motion the events that will lead to Lillian's birth and subsequent separation from her family. Because of Iris's mutilation, Matilda retaliates by murdering John Baptiste during the next Masquerade. Matilda's actions then cause police officers to investigate the Maroon settlement Noir, which results in her death. Then, Lillian is conceived from Iris's retributive sexual interaction with Winston Baptiste, who is Cecile and John Baptiste's son. As the reader gathers from these events, the "madness" of Lillian's life extends to the entire Dominican social structure because colonialist violence has infiltrated each relationship, even decades after Dominican independence.

At the end of the novel, Lillian understands that what the dominant class remembers and repeats constitutes people's sense of reality. So, she chooses how Dominicans will remember her: as a figure of abject horror. In the final scene, Lillian decides to jump from the top of Noir's mountain so that she will fall through the trees and lose her skin. She believes, "when [other Dominicans] found her she would be exactly what they wanted her to be: their nightmare come true, a *soucouyant*" (292). Originating in the legacies of slavery, the mythical *soucouyant* (also called *soucriant* or Old Higue, as in *The White Witch of Rosehall*) is a vampiric female demon who wears the skin of a woman throughout the day and discards the skin at night in order to feast on human blood. Giselle Liza Anatol's comprehensive study of female vampires in circum-Caribbean literature historicizes complex, and often contradictory, representations of the *soucouyant*. While "the skin-shedding, bloodsucking female can be interpreted as an image of cultural resistance to colonial ideology, . . . she can also be read as shoring up colonial notions of propriety and respectability" (14). Even so, the *soucouyant* in contemporary literature "is no longer frightening as an objectified 'thing' or 'beast' whose skin has been removed by a separate brutalizing force, and neither is she the subjugated being whose blood oozes because of the viciousness of the master's whip. Instead, she is horrifying because she can strip off her own skin and penetrate the skins of others; she is also the one who draws blood, not leaks it. She is a powerful actor, not acted upon" (9). Lillian gains power through hoping to embody the *soucouyant* myth. In doing so, she embraces the violent histories of Dominica and her sense of loss (since she never knew her mother). For the first time in her life, she might be able to control how Dominicans will remember her; that this ending "would be perfect for her song" signals that she claims a legacy of female fury to be passed on through folk song (John 292). Although she has done nothing "monstrous," Lillian will be remembered as such in this society that deems her—and the women who went against social norms before her—abject. Still, the racist, sexist, classist culture, with its colonial hierarchies left over from slavery, is the true monster.

Just as *soucouyant* myths carry with them gendered contexts that *Unburnable* draws on, so have vampire myths more broadly been vehicles for portraying cultural frameworks, especially in terms of sexuality. Along these lines, Bonnie Zimmerman claims that female vampires commonly illustrate fears about women's same-sex desires: "Lesbianism—love between women—must be vampirism; elements of violence, compulsion, hypnosis, paralysis, and the supernatural must be present. One woman must be a vampire, draining the life of the other woman, yet holding her in a bond stronger than the grave" (381). Connecting Zimmerman's ideas to Creed's, the lesbian vampire is popularly depicted as the monstrous-feminine, an abject figure of horror that illustrates heteropatriarchy's fears. Although there are notable exceptions to this type—such as Jewelle Gomez's *The Gilda Stories*, which is more concerned with reframing vampiric sensuality "in a less exploitative mode" that privileges vampires who strive "to share and not to rob" (Gomez, "Recasting the Mythology" 91; *Gilda Stories* 50)—the most visible narratives are those that feature violent, voracious lesbian vampires.

The myth of the violent lesbian, popularized in tropes such as "the lesbian vampire," still thrives today. For example, in the fifth season of HBO's pulpy series *True Blood* (2012), Tara, a Black Louisianan woman, is made into a vampire by Pam, a centuries-old white vampire. An enslaver/enslaved woman dichotomy characterizes their relationship, and Tara says as much— "So, basically I'm your slave"—when Pam orders her to work at the vampire-friendly bar Fangtasia ("Let's Boot and Rally"). As Pam and Tara's relationship reveals (and as the show consistently reiterates throughout its seasons), vampires solidify their bonds through violence. Later, Pam hypnotizes an overtly racist white woman to feed Tara ("Somebody That I Used to Know"). Pam orders the woman, "You will consider it a privilege to let your racist, peckerwood blood shoot into [Tara's] gorgeous cocoa mouth." Apparently, this is a means of courting, for Tara and Pam passionately embrace in the final episode of the season ("Save Yourself"). The myth of the "violent lesbian" is not new, however, as the rise of the myth correlated with the fin de siècle popularity of Bram Stoker's *Dracula*. As Lisa Duggan shows in *Sapphic Slashers*, both "the black beast rapist and the homicidal lesbian . . . appeared, in new cultural narratives at the end of the nineteenth century, as threats to white masculinity and to the stability of the white home as fulcrum of political and economic hierarchies" (3). Both "types" were deemed abject due to their threats to the white heteropatriarchal status quo. Consequently, it is no surprise that (as Zimmerman notes) the lesbian vampire is an easily identifiable horror figure, for the term "lesbian" has long been associated with monstrous violence.[13]

Though it does not directly mention magical elements like witches or vampires, as we find in the texts previously examined in this chapter, Achy Obejas's *Memory Mambo* (1996) builds on thematic concerns at hand: the novel depicts—in horrifying detail—extreme intimate violence that two women who are lovers inflict on each other. Intimate partner violence between women is a highly contentious subject, especially considering the popular equating of "lesbian" with "monster." Yet, Obejas's novel productively uses an imagery of horror to feature a protagonist—Juani Casas—who, like Lillian in *Unburnable*, fears that she has become a monster. In *Memory Mambo*, monstrousness results from characters' social stratification. The most reviled character in the novel, for example, is Jimmy, the ultra-macho, sexually aggressive, and sadistic husband of Juani's cousin Caridad. "In the context of contemporary US values," says Maria Celina Bortolotto, Jimmy "appears as a quite disenfranchised male. In a society where (monetary) power is one of the most respected indicators of normative masculinity, he works as a janitor and has trouble making ends meet" (34). While readers notice Juani's reluctant attachment to Jimmy, whom the text sets up as Juani's monstrous double, the narrative also leaves room for the violence perpetrated by Jimmy, and later between Juani and her lover Gina, to represent more than their interpersonal relationships. Indeed, the grotesque violence that erupts in *Memory Mambo* stands in for what cannot be easily eradicated: the violence of colonial and colonized histories.

Juani's thoughts about her family also come to represent much more than an individual's opinions and experiences, especially when she mentions their attitudes about race, skin tone, class, and nationality. The narrative is filtered through Juani's first-person perspective as a twenty-four-year-old lesbian who came from Cuba to the United States on a boat with her family at the age of six in 1978. Despite Juani's uncertainty and penchant for romanticism, as Linda J. Craft argues, her narration leaves open spaces to critique her parents' generation's adherence to hierarchies (371). Katherine Sugg adds that Juani's narrative voice is "permeated by the memories of others—their instrument, in fact," and as such she "gestures toward a darker underside of diasporic remembering" (470). For instance, several family members embrace the theory that their name (Casas) came directly from Bartolomé de Las Casas, and they imagine he was an ancestor. Despite the obvious problems of naming a Catholic priest as an ancestor, the family believes the name entitles them to white Spanish roots. As with many of the family's "histories," according to Kate McCullough, the story of Las Casas "demonstrates ambivalence toward, or an inability to resolve, the violence at the heart of the colonial project" (583–84). Along these lines, Juani's mother's beliefs about skin color in Cuba have influenced Juani's familial dynamic, evinced in her mother's story about how a diviner told her that she would marry someone with green eyes. Juani's mother was "delighted" because (Obejas 32), despite evidence of her mixed racial heritage (her daughter Nena's skin tone darkens in the sun, and her son Pucho has "kinky hair and full lips" [34]), she would "do just about anything to deny her real lineage" (32). When Juani's mother saw Juani's father for the first time, "she was sure their kids would be colorless and beautiful," which reflects an impossible and ironic sense of what her society's color hierarchy values (the absence of all color). Because colonialism engenders such denial to sustain and propagate racial hierarchies (McCullough 585), this preference for "colorlessness" haunts Juani's family in a midwestern U.S. city—these colonial norms are not easily forgotten, nor are they replaced by more egalitarian views. The novel thereby depicts its Chicago setting as one in tune with hierarchical, colonizing structures, for the violence that erupts between Juani and her lover Gina makes clear that the United States serves as a place for willed forgetfulness and denial of the realities of colonialization.[14]

From the beginning, Juani and Gina's relationship shows signs of inequalities that reflect their cultural backgrounds. Gina, a Puerto Rican who has traveled throughout the Caribbean and is now involved in political outreach, identifies with Caribbean anticolonial struggles for freedom rather than the sexual identity politics of the United States in the 1990s: "But for Gina, being a public lesbian somehow distracted from her *puertorriqueñismo* [Puerto Rican-ness, nationalism]" (Obejas 78). According to Ileana M. Rodríguez-Silva in *Silencing Race*, Gina's radical speech in the novel seems to indicate her allegiance to a Puerto Rican nationalism that criticizes racial and class disparities continued by a system that still privileges the prerogatives of white Creole men (3–4). However, what Gina says to and does with Juani solidifies how these aspects of identity cannot be conveniently separated from sexuality: "'That's so white, this whole business of sexual identity,' she'd say, while practically undoing my pants. 'But you Cubans, you think you're white'" (Obejas 78). Gina's position simultaneously calls out the white privilege and racism in U.S. gay and lesbian movements (McCullough 593), while also using Juani's "whiteness" (via her Cuban background) to assert sexual power. Issues of color, class, sexuality, gender, and nationality are all inextricably wound up into a tight cord of tension in Gina and Juani's relationship, and the resulting failure of their relationship comes from what Frances R. Aparicio calls "the disturbing lack of intralatino knowledge that is part and parcel of a colonial education in the United States" (634). Even before physical violence breaks out between Gina and Juani, their interactions seem to always verge on a breakup, while Gina constantly vocalizes the racialized class disparities between Puerto Ricans and Cubans in the United States.

Gina's frequent expression of Cuban and Puerto Rican difference resembles the insularity that Dara E. Goldman sees in Caribbean cultural discourses, the "repeated reproduction of the foundational topos of the island" (17). Even among Juani's extended Cuban-American family, Gina feels left out, and she uses this as fodder to try to spark reactions from Juani: "[Gina] said we were racists and classists and that we only made fun of Puerto Ricans because most of them were darker and poorer than us" (Obejas 122). Despite Juani's efforts to see her attraction to Gina as apolitical, the scene in which Gina calls out Juani's family for being elitist also indicates that she takes Gina's accusations personally.

The novel accordingly contextualizes Juani and Gina's outburst of physical violence, as unacknowledged differences (due to their cultural and colonial backgrounds) mire their relationship. Just before their violent encounter, Juani is repeatedly humiliated by Gina's *independentista* (pro-independence) friends who enjoy calling Juani a *"gusana"* — "a pejorative used to refer to Cubans exiled from the revolutionary government" (Obejas 242). This happens while they are all sitting under a romanticized portrait of Fidel Castro in Gina's apartment. After Gina's friends leave, her conversation with Juani about the term reveals much about their relationship: "Gina sat up and put her arms around me. '*Mi gusanita,*' she said softly, stroking me. . . . 'It never occurred to me that you felt so strongly about it'" (132). Here, Gina claims Juani, both with her body and her words, in a manner that regards Juani as inferior: "I was jealous that she and her friends knew so much about my country, and I knew so little, really, not just about Cuba, but about Puerto Rico and everywhere else. I was pissed that, while they'd been to Cuba, I had spent all my time working in a laundromat. . . . I hated their independence movement, not for political reasons, but because it seemed to give them direction. And hope" (133). In this revelation, Juani makes clear her feelings of exclusion — not just as a Cuban-American but also (ironically, considering Gina's political leanings) as a person from a lower class who lacks mobility. "Suddenly" Juani realizes that she "hated that [she] was just sitting there like a big black hole" (133). Juani sees she has been the void against which Gina and her *independentista* friends can define themselves through negation.

Before I look closely at the scene of violence between Gina and Juani, let me reiterate the serious social implications of describing such violence. Even in feminist discourses, battery between women has been a challenging subject to address. As Obejas indicates in an essay entitled "Women Who Batter Women," "Battering has long been one of the lesbian community's nastiest secrets. Because they either buy into myths about the inherent goodness of lesbian relationships or fear giving fuel to homophobes, many lesbians refuse to admit that domestic violence can exist between two women" (53). Furthermore, as Claudia Card explains, in relationships of battery between women, "the violence is horizontal insofar as it comes from one who does not occupy a political position of superiority (or inferiority), and yet it also gives rise to a dominance order, reproducing structures of oppression. Thus, interaction with a lesbian batterer seems horizontal in some respects but vertical in others" (124). *Memory Mambo's* depiction of violence between women who are sexual partners thereby opens another line of inquiry in *Grotesque Touch*. Juani is what Craft calls a "woman-monster, woman-out-of-control" (376), because partner battery at once conforms to stereotypes about the always already violent lesbian, but also runs counter to U.S. cultural assumptions about women's passivity in abusive relationships.

An analysis of the details of Juani's and Gina's violence is essential, for the novel describes their violence—as skin meets skin, with no mediating weapons or other actors—in a manner that makes their bodies abject. Due to the psychic weight of carrying such an event in her mind, Juani waits until a flashback halfway through the novel to show why her chest has given her pains throughout the story: she struck Gina, who in the confusion of the moment latched her teeth onto Juani's breast. Their physical violence begins after the verbal violence of calling Juani a *gusana*, when Gina, after taking Juani in her arms, "shoved [Juani] a little," what Juani later calls "just a little push with her open palm to [Juani's] shoulder" (Obejas 134). Yet, even Gina's slight movements convey their social separation to Juani. In response to this action, Juani's body—she claims not to be in control of her actions at this point—quickly escalates the scene when she pummels Gina's face with her fist: "I don't know why or how but I smashed it into her" (134). Juani's lack of understanding about the reasons for the violence define this scene, unlike Mrs. Richard's sense of social obligation in *Unburnable*. Still, Juani's body and Gina's body reflect grotesque embodiments of colonizing violence.

Juani then follows a predictable script of partner battery, as she demands submission. Both Juani and Gina are bleeding profusely, and when Gina screams, Juani replies "in a voice deep and calm and flat: 'Just shut up'" (134). Juani nevertheless believes her own response comes out of shock, because she cannot connect her sensations with "the crime on [Gina's] face" (134). In this moment, both Juani and Gina seem to have transformed into something animalistic: "*I hate you*, [Gina] said, and smeared the blood with her hands on my face, getting it all over my eyes and blinding me just long enough so she could sink her spiky nails into my wrists" (134, emphasis in original). In her memory (for readers cannot know for sure whether Gina spoke these italicized words) Juani is unfeeling, and Gina is all-feeling; in this scene they are locked in a conflict that reduces them—very literally—to blood, the surfeit expenditure that we have already noticed in colonial economies in *All*

Souls' Rising, The Book of Night Women, and—in this chapter—*American Horror Story* and *Unburnable*.

The violence in this scene is purposefully sexualized and gendered, revealing the long-lasting narratives that tie women's bodies to colonizing endeavors. Earlier in her recollection, Juani recognizes her intimate proximity to Gina when her body reacts violently: "She was just sitting next to me, her thigh pressed against my thigh, her sweat and cologne stinging my eyes she was so close—and I felt the bones of her face collapse under my hand" (Obejas 134). Juani's reading of her closeness to Gina shows how easily the erotic transforms into violence due to their repressed anger and unwillingness to address their differences. As their struggle progresses, Gina and Juani fall to the floor, predictably knocking over furniture. Then, something unpredictable happens, as the spilling of blood becomes undeniably sexual: "She coughed and lowered her mouth automatically, but she was gone now too and didn't realize what she was doing, so when her teeth clamped down again—just as hard, and angrier now—they came down on my breast, which is small and, normally, soft, not very firm at all" (135). Unlike the rape scene in *Unburnable*, this depiction of violation is narrated through Juani's eyes, as she is both perpetrator of battery and the recipient of sexual violence. Although this scene relies on Juani's description of the physicality of the violence—both the feeling of striking Gina as well as how her own body (especially her breast) responds to Gina's violent touch—the narration quickly dissolves into a more detached voice. Juani cannot continue to focus on the *feeling* of the violence: "This is the part when I left my body, when I just walked out of it and watched us from across the room, like a ghost or a spirit" (135). Reduced to bodily responses—indiscriminately striking and gnawing—the violence both women inflict now seems to be separate from who they are as people. The violence is somehow instinctual.

Immediately following this section, though, the chapter ends with an italicized (and more romanticized) account of the women's spilling and mingling blood: "*My blood like a fountain from my nipples, like a geyser, like rain—and I kiss you, my tongue running inside your bloody mouth, gums, teeth, down to your throat, then we both gasp and choke and spit—and I love you, monstrously and uselessly, but I still love—I will always love you*" (135). As Juani's body loses blood, then is filled with desire, this narrative aside reads as a grotesque, abject love scene. The eroticization of the violence within the scene further complicates what Juani achieves in retelling the incident. The narrative is reminiscent of the vampire trope already discussed in this chapter. In some ways, the complicated, romanticized (and abject) imagery of violence is similar to Jewelle Gomez's *The Gilda Stories*, as the novel admits that a sensual scene of blood exchange between two female vampires "to an outsider . . . may [be] one of horror" because "their faces [are] red and shining, their eyes unfocused and black, the sound of their bodies slick with wetness, tight with life" (Gomez 140). In *The Gilda Stories*, this mutual exchange of blood and passion is "a birth," "not death," unlike the monstrous, capitalistic, racist society that threatens death to all beings in the novel (140). While *Memory Mambo* might seem to draw on this kind of romanticized lesbian vampire imagery, the reality is that blood (which pours from Juani's breast like milk), bones, muscles, and tongue all tangle together in a way that, despite the serious physical damage the women inflict on each other, still signals a bond to Juani. To readers, however, the women's physical violence makes the psychological chasm between them undeniable—and so do their bodies show the grotesque realities of colonized histories and sexualities via this violence.

This connection between violence, sexuality, race, and the women's bodies is made clearer when we consider that Juani herself has previously described Gina's body as the land in Cuba *or* Puerto Rico. She conflates the two places: "To me, she was like the purest, blackest earth—that rich, sweet soil in which sugarcane grows. I always imagined her as hills in which I would roll around, happy and dirty" (Obejas 119). Here, the narrative connects women's bodies to the colonized land of a sugar plantation. Juani complicates this scene further, though, when she says that "when [she] was going through these revelries, [she] always forgot how sugarcane sucks the earth, makes it barren and dry, how it made [her] Tío Raúl rich but drove him insane first" (119). Passion, madness, and violence intertwine in Juani's thoughts about Gina—which readily draw on a gendered, sexualized, and ableist narrative of Caribbean peoples, like we see in the studio-produced adaptations of *Wide Sargasso Sea*.

Furthermore, Juani's relationship with Gina is not the only context that foregrounds her violence; her cousin Caridad's husband, Jimmy, serves as a complicated double for Juani's violence. Caridad's sister Pauli calls him "Jimmy Frankenstein," a "reference . . . not to the hapless monster, whom she regarded as an innocent, but to the scientist, the evil Victor who pieced together cadavers and animated them in his own earthly hell" (Obejas 59). To Pauli, "Jimmy had found a way to kill Caridad and then bring her back in his own distorted image, compliant and anesthetized" (59). On one level, Juani seems to fear her attraction to Jimmy's *machismo*, his ever-present willingness to use his sexuality to bully Caridad and Juani (he frequently flaunts his erections and makes crude jokes about Juani's sexuality). On another level, Juani fears becoming like Jimmy.

Once Jimmy gains power over Juani's story because he is the only other person who knows about the fight, he claims power over her as well. In the hospital, Jimmy readily tells police officers that it was "just a little domestic violence," and he continues to tell Juani, "That's what I told the cops—they love cat fights, you know" (Obejas 138). Despite the damaging violence Gina and Juani inflicted on each other, Jimmy's story immediately disempowers both women by trivializing their actions. Once he blackmails Gina into silence as well, Jimmy has complete control over the story (and Juani), and he then transforms the complex story of violence between women into "the incident," a tale of political violence that the women suffered when a man broke into Gina's apartment (147). Although Jimmy's version of "the incident" makes events more palatable for others, the process of reducing the women's actions to a "catfight" and then completely removing them from the actions mirrors cultural attitudes at large. Giving the power to change the story to Jimmy—a reviled character—clarifies the novel's message: telling lies to cover up the truth of violence between women is, itself, a monstrous endeavor.

Even so, *Memory Mambo* shows that power-hungry people like Jimmy cannot hide their true natures for long. Because of Jimmy's psychological power over her, Juani is understandably afraid that they are alike in their monstrosity; however, Jimmy's actions ultimately reveal to her that they are fundamentally different. In a scene of horrible revelation, Juani wakes up from a nap to discover that Jimmy is forcing her infant cousin Rosa (who is Pauli's daughter, and Jimmy's niece) to perform oral sex on him. Jimmy's "gruesome face" tells Juani everything she needs to know, and she is immediately released from his domination when the scene breaks out into utter chaos as Pauli and Ali (Rosa's father) rush inside the house upon hearing Juani's scream (221, 222). Scholars have difficulty putting this scene into words, because such violence committed on the body of a child is widely considered to be beyond the limits of the imaginable; thus, readers are likely to consider this scene to be more monstrous than Juani and Gina's fight.[15] Seeing this sexual violence, what Sugg refers to as "the last and most horrific of Juani's traumatic calls to bad witnessing" (475), allows Juani to break free from Jimmy's spell. She does not lie for Jimmy, though he repeatedly begs for her to tell everyone "what happened," as he did for her (Obejas 225). Instead, Juani kicks him in the face and runs away: "I'm out of there, out of that furnace of all their passions and tempers, out of that sucking spiral to hell, out of their circle of darkness and fire" (226).

By extracting herself from the scene, Juani attests to Jimmy's crime, and she also begins to come to terms with the violence she and Gina inflicted on each other. While Juani has a long way to go to undo her romantic notions about her violence—Gina asks, "What kind of amnesia are you suffering from? . . . Don't you remember? You beat the shit out of me" (230)—they can at least admit the irreparable damage that they have inflicted on each other. Although Juani does not explicitly think about her and Gina's violence in terms of colonial violence, readers can make this leap: the women were, and still are, in denial concerning the socially conditioned distance between them. Nevertheless, the sexual violence Jimmy enacts on Rosa's body is "undeniable" to Juani's memory, about which Juani says, "*I don't want to remember any part of this*" (234, emphasis in original). Readers connect these instances of violence, and while the novel is open-ended about whether Juani realizes how her own actions stem from the violence of colonialism, the narrative concludes with at least a gesture toward growth and admittance: Juani is about to open up to her relative Patricia; Juani has decided to travel to Cuba to expand her sense of the greater narrative; and the novel ends with the line "It's quiet now" (237).

Obejas's novel thus expels the abject male—Jimmy—and preserves Juani's sense of self in the aftermath of her monstrous actions. In terms of narrative conventions, *Memory Mambo* ends with a remarkable peace: unlike what Barbara Creed and other scholars identify in horror tropes, Obejas's novel does not classify Juani as the monstrous-feminine, nor the monstrous-lesbian. She, humanized in her narrative, shows personal growth that moves toward understanding that her violent past with Gina mirrors much larger systems of power and control in societies where racist, sexist, classist, and nationalist ideologies intersect. Unlike in *Unburnable*, then, the protagonist of *Memory Mambo* does not have to be utterly destroyed by colonization's monstrous powers. Despite her temporary embodiment of the very grotesque, abject violence that narratives tend to expel, Juani—in the end—can hope. The novel condemns a social environment where power, passion, and violence intertwine. Juani's acts of "monstrosity" thereby expose pasts of slavery and ongoing colonization; her story reframes the imageries of horror to make dominant narratives abject.

Conclusion
Plantation Settings after 2016

When I began writing a version of this project in 2013, it did not take me long to see how pervasive plantation imaginaries are in depictions of violence between women. I soon realized that iterations of plantations are manifest within and across written, visual, and audiovisual texts — because the desire to claim colonizing power is everywhere. In our present moment, cell phone videos can capture these performances as they play out. Consider, for instance, the viral videos recording white women in the United States when they call 9-1-1 because they see Black people living their lives. As Stacey Patton recently wrote in *Dame*, "Each of these women is making these calls not because they feel legitimately threatened, but because they need to bolster their deflating identities as 'mistresses of the universe,' fully aware of the very real dangers to the Black people involved at the hand of the police." "Mistresses of the universe" evokes the power struggles at work throughout this book: white women grasping for whatever power they can exert on Black women's bodies, just to feel like they matter in a culture that has conditioned them (for centuries) to believe that they should be the center of the universe.

Readers might wonder about my archive's cutoff date, 2016. I do not mean to suggest that we live in a moment set apart from our earlier history. Indeed, researching this book has set in my mind how performances of gender, sexuality, race, ethnicity, class, ability, and nationality repeat throughout time. In *Grotesque Touch*, I have shown how performances of identity and power are firmly embedded in representations of woman-on-woman violence on plantation settings — across time, media, geographies, and genres. In turn, imagined plantations continue to appear in popular culture. Post-2016, the visibility of white nationalism might make it seem like we live in a topsy-turvy time warp, but — as is evident in texts that respond to racist, sexist, ableist, classist structures throughout time — white supremacy (and its attendant prejudices and violence) never really went away. Instead, as I claim in this book, we have been (and still are) mired by narratives that proclaim white women to be exceptional (i.e., that they do not participate in or benefit from colonizing systems), while these narratives mask the actual power relationships at work.

Some imaginative texts still reflect how people attempt to access power. Ironies of power still play out in these narratives: to rephrase Elaine Scarry, the more people try to show that they are powerful through violence, the more those performances expose how shoddy the illusion actually is. What I have noticed about some texts since 2016, however, is that they might magnify the ironies of power by blending generic conventions, or they might remix generic conventions to implicate the United States as a nation in plantation violence. By way of concluding this book, I will briefly examine three texts that exemplify such ironies to various degrees through the genres of science fiction and exploitation cinema (*Bitch Planet* 2014–17), melodrama and comedy (*Insecure* 2017), and horror (*Get Out* 2017). I will show how women's plantation violence remains a narrative feature across these genres, always reminding us that white women play a central role in upholding white supremacy.

Bitch Planet, the award-winning comic book series created by Kelly Sue DeConnick and Valentine De Landro, blends, bends, and (sometimes) breaks tropes of science fiction/dystopian genres and women-in-prison exploitation films. In its depiction of a women's prison on another planet, *Bitch Planet's* setting might at first seem to defy exploitation tropes that gained popularity in the 1970s and are manifest in cinematic depictions today. For example, in a three-part forum on *The Middle Spaces*, Rebecca Wanzo claims that in the comic books "the caricatured excess creates both the pleasure and the possibility. Without the idea of the grotesque, without the sensational, the characters could not flip the script of normativity. . . . DeConnick and De Landro suggest there is no liberation without being able to grab hold of not only the representations, but the intransigent views of these representations, and wrestling them to the ground" ("What Is the Liberatory Potential"). This might be true about some exploitation film tropes in *Bitch Planet*, such as how the series implicates the reader in the voyeuristic pleasures of prison exploitation film staples, like "The Obligatory Shower Scene" in Book One. However, I contend that the series also operates within the confines of an *exceptional* plantation setting.

Book One makes apparent the comic's plantation exploitation when a white prison agent projects a southern U.S. plantation setting onto screens while she attempts to intimidate Kamau "Kam" Kogo, a Black inmate. The agent introduces herself to Kam as "Miss Whitney" while she passive-aggressively offers Kam sweet tea. The prison cell's screens surround the women and approximate a stereotypical image of a Tara-like antebellum plantation house and its verdant environs, all in an effort to force Kam into

FIGURE C.1 *Bitch Planet*, Book One, by Kelly Sue DeConnick and Valentine De Landro (Image Comics, 2015).

submission (figure C.1). Kam does not yield to call the agent "Miss Whitney"; she is aware of what this "Southern Georgia Morning" is code for—a veneer of white civility that does not actually hide the threat of physical violence against people of color. Instead, at the bottom of the page, Kam asserts, "I am not from Georgia." Then, on the next page, Whitney removes her helmet to reveal her carefully styled blond hair, and digital white birds fly around her head as she replies that *she* is from Georgia.

In a comic book so invested in disrupting a sense of planetary place, the narrative's move to situate Whitney's threat of violence as *southern* U.S. violence seems strange. After all, the dystopian Earth in *Bitch Planet* has lost most of its geographical markers, assumingly due to climate change accelerated by unabated capitalism. We might, on the one hand, want to read this scene as implicating plantation enslavement as a cornerstone of this dystopian capitalistic society that literally jettisons nonconforming people into space to labor and die on a prison planet. Nevertheless, on the other hand, I believe this reading strains the comic book's own implicit argument that makes *the plantation* an exceptional setting. The "Southern Georgia Morning" digital projection is the only rural earthly setting in *Bitch Planet*, and it is the only setting given geographic specificity. This setting, itself a digital replica of an idealized antebellum plantation house, thereby employs exploitation film shorthand to signal Whitney's white supremacist attitudes and the physical danger she poses to Kam. However apt this characterization might seem, the narrative abruptly introduces and then mitigates the "plantation" parallels. While Book Two shows Whitney's fall from power when she is framed for the murder of a prisoner (thus showing how her position was never stable in this society, much like the white women who attempt to claim power throughout *Grotesque Touch*), the series does not pursue a sustained critique of imagined plantation settings. Like in exploitation films of the 1970s (such as *Mandingo* in chapter 1), readers are made to understand—even on an unconscious level—that such attitudes are exceptional, confined to a region of the United States.[1]

Bitch Planet at once remixes genres (science fiction, dystopian, exploitation cinema) and employs a plantation setting without calling into question assumptions of regional exceptionalism. I want to shift the conversation to two audiovisual texts released after 2016 that continue to mix generic elements but also situate violence in broader national contexts. In her conclusion to *The Illustrated Slave*, Martha J. Cutter suggests that "the invocation of an empathetic response on the part of the viewer in visual treatments of slavery has not disappeared, but it has become more ironic, self-reflective, and self-questioning," which "turns the viewer toward an examination not of a debased other, but of the politics of empathy as a whole" (226). Both *Insecure* and *Get Out*, I argue, build on Cutter's observations. Their narratives reconfigure plantation settings in ironic and self-reflective ways (through elements of melodrama, comedy, and horror, respectively) to implicate a wider swath of U.S. cultures in continuations of violence.

Viewers who tuned in to season two of HBO's popular series *Insecure* (2017) witnessed the main character Issa (played by Issa Rae) struggling to find a new meaningful pattern to her life in Los Angeles after her longtime boyfriend Lawrence (Jay Ellis) moved out of their apartment. In half of the episodes, the characters watch clips from a television show called *Due North*, a parody of plantation telenovelas set inside a generic "big house" somewhere in the United States. After the final episode of *Insecure*'s second season, viewers could see extended clips from *Due North* in a six-minute mini-episode ("Ep. 111: Due North"). Here, I want to briefly trace the show-within-a-show's story arc to comment on the narratives that *Due North* draws from and adds to.

The relationships between women as enslavers and enslaved women in *Due North* are, true to the melodrama of the telenovela form, characterized by intense interactions driven by jealousy and intrigue. During the first clip characters in *Insecure* watch, the enslaved woman Ninny (Regina Hall) sits on a couch and giggles to herself while reading ("Ep. 1: Hella Great"). Her enslaver Christine Turnfellow (Katharine Leonard), whom she calls "Miss Massa," enters the room and shrilly exclaims, "Ninny, so help me, if this is

FIGURE C.2 Katharine Leonard as Christine Turnfellow and Regina Hall as Ninny in *Insecure*'s show-within-a-show *Due North* (HBO, 2017).

anything more than a cookbook, there will be consequences . . . the foot-less kind." Ninny gasps, wide-eyed, as her enslaver continues, "Who are you cooking your thick ox ass for?" (figure C.2). This exchange does not conform to conventions of antebellum melodrama like *Uncle Tom's Cabin*, for example, because *Due North* mitigates Ninny's suffering (her enslaver threatens her with amputation) with bizarrely humorous dialogue. Thus, the audience does not achieve a sense of Ninny's virtue through victimization under en-slavement, to borrow the media scholar Linda Williams's phrasing in *Playing the Race Card*.

Though the framing of Ninny's wide-eyed reactions and her calling her enslaver "Miss Massa" connote her subordinate place in the power structure, Ninny also exerts a sense of control not usually associated with melodrama. For example, in another clip Ninny pretends to dust the room before she drops poison into Christine Turnfellow's cup ("Ep. 111: Due North"). After her enslaver drinks, Ninny picks up the cup and gazes down at her with a sidelong glance and smirk. That Ninny and her enslaver are caught in a rela-tionship of jealousy is a reality lived by women in the plantation household (as chapters 1, 2, and 3 of *Grotesque Touch* examine); yet, *Due North* magni-fies this trope to an outlandish degree. During an extended scene, for in-stance, an enslaved man barges into a dinner party and tells everyone that he has "done figured it out" ("Ep. 111: Due North"): the now-deceased Chris-tine Turnfellow was carrying on an affair with another enslaver-class woman, named Lydia (Sarah Chaney); Master Turnfellow (Scott Foley) had sex with both Ninny and an enslaved woman named Nessa (Nija Okoro); and Nessa was having sex with Ninny's husband, Zeke (Michael Jai White). The characters implicated in this convoluted web begin shoving each other, with Zeke falling to the floor and crying, "I hate slavery!" The scene ends with Ninny and Nessa fighting, and the dinner party guests continuing to eat their meal, unbothered by these revelations or the brawling.

Why disrupt the story arc about thirty-something professionals living in Los Angeles with clips of a plantation melodrama parody? *Due North* depicts slavery in a manner that favors tongue-in-cheek exaggeration over creating a narrative that reveals something new about the relationships and structures of enslavement. Yet, how *Insecure* frames this show-within-a-show interests me. Watching *Due North* is an experience Issa and Lawrence share with friends. Perhaps this is a way for *Insecure* to illustrate how they still have something in common; Issa and Lawrence are apart, yet not alone in their consumption of a popular television show. More importantly, I see *Due North* as a way Issa and Lawrence can perhaps vent (through laughter at the melodrama of *Due North*) their experiences with sexist and racist social structures they deal with daily. For example, in the fourth episode, police officers stop Lawrence because he made a U-turn, and while he gets only a warning, the scene is tinged with tension. Judging from his body language and the body language of the officers, we do not know whether the scene will end in outright violence. Furthermore, after this interaction, two young women invite Lawrence to their apartment for sex; then, disappointed that he does not perform like "the other Black guys" they have had sex with, they ignore him until he leaves ("Ep. 4: Hella LA"). *Due North* may be a kind of narrative release for the main characters' daily interactions that "other" them, but the clips from *Due North* also frame *Insecure's* season *through* the plantation narrative. Lawrence's experiences at work, with the police, and with the young women are dehumanizing: they reduce him to a body. Through this show-within-a-show, I suggest that *Insecure* creates a way for plantation structures to extend to California, for the show suggests that *all* places are shaped by the racist, sexist, classist systems that exploit Black people in the United States.

This season of *Insecure* is an example of contemporary media that employ plantation settings where audiences are not likely to expect them. Through different generic conventions, Jordan Peele's film *Get Out* (2017) also gestures to how pervasive plantation structures still are in the United States. The film's use of the horror genre to show how the upper-middle-class Armitage family

FIGURE C.3 The Armitage family's house in *Get Out* (Universal Pictures, 2017).

exploits the minds and bodies of young Black people effectively works against audiences' perceptions of "exceptional" plantation settings. Instead, the film gestures toward how widespread systems of harm are throughout the nation. In doing so, the film ties together many of the narrative tropes in *Grotesque Touch*.

Early in the film, the young photographer Chris Washington (Daniel Kaluuya) travels from New York City to his girlfriend's family home somewhere in a wooded suburb. On the house's columned porch, his girlfriend Rose Armitage (Allison Williams) introduces Chris to her parents, Missy and Dean (Catherine Keener and Bradley Whitford) (figure C.3). At this point, the camera takes a wide-angle shot of the meeting; Chris appears to be swallowed by the family's embrace and the house's symmetry. Like in many horror films, the house itself forebodes harm, and its visual perfection hides (but also warns of) the dangers within.

The Armitage home looks like a plantation house, yes, but the film goes beyond the visual trappings that connote plantation settings. The Armitage house, as viewers and Chris come to understand, is a place of horror. In the parlor, Missy hypnotizes Chris and takes away his free will; in the backyard, the Armitages hold an auction for Chris's body; in the basement, Dean and his son Jeremy (Caleb Landry Jones) attempt to remove a part of Chris's brain to replace it with the brain of the man who purchased him during the auction. In the rooms and on the lawn, the Armitages and their white patrons buy and sell young Black people for their physical abilities. Their enterprise is all about *colonizing the mind*, imposing their will on the bodies of people their daughter has lured to their home. In this way, the house represents the horrors of enslavement and the continued harm posed to Black Americans at the intersections of race, class, sexuality, ability, and gender.

The Armitage family and their patrons find much pleasure in this enterprise. Indeed, like many of the enslavers throughout *Grotesque Touch*, they claim their identity in their community *through* the violence they exert on Black people's bodies and the pleasure this violence brings. We see this dynamic happening with Rose's grandparents, whose minds were placed inside the bodies of a young Black man and woman. Walter and Georgina, as the family calls them, attempt to perform tasks as household servants while they are around Chris so they may fool him; yet, the pleasure they take in their new bodies is too much to sustain a convincing performance. Chris encounters Walter (Marcus Henderson), for instance, as he sprints across the lawn at night—Walter delights in the stolen body's speed and endurance. Chris also sees Georgina (Betty Gabriel) engrossed in her reflection, as she caresses her face and smiles—she enjoys the stolen body's attractiveness (figure C.4). To make this point even clearer, the film shows what happens when the Black woman's will to live interferes with the Armitage grandmother's will to exert power. When Chris has a moment alone with Georgina, he tries to reassure her that he does not intend to "snitch" on her to the Armitages for unplugging his phone. When she (the grandmother, that is) finally understands what Chris means (she translates "snitch" to "tattletale" in her dated vocabulary), she declares, "I can assure you . . . I don't answer to anyone." To Chris, this signals Georgina's delusional sense of place in the family's household, since she is their employee; to the Armitage grandmother, however, this is her assertion of power in the household and over this stolen woman's body. The stolen woman's consciousness almost breaks through, though, when Chris continues, "All I know is sometimes if there's too many white people, I get nervous, you know?" At this point, the audience sees Georgina having an internal struggle, which the grandmother suppresses with "No, no, no, no." With tears running from Georgina's eyes, the grandmother speaks through the woman's body and forces a smile (having overpowered the woman's mind, for now): "That's not my experience. Not at all. The Armitages are so good to us. They treat us like family." This interaction works on at least two levels: first, Georgina's strange behavior and insistence that the Armitages treat her "like family" signals to Chris that something is not right—why would she start crying if all was well; second, the grandmother's words as she speaks through the stolen woman's body are deeply

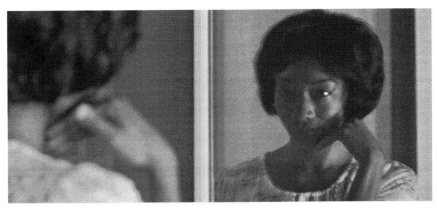

FIGURE C.4 Georgina, played by Betty Gabriel, gazes into her reflection
(Universal Pictures, 2017).

ironic. She and Walter are "like family" against their will, and they were made
into "family" through violence. The grandmother's constant internal battle
to suppress the stolen woman's consciousness continues this violence.

Moreover, Rose herself has enjoyed each victim's body before her family
steals them. Before the Armitages drag Chris into the basement to begin the
procedure, he discovers evidence of Rose's intimate involvement in her
family's scheme. He finds her collection of photographs from each relationship she formed with Black men (and one woman, Georgina) in order to lure
them to her family's home. As he shuffles through the photos, the reach of
this family's violence becomes horrifically clear—they have a system in place.
In this way, *Get Out* situates many of the themes in *Grotesque Touch* on a larger
national scale. Rose's (faked) intimacy with Black people is the mechanism
by which her family can enact violence on them, and she sadistically enjoys
this aspect of her performance. She draws a sense of identity from her role
in her family's plans because bringing physical and mental harm to Black
Americans is at the root of who she is.

The horror at the heart of *Get Out* is the horror at the heart of *Grotesque
Touch*: not taking seriously the violence of everyday racist, classist, sexist,
ableist structures means denying our collusion. What *Get Out* and *Insecure*
read together suggest is that the performances of power evident in plantation slavery are still at work today. These texts dispel a narrative of exceptionalism connoted by the plantation setting in *Bitch Planet* (for example),
which gives audiences a false sense of separation from these power structures

and the violence necessary to uphold them. In taking women's violence seriously—and not deeming such violence exceptional—*Grotesque Touch* pushes us to reevaluate how narratives reflect and shape our understandings of ourselves. This book urges us to acknowledge the violent intimacies we participate in that uphold the grotesque structures of our everyday lives.

Notes

Introduction

1. For more about "the plantation" in texts throughout time, please see (in chronological order) Rody's *Daughter's Return* (2001); B. Richardson's "South and the Caribbean" (2007); Tinsman and Shukla's introduction to *Imagining Our Americas* (2007); Duck's "Plantation/Empire" (2010); Karem's *Purloined Islands* (2010); and Wells's *Romances of the White Man's Burden* (2011).

2. Like Russ, I "understand the plantation, in a literary [and cultural] context, to be not primarily a physical location but rather an insidious ideological and psychological trope through which intersecting histories of the New World are told and retold" (3). Similarly, Handley indicates how "plantation discourse, always dependent on structures of colonialism, wedded itself to the growth of U.S. imperialism after emancipation, and therefore the stark distinctions between Caribbean and U.S. cultures that emerged in the twentieth century are, in fact, alienated cousins, as it were, of the same plantation family" (5–6). In *Wounds of Returning*, Adams also focuses on "the strange and contradictory possibilities that slavery released into the realm of the normal," which "still shape social spaces, including the reimagined plantation" (4–5).

3. As Marcus Wood claims in *Blind Memory*, "it is as if the formulaic wood-engravings are saying every whipping is like every other whipping" (120). He continues, "The reduplication of blocks suggests that there is a currency in language and in imagery for the description of pain which is accepted and familiar to the Northern abolitionist readership. There is a mythology of slave experience which for the Northern American and English reviewers constituted an unproblematic realism" (120).

4. For an overview of scholarly debates on antislavery publications' voyeurism, spectacle, and pleasure, see especially the preface and introduction to Cutter's *Illustrated Slave*. Cutter's reading of Bibb's *Narrative* complicates Wood's reading, as she acknowledges the narrative's tendency to "include . . . generic images of the torture of enslaved women and men. Sometimes these images are piled into the text without a great deal of narrative commentary beyond the mere fact of the beating itself (see page 118, for example), and sometimes they depict graphic thrashings of half-naked women. . . . On the other hand, the text also includes new images that defamiliarize such visual icons" (160–61). Cutter concludes that the visuals in Bibb's narrative "attempt to integrate a reader into the story of slavery through graphic narrative systems that are bricolaged and lacking in closure" (174).

5. "By adopting the authority and prestige of quantification," claims Goddu, "the antislavery almanac produced slavery as a social fact, intimately embedded at the heart of U.S. democracy and its systems of representation and power even as it rendered slavery a legitimate part of the national conversation about societal improvement.

Slavery, like the tides, was another complex system that relied on the revealing power of statistics to make its operations visible" ("Antislavery Almanac" 136).

6. Goddu also indicates that the visual discourse of the 1840 almanac differs from that of previous editions: "Accompanied by a title, rather than a description of the image as in the almanac's earlier editions, the heading works to generalize the image, making it representative rather than particular" ("Antislavery Almanac" 138–39).

7. Goddu argues, "The almanac's tabular and repetitive form works to systematize and regulate knowledge by making legible and understandable the complex details of an increasingly dynamic social world" so that "generalizations about the weather teach readers to make similar systematic claims about slavery" ("Antislavery Almanac" 139, 140).

8. For an overview of these stereotypes and their historiography, see White's first chapter, "Jezebel and Mammy," in *Ar'n't I a Woman?* (27–61).

9. See Young's *Disarming the Nation* for more about the Topsy/Prissy comparison in relation to Mitchell's performances of blackface (271–72).

10. In developing this methodology, I am seeking to meet the charge of scholars who focus on hemispheric American cultures before 1900, such as what Brickhouse articulates in her *Transamerican Literary Relations and the Nineteenth-Century Public Sphere*: "Remaining for the most part within this early nineteenth-century historical framework, the book thus responds to an implicit assumption in the various fields of comparative American or 'New World' studies that has often been assumed as fact: that literary transnationalism in the Americas and the critical perspectives it invites are natural outgrowths of the massive human migrations, urban pluralism, and cultural globalization the hemisphere has witnessed over the course of the twentieth century. Yet many of the literary configurations envisioned in current studies as predominately and even inherently tied to the twentieth century were in fact addressed by writers in the Americas as explicit questions and problems well before the modern and contemporary periods to which they have been cosigned" (31).

11. Neroni similarly focuses her project *The Violent Woman* on "the violent woman [who] appears at moments of ideological crisis" in U.S. cultures (18).

12. To draw attention to the continuities between past and present structures and inequalities, I hyphenate terms like "neo-colonial," "post-colonial," and "post-emancipation." Here, the hyphen puts pressure on the "new"-ness or "post"-ness of power imbalances.

13. As Monteith and Jones summarize in their introduction to the collection *South to a New Place*, "critical debate about the 'Southernization of America' has established a model whereby the South is both a cultural filter and the barometer for the health (or sickness) of the nation" via "turning assertions about the 'Americanization' of the South around" (4). Even by flipping the focus on how people usually talk about national regions, however, such ventures may in fact erase people outside the continental United States. Glissant summarizes that such theorizations of "the South" may presume that those "other people of the south, to the south of this capitalized South, never existed" (30).

14. Christina Sharpe's work also intensely traces the "transgenerational transmission" of "intimate spaces of trauma, violence, pleasure, shame, and containment" (4),

which resonates with my discussion about representations of sexual violence in chapter 3.

15. The term "circum-Caribbean" reaffirms Roach's rationale for using the term "circum-Atlantic," in that "the concept of a circum-Atlantic world (as opposed to a transatlantic one) insists on the centrality of the diasporic and genocidal histories of Africa and the Americas, North and South, in the creation of the culture of modernity. In this sense, a New World was not discovered in the Caribbean, but one was truly invented there" (4). Also see Adams's "Introduction" (5–6).

16. While I believe that the term "circum-Caribbean" best describes my project's selection of texts, I understand that various scholars have coined or mobilized other specific terms to theorize similar projects. Loichot's term "Postplantation," for example, might initially seem fitting, for she indicates that "the 'post' refers to the dynamic processes of the establishment, the lifespan, and the enduring legacy of a given structure or state" (7). As such, she believes "Postplantation" offers the most exact term for her study because "it is precisely the difference, the tension, and the violent encounter of bodies, languages, and cultures that the term Postplantation . . . encompass[es]. In short, the term Postplantation points not to a synthetic object but to a compound one built on irreconcilable differences" (7). In her work, Loichot uses these differences to bring texts together into conversation. Handley and, later, Russ use the term "Postslavery" in a similar vein. Though I do believe the prefix "post-" can draw attention to the continuities between past and present structures and inequalities (especially if the term features a hyphen, like "post-colonial" and "post-emancipation"), my project intends to focus more closely on the cultural circulations of ideologies and performances, which sometimes get lost in debates about terms like "postplantation" and "postslavery."

17. This is one of the ways my project answers and extends beyond Lowe's charge in *Calypso Magnolia*: "It is time to unlock old geographical and cultural restrictions, as we reconfigure cultural formations and interactions that have always themselves overflowed artificial boundaries" (xi).

18. In this way, my project might also be described as one of "archipelagic American Studies," as described by Roberts and Stephens's introduction to the collection by the same name: "We want to frame archipelago formation in terms of this trope of catachresis, whereby 'archipelago' itself becomes a term deployed in the attempt to name connections—the 'submarine' unities between land and sea, island and island, island and continent—that are harder to see from the shores of land-locked, above-ground, territorial epistemologies and ways of thinking" (30).

19. See McPherson's "After Authenticity," an afterword to *Creating and Consuming the American South*, for an overview of how "the South" and "authenticity" appear in that collection of essays and throughout studies of southern U.S. cultures more generally. Moreover, I would encourage readers to seek out current scholarship about regionalism in African American studies and Native American and Indigenous studies. For conversations about African American studies, see (in chronological order) R. Richardson's *Black Masculinity and the U.S. South* (2007); Robinson's *This Ain't Chicago* (2014); J. McInnis's "That 'the Land Would One Day Be Free'" (2015); and Bradley's "Re-Imagining Slavery in the Hip-Hop Imagination" (2016). For Native American

and Indigenous studies, see (in chronological order) Lowery's *Lumbee Indians in the Jim Crow South* (2010); E. Anderson's essay "Native" in *Keywords for Southern Studies* (2016); Caison's *Red States* (2018); and Lowery's *Lumbee Indians* (2018).

20. Of course, as Guterl reminds us in his epilogue to *American Mediterranean*, these connections and circulations persist in people's lived experiences today. The forced movement, captivity, and exploitation of people throughout the hemisphere presently follow processes of enslavement and colonization: "There are traces of the old exchanges of 'revolutionary commodities' in the sordid parallelisms of Mardi Gras and Carnival; in sex trade tourism to Miami, Santo Domingo, and Havana; and in the emergence of a new national trade in immigrant bodies and sex slaves through shipping lanes, ports, and railroads. There are traces of it everywhere. But we do not wish to remember, to see, or to hear" (189).

21. In this way, *Grotesque Touch* also rigorously considers the "understudied aspects of how the plantation imagination has been gendered, racialized, and eroticized in ways that oppose the domination of an ever-shifting 'North' while also reproducing the subordinate place of female experiences and literary imaginings within the Americas" (Russ 14). See also Paravisini-Gebert's essay "Alienation of Power" (esp. 9), which is a precursor to my intersectional feminist analyses of power in representations of enslavers and enslaved women.

22. Still, as Loichot summarizes from J. Michael Dash, Antonio Benítez-Rojo, and Derek Walcott, "What is at stake is not the total object, which can never be fixed in time, but an excavation of the links between its parts" (10). My study does not intend to theorize the "total object" of circum-Caribbean representations of violence.

23. As Smith and Cohn remind readers in their introduction to *Look Away!*, "it should not surprise us that many of Yaeger's concerns—gargantuas, monstrosities, throwaway or disappeared bodies, repressed trauma, landscapes of melancholy, even literal dirteating—appear in major texts by male and female Caribbean and Spanish-American writers" (7).

24. In this way, I see my project following in the steps of scholarship like Yaeger's "Circum-Atlantic Superabundance"; Cartwright's *Sacral Grooves, Limbo Gateways*; and Pinto's *Difficult Diasporas*. See my essay in *south: a scholarly journal* (2016) for more about these comparisons.

25. Benítez-Rojo, rephrasing Derek Walcott's ideas, asserts that violence is persistent in the Caribbean: "What is the problem that, according to Walcott, remains constant in the Caribbean? Violence, sheer violence, historic violence. It does not matter whether the theme is 'War and Rebellion' or any other: in the end its ultimate meaning will be violence, whether this is called discovery, conquest, slavery, or colonialism" (Benítez-Rojo 300).

26. Hartman voices this concern in the first pages of *Scenes of Subjection*: "I have chosen not to reproduce Douglass's account of the beating of Aunt Hester in order to call attention to the ease with which such scenes are usually reiterated, the casualness with which they are circulated, and the consequences of this routine display of the slave's ravaged body. Rather than inciting indignation, too often they immure us to pain by virtue of their familiarity—the oft-repeated or restored character of these accounts and our distance from them are signaled by the theatrical language usually resorted

to in describing these instances—and especially because they reinforce the spectacular character of black suffering" (3).

27. Of course, I hesitate to collect such images and performances here. I would never encourage anyone to create a digital, public-facing project around the racist, sexist imagery I will explore throughout this book. These images are already readily available in popular culture, so why perpetuate the violence decontextualized images would reproduce, just to make a shiny digital project? Lambert cautions scholars who study "the visual culture of Atlantic slavery (and indeed the Caribbean more generally)," which was "a relatively new field" when he was writing in 2004 (9). Scholars should be wary of how they "might be complicit in the colonial archive; how they might rehearse the terror, violence and brutality of racial subjection in their work; and the extent to which they keep in circulation negative images of colonized people, of enslaved people, that continue to have disempowering effects today" (3). As Lambert urges, I intend to reframe the conversation about women's agency in order to ensure that "the enslaved black body is not the sole object of display and scrutiny . . . to avoid the dangers of representational practices that are deadening, voyeuristic and reiterative" (9).

28. For example, in *Exceptional Violence*, Thomas intends to uproot the cliché of "Jamaica's reputation as the most violent Caribbean nation" in "more general contemporary migratory circuits and popular cultural representations that bounce between Jamaica and the United States" (3). Not denying that violence marks the daily lives of Jamaicans, Thomas takes a long historical perspective that asserts "predatory, violent, and illegal forms of rule are the legacies of colonial state formation and plantation-based extraction and so could not but be incorporated within—indeed, were foundational to—postcolonial state formation in Jamaica. It is not, in other words, that we have incomplete, imperfect democracies, but that democracy in the Americas has been founded on a house of cards, as it were" (13).

29. In this way, my methods are also influenced by Sheller's reflexivity in *Consuming the Caribbean*. In a section titled "Power and Positionality in Caribbean Research," Sheller says, "I am far away, yet I have been licensed to write about the Caribbean, to represent it to others, or in this case to write about how others have represented it. That is why I say this is not a book about the Caribbean, but is one about 'The Caribbean'—the invention, the fantasy, the idea, the context for my writing. Yet I write this knowing all along (it is impossible to ignore) the material effects of all that has been said and done in the name of this Caribbean" (200–201).

30. A foundational principle of intersectional feminist analysis asserts, as Margaret L. Andersen reminds us, "that even the most privileged groups are situated in the nexus of race, class and gender" and that "race, class and gender studies are *both* about untangling the race, class and gender dimensions within the experiences of a given group *and* untangling the racialised, gendered, and class processes that shape structures of domination across groups" (168, 172, emphasis in original). For more about debates and issues, see Hancock's introduction to *Intersectionality*, in which she asks, "How do intersectionality scholars find a middle ground between an impossible conceptualization of intersectionality as intellectual property, and a destructive conceptualization of intersectionality as meme, which shape-shifts so much as to no longer be recognizable as anything other than a meme gone viral?" (17). See May's

introduction to *Pursuing Intersectionality, Unsettling Dominant Imaginaries* for an overview of intersectionality's political work and backlashes against it (1–17). I also seek to be mindful of Nash's argument in *Black Feminism Reimagined*: "As part of my contribution to theorizing the field and its racialized 'stories,' I make two intimately related arguments about women's studies: First, women's studies has long constructed black feminism as a form of discipline inflicted on the field and has imagined black feminists as a set of disciplinarians who quite literally whip the field into shape with their demands for a feminism that accounts for race generally, and for black women specifically. Of course, in an account where black women's primary labor is to remedy — and perhaps even to save — the field from itself, the discipline treats black women, and black feminism, as a finite resource. Once the field has effectively reconfigured itself, black feminism is imagined as no longer necessary or vital. Nowhere has this simplistic construction unfolded more visibly than in the context of intersectionality, a term that is obsessively signaled by the field as precisely what is required to remedy feminism's histories of racism and exclusion. In other words, intersectionality is imagined as the flip side of 'white feminism,' the kind of ethical, inclusive, and complex feminism required for feminists to revise — and to complete — their political project. Second, intersectionality has become far more than a term with an intellectual history, a term that emerged out of a cohort of black feminist engagements with the 'interlocking' nature of structures of domination. It has become women's studies' primary program-building goal. As I argue later in this introduction, black feminist defensiveness emerges from these institutional conditions, from a milieu where black women are imagined as both saviors and world-ending figures, and where intersectionality is both peril and promise" (13).

31. Audre Lorde famously asked a group of women at a gender studies conference, "What does it mean when the tools of a racist patriarchy are used to examine the fruits of that same patriarchy?"; she answered her question with, "It means that only the most narrow perimeters of change are possible and allowed" ("The Master's Tools" 110–11).

32. I hope to respond to Imani Perry's call to "insist that the root of the architecture of patriarchy is found in those places underneath layers of domination" (96). In the words of Hortense J. Spillers, I intend to "embrace the monstrosity" (qtd. in Perry 97), which is "to wrestle with the world from the status of the outside. The task is hard and demands that we read the world we occupy rigorously" (Perry 97).

33. According to Motz, "Two important reasons for ignoring female violence are, on the one hand, the widespread denial of female aggression and, on the other, the idealisation of motherhood. A further reason is the secretive or personal nature of much female violence" (4). A foundational concept for her study, then, is that "it is . . . essential to recognise the violence that is done to [women] through the denial of their capacity for aggression, and the refusal to acknowledge their moral agency" (4). However, Motz's work also succumbs to the popular notion that women mainly enact expressive violence: "I consider the acts of violence typically committed by women, against their own bodies and against their children, to be essential tools of communication" (6). Burfoot and Lord's introduction to *Killing Women* comments on this typical representation of women's violence: "When women murderers (fictional and actual) make a rare appearance, their representation tends to be restricted to reactive roles,

such as the vengeful wronged woman and the maternal protector" (xiii). Pearson argues against this stereotype associated with violence committed by women: "Every now and then, when scholars in criminology and sociology concede the possibility of female aggression, they hasten to add that women only engage in 'expressive' aggression, which means giving vent impulsively to bottled-up feelings. Women do not, these scholars maintain, engage in 'instrumental' aggression, the kind that is cool and calculating. By maintaining this distinction between impulsive and strategic violence, the basic paradigm of female virtue holds" (15). One such attempt to break free from these common tropes is found in Hendin's interdisciplinary study *Heartbreakers*, which states that "in fiction, film, and media, violent women are new icons who dramatize in extreme ways transformations in intimacy, social life, and public attitudes" (1). Similarly, but with a more specific focus on violent women in film, King and McCaughey assert in their introductory essay to the collection *Reel Knockouts*, "The essays in this volume look at films not simply in terms of whether they properly represent women or feminist principles, but also as texts with social contexts and possible uses in the reconstruction of masculinity and femininity. We can use these images, whether they're lies or not" (3).

34. I am indebted to scholars who approach historical, cultural, film, and literary studies through intersectional feminist lenses. For example, Fuentes's *Dispossessed Lives* reads against and through the grain of historical archives about enslaved women in Barbados. *Dispossessed Lives* is essential to my own project, for it bears repeating that archives themselves are violent: "Enslaved women appear as historical subjects through the form and content of archival documents in the manner in which they lived: spectacularly violated, objectified, disposable, hypersexualized, and silenced" (5). Later, Fuentes asks, "How do we write a history of the voiceless and the violated?" (126). Her answer: "While it is not possible to avoid reproducing the violence of slavery and the archive if one wants to account for violated lives, we can interrogate the meaning and consequences of such images" (139). Moreover, I build on bell hooks's claim, "Although women do not have the power ruling groups of men often exert, they do not conceptualize power differently. Like most men, most women are taught from childhood on that dominating and controlling others is the basic expression of power" (*Feminist Theory* 85). Thus, a society organized by women would not look markedly different, because women "would organize it differently only if they had a different value system" (86). McClintock goes on to frame this idea of women's collusion with European imperial power structures: "Barred from the corridors of formal power, [colonial women] experienced the privileges and social contradictions of imperialism very differently from colonial men. . . . Nonetheless, the rationed privileges of race all too often put white women in positions of decided—if borrowed—power, not only over colonized women but also over colonized men. As such, white women were not the hapless onlookers of empire but were ambiguously complicit both as colonizers and colonized, privileged and restricted, acted upon and acting" (6).

35. One type of relationship that *Grotesque Touch* does not examine in depth is familial violence. These tropes of violence require careful contextualization in terms of race, class, gender, ethnicity, sexuality, skin tone, ability, and nationality that extend beyond my present project. For more viewpoints on this subject, please see

(in alphabetical order) hooks's chapter "Revolutionary Black Women" in *Black Looks* (41–60); Kalisa's *Violence in Francophone African and Caribbean Women's Literature*; Lancaster's *Angelic Mother and the Predatory Seductress*; O'Callaghan's "Caribbean Migrations" and *Women Writing the West Indies, 1804–1939*; Rody's *Daughter's Return*; Rousseau's *Black Woman's Burden*; and Spillers's "Mama's Baby, Papa's Maybe."

36. In this way, *Grotesque Touch* follows studies like Guillermina De Ferrari's *Vulnerable States* to create spaces to contemplate the importance of narratives that describe the body in ways that seem sensationalistic. To De Ferrari, "an exhibitionist attitude toward the body in its most vulnerable states," as depicted in Caribbean literature, adds to a narrative's criticisms of imperialism's violent relationship to colonized bodies (2). Narratives do this by "respond[ing] to the same foundational gesture of deriving legitimacy for the colonial enterprise from the body of the colonized" (2).

Chapter One

1. See chapter 3's examination of Harriet Jacobs's autobiography (1861), for example.

2. Though *Mandingo* was a Hollywood studio film, its depictions of nudity, rape, and other forms of violence easily classify it as an "exploitation" film. Clark provides a more general definition of exploitation films, as they "might be viewed as peculiar hybrids of the art and the commercial pictures. Like the art film, exploitation pictures are made cheaply, by independent filmmakers, and reflect no studio control. They are aimed at a small, exclusive audience who might avoid mainstream Hollywood product. Like the commercial film, exploitation pictures are produced by individuals who are more concerned with making a dollar than with making a work of art" (4). Yet, my use of the term "exploitation film" is mirrored in Quentin Tarantino's statement that *Mandingo* and *Showgirls* are the only two "full-on, gigantic, big-budget exploitation movie[s]" (qtd. in Udovitch 172).

3. See Rabinowitz's *American Pulp* for an examination of pulp in earlier years: "What is pulp? Steamy fiction? Sleazy magazines? Cheap paper? Or might it be a technology, a vehicle that once brought desire—for sex, for violence—into the open in cheap, accessible form? Or, and this is the question that motivates this book, might it be part of a larger process by which modernism itself, a high literature and art but also a mass consumer practice, spread across America?" (22).

4. Harrison refers to these pulp novels as "'slave plantation' titles" (182). I use the term "plantation pulp novel" to connote their setting as well as the quantity and quality of their production.

5. Currently, you can easily find hundreds of plantation pulp novels (cheaply made, used, worn, water- or otherwise stained) for sale for a penny each online. Collectors also maintain online forums to offer suggested reading for plantation pulp fans.

6. The scholar Joyce L. Sparer wrote in 1968 that Mittelhölzer's "fascination with the merely bizarre and sensational is excessive. His novels abound in 'sextravaganzas,' products of adolescent-like fantasying" (25).

7. Edmondson provides an overview of how paperback publication transformed the way Mittelhölzer's novels were advertised, in comparison to his hardback novels in the

1940s and 1950s: "His paperback novels, however, were published by commercial publishers and aimed for a whole new audience, the kind of audience that might not have been otherwise interested in stories that illustrate grand national themes. Their covers are instructive: mixed-race Amerindian women with bare breasts; a white creole woman holding a whip over a black, half-naked servant who lies at her feet; two white creole women fighting off threatening black men. Sex and miscegenation were, and are, irresistible topics. Much has been made of the 'new' sexuality that pervades so much of today's popular culture, but as the covers of Mittelhölzer's books illustrate, there is nothing new about it. It is a question of what is emphasized" (10).

8. See Margaret Walker's *Jubilee* (1966) for an early example, as the enslaver Salina Dutton conducts sadistic whippings, beatings, and purgings of enslaved people. Other literary examples of sadistic white women who enslave include Jane's enslaver in the early pages of Ernest J. Gaines's *Autobiography of Miss Jane Pittman* (1971), Hortense in Isabel Allende's *Island beneath the Sea* (2009), Mrs. Charles in Delia Sherman's *Freedom Maze* (2011), and Miss Emmaline in Jessica Maria Tuccelli's *Glow* (2012).

9. I will address this topic in more detail when discussing law and sadism in the context of the Code Noir in chapter 2.

10. See Marcus Wood's *Slavery, Empathy, and Pornography* for how "the whole *Mandingo* phenomenon" was "firmly implanted in the European cultural imagination by the end of the eighteenth century" and has "proved remarkably resilient, and remarkably unstudied" (89).

11. Movie critic Roger Ebert's 1975 review calls Onstott's novel a "wretched potboiler" and the film a "piece of manure," "racist trash, obscene in its manipulation of human beings and feelings." See DeVos for a study on the reception of the film.

12. Shimizu aptly observes that in the film "mastery is contradictory for white women in slavery because they undergo injury in white patriarchy as they benefit from white supremacy" (49). Yet, she offers this insight specifically in terms of Blanche's rape of Mede; Shimizu does not address Blanche's attempted mastery of Ellen's body.

13. Robin Wood reads the scene of violence between Blanche and Ellen in this vein because it comes just before Hammond and his father attend Mede's fight in New Orleans, as "both instances [are] either directly provoked or actually supervised by the Great White Male" (279).

14. See Li's essay "*12 Years a Slave* as a Neo-Slave Narrative" for how "differences and cinematic embellishments highlight McQueen's unique vision and his notable concern for exploring the experiences of black women" (326). Li also concludes that (as evinced by Patsey's final scene) Northup's "only power, like that of McQueen, lies in his ability to chronicle, not alleviate, the sufferings of others" (330).

Chapter Two

1. Gyssels, for example, claims that Claudine and other white French/Creole women in recent fictions are "monsters who display sadistic behaviour, pitiless creatures who slaughter their husband's [sic] concubines. But as the narratives unfold, the reader learns how prior to these bestialities, they repeatedly had to deal with the infidelity

and betrayal by their husband, with excesses of interracial sex and violence in the household and plantation" (116).

2. Describing this violence in terms of a sacrament, here the narration resembles Girard's philosophizing in *Violence and the Sacred*, as the Saint-Domingue society of enslavers "sacrifice" those people unlike them (those who are enslaved), a thought process that "prompts the entire community to choose victims outside itself" (Girard 8). Enslaved people are "sacrificial" in Bell's work because—before the revolution begins—there seems to be no chance of reprisal, as in Girard's theorizing of violence (Girard 13).

3. My argument follows Lowe's claim that Claudine "understand[s] that even her brutalities have not penetrated into the inner being of the slave, who is, indeed, singing a 'song of resistance'" (130). Unlike Lowe, I do not see Claudine's resulting actions as "madness," considering how her violence echoes corrupt social norms.

4. Baron de Vastey's list of women's violence (see esp. 118–21) ends with how such violence was intrinsic to enslavement: "No, it is impossible for me to keep on describing such atrocities. What courage and what strength of spirit it would require to write down the innumerable misdeeds of the colonists during the colonial regime. It would take me entire volumes. The slight account I have just given of the atrocities of which we have been the victims will suffice to give an idea of the colonists' character. The wives of these monsters proved equally proficient in the commission of such deeds: when it comes to debauched and indecent conduct, several of those furies—the shame and dishonour of their sex—equalled and even surpassed the men, committing the most abominable excesses, the most unimaginable crimes and unparalleled acts of cruelty" (123).

5. The plantation's name Coulibre connects James's novel to Jean Rhys's *Wide Sargasso Sea*, which is partially set on the dilapidated Jamaican sugar plantation Coulibri after emancipation. Chapter 4 will elaborate on these connections.

6. Vásquez addresses this trope in *The Book of Night Women*: "Both [Isobel's] sexual predilections and cross-dressing emphatically counter heteronormative expectations of white colonial female sexuality. Nevertheless, when it suits her, Isobel blames her 'degeneracy' on her creole status" (56).

7. The film *Hoe Duur Was de Suiker* does not depict a clear sense of ethnic social stratification between non-Jewish Dutch and Sephardic Jewish plantation owners in Suriname, who are the focus of both the novel and the film adaptation. However, the film's treatment of Jewish enslavers is consistent with what Casteel observes about the novel: "The novel gives voice to marginalized Jewish historical subjects, but only at the cost of suppressing the voices of their slaves, echoing a historical pattern in which Jews obtained opportunities in the colonies that were denied to them in Europe, but only by participating in a system that negated the humanity of slaves" (146). For more about Suriname's Jewish communities and their participation in slavery, see Ben-Ur.

8. This oft-paraphrased line is from Zora Neale Hurston's *Their Eyes Were Watching God* (1937), when Nanny instructs Janie about the bodily lessons she learned during enslavement.

9. For a similar literary example, see Évelyne Trouillot's *Infamous Rosalie* (2003), in which the young enslaved woman Lisette explicitly articulates her understanding of how power, intimacy, and violent touch intertwine: "As a Creole [someone born in

Saint-Domingue, instead of Africa], I can barely imagine a plantation without whites, without a master and a mistress. I grew up as Mademoiselle Sarah's Negress, always ensconced in the masters' room, with my mistress's perfume on my skin, traces of her powder on my fingers, and the imprint of her hand on my cheek" (51).

10. The relative ease of Mini-Mini's cohabitation with her former enslaver (when compared with other narratives in *Grotesque Touch*) might have historical precedence in the practice known as "Suriname marriage." According to Ben-Ur, "Like Dutch co-lonial law, Suriname's Jewish laws included no restrictions against extramarital mis-cegenation between white males and blacks or Eurafrican slaves. Only when Sephardic men attempted to formalize unions with former slaves did strict penalties accrue" (155). Hoefte and Vrij conclude that these "often long-lasting common-law relation-ships were an important element of Suriname colonial society. The low number of legal unions is not only to be explained on the basis of color codes. A Suriname marriage was accepted by all social strata (including the church) and by both sexes by the late eighteenth century" (162).

11. See Lindon Barrett's essay "African-American Slave Narratives" for an over-view of twentieth-century scholarship dealing with literacy, agency, and embodiment in slave narratives. For more recent studies, see (in chronological order) Aravamu-dan's *Tropicopolitans* (1999), H. Williams's *Self-Taught* (2005), and Hager's *Word by Word* (2013).

12. For more on the trope of concubinage and agency in narratives about Suri-name, see J. Sharpe. We can also think about Mini-Mini's romantic story arc in light of Winters's *The Mulatta Concubine*: "Read against the ubiquity of visual and written depictions of the free(d) mulatta concubine across diasporic time and space, her presence demands a consideration of how these women, whom the official archive consistently depicts as free and authoritative over their bodies and sexuality, fit into an African diasporic community produced by and through its subjection to the trans-atlantic slave trade" (2).

Chapter Three

1. Following Girshick's research in *Woman-to-Woman Sexual Violence*, I am defin-ing sexual assault and sexual violence to mean "any unwanted sexual activity" (Girshick 19).

2. For a historical account of the concepts of consent and coercion throughout U.S. history, see Haag's *Consent*.

3. See Brison's *Aftermath* for a detailed account of how she was silenced (and strug-gled to find her voice) as a survivor of sexual violence, even though her case was rela-tively clear-cut according to French and U.S. laws alike (the assailant was a stranger who nearly murdered her when she was going for a walk).

4. See Deer's "Decolonizing Rape Law" for an overview.

5. *Queering Sexual Violence*, edited by Patterson, offers a chorus of voices that dis-rupt such binary thinking about sexual violence.

6. See Girshick's *Woman-to-Woman Sexual Violence* for an in-depth analysis of how systems of oppression and myths intersect in women's experiences of same-sex

violence. Chapter 5 will go into more depth about the stereotype of violent lesbians in popular culture.

7. For reviews contemporary to ABC's initial broadcasts, see V. Jarrett's "An Epic TV Tale of Our Heritage" and Trescott's "An Emotional Preview of Haley's 'Roots.'" See Dayan and Katz's *Media Events* for their analysis of *Roots* as a "media event."

8. For an overview of the critical responses to the masculinist focus of *Roots*, see Ryan (124–25). Also see Mellis's "Roots of Violence" for a comprehensive analysis of the intersections of gender and race in *Roots*.

9. See also my discussion of pulp novel cover artwork in chapter 1.

10. Washington, on the other hand, reads these silences as deflecting from Truth's lived experience of "sexual involvement" with a man who enslaved her (44). Washington claims, "If she had admitted 'sinning' with her former master, her credentials would have been suspect" in abolitionist circles (47).

11. In her essay "Valerie Martin's *Property*," Li adds to a discussion of how the novel's narrative strategies create a "neo-enslaver narrative."

12. See the novel *Dessa Rose* by Sherley Anne Williams (1986) for a more realistically hopeful portrayal of interracial women's bonds during slavery. As Suzanne W. Jones claims, "the relationship between Dessa Rose and Ruth Elizabeth (Rufel) Sutton begins by accident and continues out of self-interest and necessity," as the women "are outside of their accustomed social roles and physical spaces" and are "thus interacting with each other in new ways" (88, 91).

13. I extend this interrogation of "grand narratives" into post-emancipation domestic spaces in chapter 4.

14. At first glance, there might not be much to my categorizing of some texts as "plantation pulp novels" and others as "plantation erotica." The characteristics of these categories lie in the degree of descriptions of sexual arousal and touch. Plantation pulp novels of the twentieth century have given way to full-on works of erotica due to lax censorship. In the current age of online and self-publishing, any online search for plantation erotica will yield more results than a human being could read. I do not focus on these types of fictions because of their persisting simplistic narratives that revel in racist tropes. For instance, works of erotica such as Laurinda D. Brown's *Highest Price for Passion* (2008) create racist depictions of enslaved women. In *Passion's* account of her sexual relationship with Miss Annie, her enslaver, "arousal merges with imagery of torture and fear as Passion associates her heart beating with running from the slave catchers' horses and Miss Annie's nails in her flesh 'like the whip'" (M. Richardson 51). Such representations undoubtedly originate from earlier plantation pulp novel tropes, but they do not add anything new to my argument.

15. Holland's claims in *Erotic Life of Racism* inspire my own here: "So often our 'racist' culture is held as separate and apart from our desiring selves. To think about desire is to arrive at a queer place. But I do not mean for that queer place to become overdetermined by its association with desire, with the erotic. In essence, I am opening the door to a notion of the 'erotic' that oversteps the category of the autonomous so valued in queer theory so as to place the erotic—the personal and political dimension of desire—at the threshold of ideas about quotidian racist practice" (9).

16. See Stallings for a summary of these criticisms (67–70).

17. For example, see Green's "What the Eyes Did Not Wish to Behold," Melancon's "Towards an Aesthetic of Transgression," and L. Walker's *Looking Like What You Are*.

18. Stallings uses the term "females" most often to mean "women."

19. For more about Naiad's publication strategies, see Harker's *Lesbian South*, especially the section titled "Lesbian Feminist Trash: Naiad Press and Lesbian Genre Fiction" (48–52).

20. Monteith briefly references the connection between the two stories in *Advancing Sisterhood?* when she claims that "by preceding this story with one entitled 'The Mistress and the Slave Girl,' the predication of the one relationship in the other is made overt" (173).

21. While beyond the geographic scope of this chapter, Ellen Ombre's short story "Flarden" (published in 1992 and translated to English as "Shreds") depicts continuations of sexual violence between slavery and post-emancipation domestic labor in Suriname. Ombre's narrative draws these connections via the mythos around the enslaver Susanna de Plessis, referred to as "Mrs. Du Plessis," who ordered "the plantation flogger . . . to cut off [a] young slave's breasts. That would teach her to make eyes at her master. Boiling with rage, she personally fried up the breasts for her husband." In the story, an upper-class woman named Mrs. Miskin tells this story to Hannah, a young woman placed in foster care in the Miskins' urban home. The tale might be a warning to Hannah, as Mr. Miskin sexually assaults her by the end of story, creating parallels between sexual violence throughout time.

Chapter Four

1. A genealogy of such academic work extends from Du Bois's essay "The Servant in the House" (1920) to contemporary in-depth studies of the intersecting structures of power in domestic labor in the United States. Works in this category include (in chronological order) Thornton Dill's *Across the Boundaries of Race and Class* (1979); A. Davis's *Women, Race, and Class* (1981); Rollins's *Between Women* (1985); Collins's *Black Feminist Thought* (2000); Bapat's *Part of the Family?* (2014); and Nadasen's *Household Workers Unite* (2015). Additionally, studies based on oral histories of Black domestic workers in southern U.S. locations profess to give voice to women's experiences, such as Tucker's *Telling Memories among Southern Women* (1988); Clark-Lewis's *Living In, Living Out* (1994); Hunter's *To 'Joy My Freedom* (1997); and most recently Van Wormer, Jackson, and Sudduth's *Maid Narratives* (2012).

2. For overviews and syntheses of debates ranging from the twentieth century to the 2010s, see (in alphabetical order) Cobble's *Other Women's Movement*; Federici's *Revolution at Point Zero*; Fraser's *Fortunes of Feminism*; K. Jarrett's "Relevance of 'Women's Work'"; and Weeks's *Problem with Work*.

3. For more on how some feminist movements replicate colonizing thought and power structures, see (in alphabetical order) Ahmed's *Living a Feminist Life*; Alarcón's "Theoretical Subject(s) of *This Bridge Called My Back* and Anglo-American Feminism"; hooks's *Ain't I a Woman*; Hull, Bell Scott, and Smith's *All the Women Are White, All the Blacks Are Men, but Some of Us Are Brave*; Lorde's "Age, Race, Class, and Sex" and "Master's

Tools"; Mohanty's "Under Western Eyes"; Moraga and Anzaldúa's *This Bridge Called My Back*; and Newman's *White Women's Rights*.

4. McRae's *Mothers of Massive Resistance* offers a compelling argument about white women's racist political activity to uphold segregation: "Moving from the 1920s into the 1970s, the book charts the long era of massive support for racial segregation and the white women who served as its crucial workforce" through "employing a politicized formulation of motherhood" (10, 14).

5. For example, see Kaye Gibbons's novel *Ellen Foster* (1987) and Anna Jean Mayhew's novel *The Dry Grass of August* (2011) for narratives that assume only white men, not white women, enact violence. For a discussion of similar tropes, read Monteith's chapter "Across the Kitchen Table" in *Advancing Sisterhood?* (102–12).

6. First published in 1985, J. Jones's *Labor of Love, Labor of Sorrow* makes these connections clear: "Domestic service recapitulated the mistress-slave relationship in the midst of late nineteenth-century industrializing America. As paid labor became increasingly associated with the time-oriented production of goods, the black nurse, maid, and cook remained something of a labor-force anachronism in a national if not regional (southern) context" (127). In this environment, "service made manifest all the tensions and uncertainties inherent in personal interaction between the female members of two different classes and races," so that "in the kitchen, bedroom, and parlor, in the course of a fourteen-hour day, a 'disordered temperament' could find a multitude of opportunities to wreak emotional and physical violence upon another human being so similar yet so different from herself" (127, 130–31). More recently, Sharpless's study *Cooking in Other Women's Kitchens* claims that the practice of physical punishment "continued, although in a more limited way, after emancipation" (137). Though they were no longer enslavers by law, and thereby did not have the same structures of power available to them, "employers could be horrifically creative in their punishments for their employees" (137). The idea that the employer/employee relationship can mirror that of enslaver/enslaved also appears in a study about migrant domestic workers. In her *Doing the Dirty Work?*, B. Anderson suggests that "it is perhaps in the area of mistress/employer–slave/worker relations that the comparison with slavery proves most useful" (136). Anderson goes on to elaborate, "Of course workers and slaves throughout the world and over generations have been beaten and had their teeth torn out by their masters and their owners, but as with the experiences of household slaves in the American South, *routine physical violence perpetrated by the female employer is characteristic of many of the narratives of migrant domestic workers*" (136, emphasis mine).

7. I would add Sue Monk Kidd's novel *The Secret Life of Bees* (2002) to this category. The novel describes the "love" August (a Black woman who was formerly a nanny) holds for Lily and her deceased mother (August's white charge) in 1964. August says to Lily, "Mostly, though, I want you to know, *I* love you. Just like I loved your mother" (243, emphasis in original). The novel was also adapted into a Hollywood-produced film (2008).

8. For more on *Can't Quit You, Baby*, see Shoemaker (84) and Monteith (116).

9. See also Collins's chapter "Mammies, Matriarchs, and Other Controlling Images" in *Black Feminist Thought* for an overview of such representations of Black women (69–96).

10. For an overview of how these issues persist today, see Enloe, esp. chap. 7, "Scrubbing the Globalized Tub" (305–42).

11. See S. Haley's *No Mercy Here* for how Georgia adopted this form of imprisonment: "Moreover, a gendered system of labor exploitation emerged in 1908, under which imprisoned women were forced to work for private white families before their prison sentences were complete. This system of gendered and racialized exploitation and social control helped to maintain the notion that a white woman's social and economic role was a domestic manager, a position perceived to be necessary for capitalist expansion. The new system established a public-private partnership whereby both state employees and ordinary women became wardens, controlling the social lives, labors, and futures of imprisoned African American women" (4).

12. This type of threatened violence occurs in another story by Alice Walker, "The Revenge of Hannah Kemhuff" (1967). Yet, in this story the violence against a white woman is only implied in a Black woman's speech. The white woman inflicts violence on herself.

13. The most militant type of servants—those who directly murder their employers—are, due to the radical nature of this trope, seen in very few U.S. texts. For example, see Ted Shine's *Contribution* (1968) and Ed Bullins's *The Gentleman Caller* (1969), two Black Arts plays that depict women who kill their employers. Through this staging of violence, the playwrights "move beyond stirring the water to draining the lake. They create characters who, directly and indirectly, work to overthrow the society which has fostered oppression of Blacks and particularly of black domestics" (Harris 155).

14. Silvera's oral history of domestic workers in Canada, *Silenced*, for example, "was the first of its kind; that is, the first account in Canadian history of Caribbean domestic workers talking about their work experiences and living conditions in Canada" (v).

15. See Sheller for an analysis of how narratives advertise Black and brown bodies for tourists' consumption (156–66). Also see Tompkins's *Racial Indigestion* and hooks's chapter "Eating the Other" in *Black Looks* (21–39).

16. Edmondson summarizes that de Lisser's novel "was, as even his critics acknowledge, an early precursor to the proletarian, anticolonial barracks-yard novel" (34). For another example of an early narrative that shows violence between women as employers and servants, see Thomas Henry MacDermot's novel *One Brown Girl And—* (1909).

17. As Higman claims in "Domestic Service in Jamaica since 1750," the context of Jamaican domestic labor is one rooted in the norm of privileging lighter skin color, which was established during slavery (48–49). As mixed-race Jamaicans later "came in turn to predominate in the emerging servant-employing middle class at the end of the nineteenth century, so they gave way to the black domestic" (49). Servants continued to have a "role in giving 'dignity' to Jamaican households," which "remained of central importance to those of the middle class" throughout the twentieth century (62).

18. Spivak also discusses mirroring in her foundational essay "Three Women's Texts and a Critique of Imperialism."

19. Although Antoinette's relationship with Christophine is important to her narrative, it does not feature clear violence between the two women. See Jaising's "Who Is Christophine?" for popular critical commentary about Christophine (816–17).

20. Michelle Cliff's novel *Abeng* (1984) is a clear literary response to *Wide Sargasso Sea* in this respect, as the protagonist Clare Savage (a mixed-race middle-class Jamaican adolescent in the mid-twentieth century) learns about her society's classist, racist, sexist norms, especially through her relationship with Zoe, who is poorer and has a darker skin tone. Like in *Wide Sargasso Sea*, the final scene of *Abeng* features Clare's dream, in which she injures Zoe and then tries to doctor her wound (166). The dream signals Clare's entrance into a womanhood (her menstruation begins) that requires her (albeit reluctant) injury of women who belong to lower classes. Clare starts to unlearn this conditioning about class, race, gender, and sexuality in Cliff's later novel *No Telephone to Heaven* (1987), in which she becomes a revolutionary figure that Antoinette's social position can never allow her to be in the 1800s.

21. The film is funded in part by the International Fund for the Promotion of Culture (UNESCO) and the Caribbean Community Secretariat (CARICOM). The film is distributed in the Caribbean by Banyan Limited and internationally by Caribbean Tales Worldwide Distribution.

Chapter Five

1. Morales-Franceschini's essay "Tropics of Abjection" also offers insight into the generative and limiting aspects of applying Kristeva's theories of the abject and the semiotic to Caribbean studies. Specifically, he "consider[s] how such figures [such as refuse and the corpse] are resignified to denounce (rather than exonerate) colonial violence," and his essay traces "the tropes of bareness and monstrosity" as well as "the relation of the abject to the maternal" (513).

2. Cinema studies scholars have widened their applications of Creed's theories, such as those studies that consider Asian horror cinema. For instance, see Seet's "Mothers and Daughters" and Wee's "Patriarchy and the Horror of the Monstrous Feminine." Still, the appearance of the monstrous-feminine in scripted television programming is undertheorized, and my study is one of a handful that deals with scripted U.S. television shows: see Cuklanz and Moorti's "Television's 'New' Feminism" and Subramanian's "Monstrous Makeover," for example.

3. For discussions of the spectacle of the LaLaurie mythology, look to C. Baker's chapter "Slavery's Suffering Brought to Light—New Orleans, 1834" in *Humane Insight* (18–34), Miles's chapter "Madame Lalaurie: French Quarter Fiend" in *Tales from the Haunted South* (48–79), Long's *Madame LaLaurie*, and de Caro's "LaLaurie Haunted House, Ghosts, and Slavery."

4. Much of LaLaurie's relationship with her three daughters reflects Creed's theory of the monstrous-feminine mother in horror films. Although this relationship is beyond the scope of my argument, LaLaurie's tutelage (she forces one daughter to regularly "harvest" organs) and imprisonment of her daughters obviously show horrific abjection. She keeps them in her torture chamber for a year and promises the eldest, "On Christmas morning, I'm going to stuff your conniving mouth full of shit," because they were planning to kill her ("Coven: Burn, Witch. Burn!"). This relationship of familial violence illustrates LaLaurie's extreme efforts to force her daughters

into conforming to her ideals of power via racialized violence, which reflects her culture at large.

5. I read this scene of abjection in accordance with D. Scott's thoughts in *Extravagant Abjection*. Scott approaches "the abject" in terms of what dominant discourses have deemed necessary to expel in order to maintain the status quo: "We see an example of this attribution of abjection and its avoidance as we follow the trajectory from Fanon's essential point in *Black Skin, White Masks* that blackness functions in Western cultures as a repository for fears about sexuality and death—fears, in other words, about the difficulty of maintaining the boundaries of the (white male) ego, and fears about acknowledging the repressions and renunciations on which Western civilization depends" (4).

6. For an interrogation of ghost tours, see Miles's *Tales from the Haunted South*.

7. For a wide-ranging examination of racialized horror in Blaxploitation films, including *Sugar Hill*, see chapter 5 of Means Coleman's *Horror Noire*, "Scream, Whitey, Scream" (118–44).

8. For an overview of de Lisser's complicated class, ethnic, and national identities in the context of Jamaican historical narratives, see pages 54–55 of Edmondson's *Caribbean Middlebrow*.

9. Thomas situates the "White Witch" tale as "a story that would be familiar to any Jamaican, because it is one of the legends one learns as a school-age child, the details of which—and especially those details related to how she mistreated her slaves—are indelibly imprinted on one's consciousness" (113). Repetitions of the "White Witch" legend over time, she says, "renders legible and repeats many" tropes of violence in Jamaica, such as "the corruption of plantation societies; the complex but fundamentally unequal relationships that develop within them; the violence that structures these relationships; the obscuring of violent structural inequalities by such means as (black) magic and fetishization; and the ultimate vindication and redemption of those 'at the bottom.' In other words, this cultural myth-cum-performance event reminds us not only of what we already know but also of what we are in constantly in danger of forgetting, and this reminder is perhaps all the more powerful because of the gendered 'twist' in the story" (113–14).

10. The perceived collective power that women can derive from witchcraft also factors into *American Horror Story's* tropes. For an overview of the long-standing ties between feminism and witchcraft, see especially pages 409–11 in Moseley's "Glamorous Witchcraft."

11. Both Queenie's and Laveau's characterizations (their disposability, bitterness, etc.) in *American Horror Story* ultimately fall back on the limited roles that have historically been available to African American women on television. For more on these types, see especially the seventh chapter, "The Oppositional Gaze," in hooks's *Black Looks* (115–31) and Springer's "Divas, Evil Black Bitches, and Bitter Black Women."

12. See Kalisa's *Violence in Francophone African and Caribbean Women's Literature* for similar explorations in Francophone literary contexts. She focuses on "the specificity of women's narratives by exploring female victimization through socially sanctioned

patriarchal violence. . . . Central to [her] analysis is the dynamics of female generational relationships" (78).

13. See also (in chronological order) Hart's *Fatal Women* (1994), Mayne's *Framed*
(2000), the chapter "Romancing Trauma" in Neroni's *The Violent Woman* (2005, 83–112),
and the chapter "Lethal Lesbians" in B. R. Rich's *New Queer Cinema* (2013, 103–22).

14. Though beyond the scope of this chapter, real and perceived violence in Chicago remains a staple of popular media, including current 24/7 cable news cycles. For
an introduction to the phenomenon of perceived violence and its relation to news cycles, see the NPR segment "Why the Public Perception of Crime Exceeds the Reality."
For a popular film representation of Chicago as a violent place in particular, see the
horror film *Candyman* (1992). As Oakley and Fraser point out, though the film is set
in a dilapidated public housing complex called Cabrini-Green, "Ironically, this box-
office blockbuster was released around the same time the federal government initi-
ated HOPE VI," Housing Opportunities for People Everywhere, which was "part of a
larger urban imaginary that focused on bringing more affluent populations to the city,
leading some urban scholars to dub the strategy gentrification by stealth" (353–54).
The film thereby creates an easily accessible and static image of violent Chicago.

15. Craft posits that the shocking instances of violence in the novel are so beyond
the reaches of human action that they could be considered instances of demonic possession: "Perhaps Jimmy's performance of the unspeakable on the body of his infant
niece results from possession, just as does Juani's incomprehensible aggression against
her lover. How else can these outrageous acts be explained?" (382). La Fountain-Stokes
takes a more oblique approach to labeling Jimmy's violence: "The novel's rather violent conclusion settles what appears as a parallel narrative or thematic axis: Juani's violence against Gina reproduces the daily domestic physical violence inflicted on
Caridad by Jimmy and unfortunately foreshadows a more distasteful episode of child
sexual abuse" (89). Going a step further, Ramírez points out that in the narrative Jimmy's action is "un acto innombrable (realmente nadie llega a nombrarlo) [an unnam-
able/unspeakable act (nobody really gets to name it)]" (131).

Conclusion

1. To give a more recent example, this pattern of exceptional plantation violence appears in Gerard Bush and Christopher Renz's 2020 film *Antebellum*. In many ways, the
film embraces exploitation film tropes to linger on how Veronica, a modern-day woman
(played by Janelle Monáe), experiences abuse when she is held captive at a neo-
Confederate theme park. Given that *Antebellum* is set in present-day Louisiana, the
film's focus on exploitation tropes of torture and sexual violence narrows social critique down to regional exceptionalism. Though Veronica kills the white woman who
orchestrated her capture (played by Jena Malone) by bashing her head on a Confederate monument, this scene does not quite critique white women's participation in racist systems. Instead, the film makes Malone's character out to be an outlandish
caricature that does not prompt self-reflection from the audience, much like the pulp
novels and exploitation films in chapter 1.

Works Cited

12 Years a Slave. Dir. Steve McQueen. Perf. Chiwetel Ejiofor, Michael Fassbender, Lupita Nyong'o, and Sarah Paulson. Twentieth Century Fox, 2013. DVD.

Abdur-Rahman, Aliyyah I. *Against the Closet: Black Political Longing and the Erotics of Race.* Durham: Duke UP, 2012.

Adams, Jessica. "Introduction: Circum-Caribbean Performance, Language, History." *Just Below South: Intercultural Performance in the Caribbean and the U.S. South.* Eds. Jessica Adams, Michael P. Bibler, and Cécile Accilien. Charlottesville: U of Virginia P, 2007. 1–24.

———. *Wounds of Returning: Race, Memory, and Property on the Postslavery Plantation.* Chapel Hill: U of North Carolina P, 2007.

Ahmed, Sara. *Living a Feminist Life.* Durham: Duke UP, 2017.

Alarcón, Norma. "The Theoretical Subject(s) of *This Bridge Called My Back* and Anglo-American Feminism." *Criticism in the Borderlands: Studies in Chicano Literature, Culture and Ideology.* Eds. Héctor Calderón and José David Saldívar. Durham: Duke UP, 1991. 28–39.

Allende, Isabel. *Island beneath the Sea: A Novel.* 2009. Trans. Margaret Sayers Peden. New York: Harper Perennial, 2011.

The American Anti-Slavery Almanac for 1840. New York: The American Anti-Slavery Society; Boston: J. A. Collins, n.d.

Anatol, Giselle Liza. *The Things that Fly in the Night: Female Vampires in Literature of the Circum-Caribbean and African Diaspora.* New Brunswick: Rutgers UP, 2015.

Andersen, Margaret L. "The Nexus of Race and Gender: Parallels, Linkages, and Divergences in Race and Gender Studies." *The SAGE Handbook of Race and Ethnic Studies.* Eds. Patricia Hill Collins and John Solomos. Los Angeles: SAGE, 2010. 166–87.

Anderson, Bridget. *Doing the Dirty Work?: The Global Politics of Domestic Labour.* New York: Zed Books, 2000.

Anderson, Eric Gary. "Native." *Keywords for Southern Studies.* Eds. Scott Romine and Jennifer Rae Greeson. Athens: U of Georgia P, 2016. 166–78.

Antebellum. Dir. Gerard Bush and Christopher Renz. Perf. Janelle Monáe and Jena Malone. Lionsgate, 2020. DVD.

Aparicio, Frances R. "Cultural Twins and National Others: Allegories of Intralatino Subjectivities in U.S. Latino/a Literature." *Identities: Global Studies in Culture and Power* 16.5 (2009): 622–41.

Aravamudan, Srinivas. *Tropicopolitans: Colonialism and Agency, 1688-1804.* Durham: Duke UP, 1999.

Bailey, Carol. "Destabilising Caribbean Critical Orthodoxies: Interrogating Orality in Marie-Elena John's *Unburnable*." *Caribbean Quarterly: A Journal of Caribbean Culture* 59.1 (2013): 31–49.

Baker, Courtney R. *Humane Insight: Looking at Images of African American Suffering and Death*. Champaign: U of Illinois P, 2017.

Baker, Patrick L. *Centring the Periphery: Chaos, Order, and the Ethnohistory of Dominica*. Montreal: McGill-Queen's UP, 1994.

Ball, Erica L., and Kellie Carter Jackson. "Kunta Kinte: The Power of a Name." *Transition* 122 (2017): 42–46.

Bapat, Sheila. *Part of the Family?: Nannies, Housekeepers, Caregivers and the Battle for Domestic Workers' Rights*. Brooklyn: IG Publishing, 2014.

Baptist, Edward E. *The Half Has Never Been Told: Slavery and the Making of American Capitalism*. 2014. New York: Basic Books, 2016.

Barrett, Lindon. "African-American Slave Narratives: Literacy, the Body, Authority." *American Literary History* 7.3 (1995): 415–42.

Bell, Madison Smartt. *All Souls' Rising*. 1995. New York: Vintage, 2004.

Benítez-Rojo, Antonio. *The Repeating Island: The Caribbean and the Postmodern Perspective*. Trans. James E. Maraniss. 2nd ed. Durham: Duke UP, 1996.

Ben-Ur, Aviva. "A Matriarchal Matter: Slavery, Conversion, and Upward Mobility in Suriname's Jewish Community." *Atlantic Diasporas: Jews, Conversos, and Crypto-Jews in the Age of Mercantilism, 1500–1800*. Eds. Richard L. Kagan and Philip D. Morgan. Baltimore: Johns Hopkins UP, 2009. 152–69.

Bibb, Henry. *The Life and Adventures of Henry Bibb: An American Slave*. Madison: U of Wisconsin P, 2001. Originally published as *Narrative of the Life and Adventures of Henry Bibb, An American Slave; Written by Himself*. 1849.

Bibler, Michael P. *Cotton's Queer Relations: Same-Sex Intimacy and the Literature of the Southern Plantation, 1936–1968*. Charlottesville: U of Virginia P, 2009.

Bolles, A. Lynn. "'The Caribbean Is on Sale': Globalization and Women Tourist Workers in Jamaica." *The Gender of Globalization: Women Navigating Cultural and Economic Marginalities*. Eds. Nandini Gunewardena and Ann Kingsolver. Santa Fe: School for Advanced Research P, 2007. 215–31.

Bortolotto, Maria Celina. "Dirty Laundry: Narratives, Secrets, and Shame in Obejas's *Memory Mambo*." *SECOLAS Annals* 52 (2008): 29–41.

Bradley, Regina N. "Re-Imagining Slavery in the Hip-Hop Imagination." *south: a scholarly journal* 49.1 (2016): 3–24.

Breines, Winifred. *The Trouble between Us: An Uneasy History of White and Black Women in the Feminist Movement*. New York: Oxford UP, 2006.

Brickhouse, Anna. *Transamerican Literary Relations and the Nineteenth-Century Public Sphere*. New York: Cambridge UP, 2004.

Brison, Susan J. *Aftermath: Violence and the Remaking of a Self*. Princeton: Princeton UP, 2002.

Brooks, Kinitra D. *Searching for Sycorax: Black Women's Hauntings of Contemporary Horror*. New Brunswick: Rutgers UP, 2018.

Brown, Kimberly Juanita. *The Repeating Body: Slavery's Visual Resonance in the Contemporary*. Durham: Duke UP, 2015.

Brown, Laurinda D. *The Highest Price for Passion*. New York: Strebor Books, 2008.

Bullins, Ed. *The Gentleman Caller*. 1969. *Illuminations* 5 (1971): 1–15.

Burfoot, Annette, and Susan Lord. "Introduction." *Killing Women: The Visual Culture of Gender and Violence*. Eds. Annette Burfoot and Susan Lord. Waterloo: Wilfrid Laurier UP, 2006. xi–xxii.

Burnard, Trevor, and John Garrigus. *The Plantation Machine: Atlantic Capitalism in French Saint-Domingue and British Jamaica*. Philadelphia: U of Pennsylvania P, 2016.

Bush, Barbara. "Hard Labor: Women, Childbirth, and Resistance in British Caribbean Slave Societies." *More than Chattel: Black Women and Slavery in the Americas*. Eds. David Barry Gaspar and Darlene Clark Hine. Bloomington: Indiana UP, 1996. 193–217.

Butler, Octavia. *Kindred*. 1979. Boston: Beacon, 2003.

Caison, Gina. *Red States: Indigeneity, Settler Colonialism, and Southern Studies*. Athens: U of Georgia P, 2018.

Candyman. Dir. Bernard Rose. Perf. Virginia Madsen and Tony Todd. 1992. Columbia TriStar Home Entertainment, 2004. DVD.

Carby, Hazel V. *Reconstructing Womanhood: The Emergence of the Afro-American Woman Novelist*. New York: Oxford UP, 1987.

Card, Claudia. *Lesbian Choices*. New York: Columbia UP, 1995.

Cartwright, Keith. *Sacral Grooves, Limbo Gateways: Travels in Deep Southern Time, Circum-Caribbean Space, Afro-Creole Authority*. Athens: U of Georgia P, 2013.

Cary, Lorene. *The Price of a Child: A Novel*. 1995. New York: Vintage, 1996.

Casteel, Sarah Phillips. *Calypso Jews: Jewishness in the Caribbean Literary Imagination*. New York: Columbia UP, 2016.

Cather, Willa. *Sapphira and the Slave Girl*. 1940. New York: Vintage, 1975.

Childress, Alice. *Like One of the Family: Conversations from a Domestic's Life*. 1956. Boston: Beacon, 1986.

Chopin, Kate. "La Belle Zoraïde." 1894. *Bayou Folk*. Ed. Bernard Koloski. New York: Penguin, 1999. 152–57.

Christian, Barbara. "Images of Black Women in Afro-American Literature: From Stereotype to Character." 1975. *Black Feminist Criticism: Perspectives on Black Women Writers*. New York: Teachers College P, 1997. 1–30.

Clark, Randall. *At a Theater or Drive-In Near You: The History, Culture, and Politics of the American Exploitation Film*. New York: Garland, 1995.

Clark-Lewis, Elizabeth. *Living In, Living Out: African American Domestics in Washington, D.C., 1910–1940*. Washington, DC: Smithsonian Institution Press, 1994.

Cliff, Michelle. *Abeng*. 1984. New York: Plume, 1995.

———. *No Telephone to Heaven*. 1987. New York: Plume, 1996.

Cobble, Dorothy Sue. *The Other Women's Movement: Workplace Justice and Social Rights in Modern America*. Princeton: Princeton UP, 2004.

Collins, Patricia Hill. *Black Feminist Thought: Knowledge, Consciousness, and the Politics of Empowerment*. 2nd ed. New York: Routledge, 2000.

Coser, Stelamaris. *Bridging the Americas: The Literature of Paule Marshall, Toni Morrison, and Gayl Jones*. Philadelphia: Temple UP, 1995.

"Coven: Bitchcraft." *American Horror Story*. FX. 9 Oct. 2013. Television.

"Coven: Boy Parts." *American Horror Story*. FX. 16 Oct. 2013. Television.

"Coven: Burn, Witch. Burn!" *American Horror Story*. FX. 6 Nov. 2013. Television.

"Coven: Go to Hell." *American Horror Story*. FX. 22 Jan. 2014. Television.

"Coven: Head." *American Horror Story*. FX. 11 Dec. 2013. Television.

"Coven: Protect the Coven." *American Horror Story*. FX. 15 Jan. 2014. Television.

"Coven: The Dead." *American Horror Story*. FX. 20 Nov. 2013. Television.

"Coven: The Replacements." *American Horror Story*. FX. 23 Oct. 2013. Television.

"Coven: The Seven Wonders." *American Horror Story*. FX. 29 Jan. 2014. Television.

Craft, Linda J. "Truth or Consequences: Mambos, Memories and Multiculturalism in Achy Obejas's Chicago." *Revista de Estudios Hispánicos* 35 (2001): 369–87.

Creed, Barbara. "Horror and the Monstrous-Feminine: An Imaginary Abjection." 1986. *The Dread of Difference: Gender and the Horror Film*. Ed. Barry Keith Grant. Austin: U of Texas P, 1996. 35–65.

Cuklanz, Lisa M., and Sujata Moorti. "Television's 'New' Feminism: Prime-Time Representations of Women and Victimization." *Critical Studies in Media Communication* 23.4 (2006): 302–21.

Cutter, Martha J. *The Illustrated Slave: Empathy, Graphic Narrative, and the Visual Culture of the Transatlantic Abolition Movement, 1800–1852*. Athens: U of Georgia P, 2017.

Dalton, Anne B. "The Devil and the Virgin: Writing Sexual Abuse in *Incidents in the Life of a Slave Girl*." *Violence, Silence, and Anger: Women's Writing as Transgression*. Ed. Deirdre Lashgari. Charlottesville: U of Virginia P, 1995. 38–61.

Danticat, Edwidge. *Breath, Eyes, Memory*. New York: Vintage, 1994.

Davis, Angela Y. *Women, Race and Class*. 1981. New York: Vintage, 1983.

Davis, Cynthia J. "Speaking the Body's Pain: Harriet Wilson's *Our Nig*." *African American Review* 27.3 (1993): 391–404.

Dayan, Colin. *Haiti, History, and the Gods*. Berkeley: U of California P, 1995.

Dayan, Daniel, and Elihu Katz. *Media Events: The Live Broadcasting of History*. Cambridge: Harvard UP, 1992.

de Caro, Frank. "The LaLaurie Haunted House, Ghosts, and Slavery: New Orleans, Louisiana." *Putting the Supernatural in Its Place: Folklore, the Hypermodern, and the Ethereal*. Ed. Jeannie B. Thomas. Salt Lake City: U of Utah P, 2015. 24–48.

DeConnick, Kelly Sue, and Valentine De Landro. *Bitch Planet*. Book One. 2014–15. Berkeley: Image Comics, 2015.

———. *Bitch Planet*. Book Two. 2016–17. Portland, OR: Image Comics, 2017.

Deer, Sarah. "Decolonizing Rape Law: A Native Feminist Synthesis of Safety and Sovereignty." *Wíčazo Ša Review* 24.2 (2009): 149–67.

De Ferrari, Guillermina. *Vulnerable States: Bodies of Memory in Contemporary Caribbean Fiction*. Charlottesville: U of Virginia P, 2007.

de Lisser, Herbert G. *Jane's Career: A Story of Jamaica*. 1913. Exeter: Heinemann, 1981.

———. *The White Witch of Rosehall*. 1929. London: Macmillan Education, 1982.

de Vastey, Baron. *The Colonial System Unveiled*. 1814. Trans. and ed. Chris Bongie. Liverpool: Liverpool UP, 2014.

DeVos, Andrew. "'Expect the Truth': Exploiting History with *Mandingo*." *American Studies* 52.2 (2013): 5–21.

Douglas, Ellen. *Can't Quit You, Baby*. New York: Atheneum, 1988.

———. *Hold On*. *Black Cloud, White Cloud: Two Novellas and Two Stories*. Boston: Houghton Mifflin, 1963. 143–232.

Down, Lorna. "'Flying inna massa face': Woman, Nature, and Sacred Rites/Rights in Marie-Elena John's *Unburnable*." *Experiences of Freedom in Postcolonial Literatures and Cultures*. Eds. Annalisa Oboe and Shaul Bassi. New York: Routledge, 2011. 231–41.

Dragonard. Dir. Gérard Kikoïne. Perf. Eartha Kitt, Oliver Reed, and Patrick Warburton. 1987. Warner Home Video, 1995. VHS.

Drake, Sandra. "All That Foolishness/That All Foolishness: Race and Caribbean Culture as Thematics of Liberation in Jean Rhys's *Wide Sargasso Sea*." *Critica* 2.2 (1990): 97–112.

Du Bois, W. E. B. "The Servant in the House." *Darkwater: Voices from within the Veil*. New York: Harcourt, Brace and Howe, 1920. 109–21.

Duck, Leigh Anne. "Plantation/Empire." *CR: New Centennial Review* 10.1 (2010): 77–87.

Duggan, Lisa. *Sapphic Slashers: Sex, Violence, and American Modernity*. Durham: Duke UP, 2000.

Ebert, Roger. Rev. of *Mandingo*. Dir. Richard Fleischer. *Chicago Sun-Times* 25 July 1975.

Edmondson, Belinda. *Caribbean Middlebrow: Leisure Culture and the Middle Class*. Ithaca: Cornell UP, 2009.

Enloe, Cynthia. *Bananas, Beaches and Bases: Making Feminist Sense of International Politics*. 2nd ed. Berkeley: U of California P, 2014.

Enszer, Julie R. "'The Black and White of It': Barbara Grier Editing and Publishing Women of Color." *Journal of Lesbian Studies* 18 (2014): 346–71.

"Ep. 1: Hella Great." *Insecure*. HBO. 23 July 2017. Television.

"Ep. 4: Hella LA." *Insecure*. HBO. 13 Aug. 2017. Television.

"Ep. 111: Due North." *Insecure*. HBO. 10 Sept. 2017. Television.

Fanon, Frantz. *The Wretched of the Earth*. 1961. Trans. Richard Philcox. New York: Grove, 1963.

Faulkner, William. *Absalom, Absalom!* 1936. New York: Vintage, 1972.

Faust, Drew Gilpin. *Mothers of Invention: Women of the Slaveholding South in the American Civil War*. Chapel Hill: U of North Carolina P, 1996.

Federici, Silvia. *Revolution at Point Zero: Housework, Reproduction, and Feminist Struggle*. Oakland: PM Press, 2012.

Francis, Donette A. "'Silences Too Horrific to Disturb': Writing Sexual Histories in Edwidge Danticat's *Breath, Eyes, Memory*." *Research in African Literatures* 35.2 (2004): 75–90.

Fraser, Nancy. *Fortunes of Feminism: From State-Managed Capitalism to Neoliberal Crisis*. London: Verso, 2013.

Fuentes, Marisa J. *Dispossessed Lives: Enslaved Women, Violence, and the Archive*. Philadelphia: U of Pennsylvania P, 2016.

Fulton, DoVeanna S. *Speaking Power: Black Feminist Orality in Women's Narratives of Slavery*. Albany: State U of New York P, 2006.

Gaines, Ernest J. *The Autobiography of Miss Jane Pittman*. 1971. Evanston: McDougal Littell, 1998.

Garraway, Doris. *The Libertine Colony: Creolization in the Early French Caribbean*. Durham: Duke UP, 2005.

Gebreyes, Rahel. "'Roots' Remake to Highlight Strong Black Female Narratives." *Huffington Post* 26 May 2016. Web. 21 June 2017.

Get Out. Dir. Jordan Peele. Perf. Betty Gabriel, Marcus Henderson, Daniel Kaluuya, and Allison Williams. Universal Pictures, 2017. DVD.

Gibbons, Kaye. *Ellen Foster*. Chapel Hill: Algonquin Books of Chapel Hill, 1987.

Gilchrist, Rupert. *Dragonard Blood*. 1977. New York: Bantam Books, 1978.

Gilley, Jennifer. "This Book Is an Action: A Case for the Study of Feminist Publishing." *International Journal of the Book* 9.1 (2012): 1–9.

Gilroy, Paul. *The Black Atlantic: Modernity and Double Consciousness*. Cambridge: Harvard UP, 1993.

Girard, René. *Violence and the Sacred*. 1972. Trans. Patrick Gregory. Baltimore: Johns Hopkins UP, 1979.

Girshick, Lori B. *Woman-to-Woman Sexual Violence: Does She Call It Rape?* Boston: Northeastern UP, 2002.

Glissant, Édouard. *Faulkner, Mississippi*. 1999. Trans. Barbara Lewis and Thomas C. Spear. Chicago: U of Chicago P, 2000.

Glymph, Thavolia. *Out of the House of Bondage: The Transformation of the Plantation Household*. New York: Cambridge UP, 2008.

Goddu, Teresa A. "The Antislavery Almanac and the Discourse of Numeracy." *Book History* 12 (2009): 129–55.

———. "Anti-Slavery's Panoramic Perspective." *MELUS* 39.2 (2014): 12–41.

Goldman, Dara E. *Out of Bounds: Islands and the Demarcation of Identity in the Hispanic Caribbean*. Lewisburg: Bucknell UP, 2008.

Gomez, Jewelle. *The Gilda Stories: A Novel*. Ithaca: Firebrand Books, 1991.

———. "Recasting the Mythology: Writing Vampire Fiction." *Blood Read: The Vampire as Metaphor in Contemporary Culture*. Eds. Joan Gordon and Veronica Hollinger. Philadelphia: U Pennsylvania P, 1997. 85–92.

Gone with the Wind. Dir. Victor Fleming. Perf. Clark Gable, Vivien Leigh, Hattie McDaniel, and Butterfly McQueen. 1939. Warner, 2014. DVD.

Green, Kai M. "'What the Eyes Did Not Wish to Behold': Lessons from Ann Allen Shockley's *Say Jesus and Come to Me*." *South Atlantic Quarterly* 112.2 (2013): 285–302.

Guterl, Matthew Pratt. *American Mediterranean: Southern Slaveholders in the Age of Emancipation*. Cambridge: Harvard UP, 2008.

Gwin, Minrose C. *Black and White Women of the Old South: The Peculiar Sisterhood in American Literature*. Knoxville: U of Tennessee P, 1985.

Gyssels, Kathleen. "'Les Créoles Galantes?': White Women and the Haitian Revolution." *Echoes of the Haitian Revolution, 1804-2004*. Eds. Martin Munro and Elizabeth Walcott-Hackshaw. Kingston: U of West Indies P, 2008. 109–24.

Haag, Pamela. *Consent: Sexual Rights and the Transformation of American Liberalism*. Ithaca: Cornell UP, 1999.

Hager, Christopher. *Word by Word: Emancipation and the Act of Writing*. Cambridge: Harvard UP, 2013.

Haley, Alex. *Roots*. Garden City: Doubleday, 1976.

———, creator. *Roots*. David L. Wolper Productions and Warner Bros., 1977. Television.

Haley, Sarah. *No Mercy Here: Gender, Punishment, and the Making of Jim Crow Modernity*. Chapel Hill: U of North Carolina P, 2016.

Hancock, Ange-Marie. *Intersectionality: An Intellectual History*. New York: Oxford UP, 2016.

Handley, George B. *Postslavery Literatures in the Americas: Family Portraits in Black and White*. Charlottesville: UP of Virginia, 2000.

Harker, Jaime. *The Lesbian South: Southern Feminists, the Women in Print Movement, and the Queer Literary Canon*. Chapel Hill: U North Carolina P, 2018.

Harper, Frances E. W. *Iola Leroy, or Shadows Uplifted*. 1892. New York: Oxford UP, 1988.

Harris, Trudier. *From Mammies to Militants: Domestics in Black American Literature*. Philadelphia: Temple UP, 1982.

Harrison, John. *Hip Pocket Sleaze: The Lurid World of Vintage Adult Paperbacks*. London: Headpress, 2011.

Hart, Lynda. *Fatal Women: Lesbian Sexuality and the Mark of Aggression*. Princeton: Princeton UP, 1994.

Hartman, Saidiya V. *Scenes of Subjection: Terror, Slavery, and Self-Making in Nineteenth-Century America*. New York: Oxford UP, 1997.

Heffelfinger, Elizabeth, and Laura Wright. *Visual Difference: Postcolonial Studies and Intercultural Cinema*. New York: Peter Lang, 2011.

The Help. Dir. Tate Taylor. Perf. Viola Davis, Octavia Spencer, and Emma Stone. Touchstone/Disney, 2011. DVD.

Hendin, Josephine G. *Heartbreakers: Women and Violence in Contemporary Culture and Literature*. New York: Palgrave Macmillan, 2004.

Higman, B. W. "Domestic Service in Jamaica since 1750." 1983. *Muchachas No More: Household Workers in Latin America and the Caribbean*. Eds. Elsa M. Chaney and Mary Garcia Castro. Philadelphia: Temple UP, 1989. 37–66.

Hoe Duur Was de Suiker. Dir. Jean Van de Velde. Perf. Gaite Jansen and Yootha Wong-Loi-Sing. Entertainment One, 2013. DVD.

Hoefte, Rosemarijn, and Jean Jacques Vrij. "Free Black and Colored Women in Early-Nineteenth-Century Paramaribo, Suriname." *Beyond Bondage: Free Women of Color in the Americas*. Eds. David Barry Gaspar and Darlene Clark Hine. Champaign: U of Illinois P, 2004. 145–68.

Holland, Sharon Patricia. *The Erotic Life of Racism*. Durham: Duke UP, 2012.

hooks, bell. *Ain't I a Woman: Black Women and Feminism*. Boston: South End Press, 1981.

———. *Black Looks: Race and Representation*. Boston: South End Press, 1992.

———. "Eating the Other: Desire and Resistance." *Black Looks: Race and Representation*. Boston: South End Press, 1992. 21–39.

———. *Feminist Theory: From Margin to Center*. 1984. 2nd ed. Boston: South End Press, 2000.

———. "The Oppositional Gaze: Black Female Spectators." *Black Looks: Race and Representation*. Boston: South End Press, 1992. 115–31.

———. "Rethinking the Nature of Work." *Feminist Theory: From Margin to Center*. 1984. 2nd ed. Boston: South End Press, 2000. 96–107.

———. "Revolutionary Black Women: Making Ourselves Subject." *Black Looks: Race and Representation*. Boston: South End Press, 1992. 41–60.

Hull, Akasha Gloria, Patricia Bell Scott, and Barbara Smith, eds. *All the Women Are White, All the Blacks Are Men, but Some of Us Are Brave: Black Women's Studies*. Old Westbury: Feminist Press, 1982.

Hunter, Tera W. *To 'Joy My Freedom: Southern Black Women's Lives and Labors after the Civil War*. Cambridge: Harvard UP, 1997.

Hurston, Zora Neale. *Their Eyes Were Watching God*. 1937. New York: Harper Perennial, 2006.

Jacobs, Harriet. *Incidents in the Life of a Slave Girl*. 1861. New York: Oxford UP, 1988.

Jaising, Shakti. "Who Is Christophine?: The Good Black Servant and the Contradictions of (Racial) Liberalism." *MFS Modern Fiction Studies* 56.4 (2010): 815–36.

James, C. L. R. *The Black Jacobins: Toussaint L'Ouverture and the San Domingo Revolution*. 1963. 2nd ed. New York: Vintage, 1989.

James, Marlon. *The Book of Night Women*. New York: Riverhead Books, 2009.

Jarrett, Kylie. "The Relevance of 'Women's Work': Social Reproduction and Immaterial Labor in Digital Media." *Television and New Media* 15.1 (2014): 14–29.

Jarrett, Vernon. "An Epic TV Tale of Our Heritage." *Chicago Tribune* 30 Jan. 1977: A6.

John, Marie-Elena. *Unburnable*. New York: Amistad, 2006.

Johnson, Michele A. "'Young Woman from the Country': A Profile of Domestic Servants in Jamaica, 1920–1970." 2001. *Working Slavery, Pricing Freedom: Perspectives from the Caribbean, Africa and the African Diaspora*. Ed. Verene A. Shepherd. New York: Palgrave, 2002. 396–415.

Johnson, Walter. *Soul by Soul: Life inside the Antebellum Slave Market*. Cambridge: Harvard UP, 1999.

Jones, Edward P. *The Known World: A Novel*. New York: Amistad, 2003.

Jones, Gayl. *Corregidora*. 1975. Boston: Beacon, 1986.

———. "The Machete Woman." *The Hermit-Woman*. Detroit: Lotus, 1983. 50–69.

Jones, Jacqueline. *Labor of Love, Labor of Sorrow: Black Women, Work, and the Family, from Slavery to the Present*. 1985. New York: Vintage, 1986.

Jones, Suzanne W. *Race Mixing: Southern Fiction since the Sixties*. Baltimore: Johns Hopkins UP, 2004.

Jones-Rogers, Stephanie E. *They Were Her Property: White Women as Slave Owners in the American South*. New Haven: Yale UP, 2019.

Kalisa, Chantal. *Violence in Francophone African and Caribbean Women's Literature*. Lincoln: U of Nebraska P, 2009.

Karem, Jeff. *The Purloined Islands: Caribbean-U.S. Crosscurrents in Literature and Culture, 1880–1959*. 2010. Charlottesville: U of Virginia P, 2011.

Keeling, Kara. *The Witch's Flight: The Cinematic, the Black Femme, and the Image of Common Sense*. Durham: Duke UP, 2007.

Keizer, Arlene R. *Black Subjects: Identity Formation in the Contemporary Narrative of Slavery*. Ithaca: Cornell UP, 2004.

Kidd, Sue Monk. *The Secret Life of Bees*. New York: Viking, 2002.

King, Amy K. "Circling Back and Expanding Beyond: Theorizing Excess in Circum-Atlantic Contexts." *south: a scholarly journal* 48.2 (2016): 212–24.

———. "Valerie Martin's *Property* and the Failure of the Lesbian Counterplot." *Mississippi Quarterly* 63.2 (2010): 211–31.

King, Martin Luther, Jr. "Letter from a Birmingham Jail." 1963. *Ethics: The Essential Writings*. Ed. Gordon Marino. New York: Modern Library, 2010. 356–77.

King, Neal, and Martha McCaughey. "What's a Mean Woman like You Doing in a Movie like This?" *Reel Knockouts: Violent Women in the Movies*. Eds. Martha McCaughey and Neal King. Austin: U of Texas P, 2001. 1–24.

Kousha, Mahnaz. "Race, Class, and Intimacy in Southern Households: Relationships between Black Domestic Workers and White Employers." *Neither Separate nor Equal: Women, Race, and Class in the South*. Ed. Barbara Ellen Smith. Philadelphia: Temple UP, 1999. 77–90.

Kristeva, Julia. *Powers of Horror: An Essay on Abjection*. Trans. Leon S. Roudiez. New York: Columbia UP, 1982.

La Fountain-Stokes, Lawrence. "Pop-Shock: Shifting Representations of Diasporic Puerto Rican Women's Queer Sexualities in US Latina Cultural Texts." *Letras Femeninas* 31.1 (2005): 79–98.

Lambert, David. "Deadening, Voyeuristic and Reiterative?: Problems of Representation in Caribbean Research." *Beyond the Blood, the Beach & the Banana: New Perspectives in Caribbean Studies*. Ed. Sandra Courtman. Kingston: Ian Randle, 2004. 3–14.

Lamming, George. *In the Castle of My Skin*. 1970. Ann Arbor: U of Michigan P, 1994.

Lancaster, Ashley Craig. *The Angelic Mother and the Predatory Seductress: Poor White Women in Southern Literature of the Great Depression*. Baton Rouge: Louisiana State UP, 2012.

LeBlanc, Amanda Kay. "'There's Nothing I Hate More than a Racist': (Re)centering Whiteness in *American Horror Story: Coven*." *Critical Studies in Media Communication* 35.3 (2018): 273–85.

"Let's Boot and Rally." *True Blood*. HBO. 8 July 2012. Television.

Li, Stephanie. "*12 Years a Slave* as a Neo-Slave Narrative." *American Literary History* 26.2 (2014): 326–31.

———. "Valerie Martin's *Property*: A Neo-Enslaver Narrative." *Mississippi Quarterly* 68.2 (2015): 235–55.

Loichot, Valérie. *Orphan Narratives: The Postplantation Literature of Faulkner, Glissant, Morrison, and Saint-John Perse*. Charlottesville: U of Virginia P, 2007.

Long, Carolyn Morrow. *Madame LaLaurie: Mistress of the Haunted House*. Gainesville: UP of Florida, 2012.

Lorde, Audre. "Age, Race, Class, and Sex: Women Redefining Difference." 1980. *Sister Outsider: Essays and Speeches*. Berkeley: Crossing, 2007. 114–23.

———."The Master's Tools Will Never Dismantle the Master's House." 1984. *Sister Outsider: Essays and Speeches*. Berkeley: Crossing, 2007. 110–14.

Lowe, John Wharton. *Calypso Magnolia: The Crosscurrents of Caribbean and Southern Literature*. Chapel Hill: U of North Carolina P, 2016.

Lowery, Malinda Maynor. *The Lumbee Indians: An American Struggle*. Chapel Hill: U of North Carolina P, 2018.

———. *Lumbee Indians in the Jim Crow South: Race, Identity, and the Making of a Nation*. Chapel Hill: U of North Carolina P, 2010.

MacDermot, Thomas Henry. *One Brown Girl And—*. Kingston: Jamaica Times Printery, 1909.

Machado Sáez, Elena. *Market Aesthetics: The Purchase of the Past in Caribbean Diasporic Fiction*. Charlottesville: U of Virginia P, 2015.

Mandinga. Dir. Mario Pinzauti. Perf. Antonio Gismondo, Serafino Profumo, and Maria Rosaria Riuzzi. 1976. SEFI, 2011. DVD.

Mandingo. Dir. Richard Fleischer. Perf. Susan George, Perry King, and James Mason. 1975. Legend Films, 2008. DVD.

Mardorossian, Carine M. "Rape by Proxy in Contemporary Caribbean Women's Fiction." *Feminism, Literature and Rape Narratives: Violence and Violation*. Eds. Sorcha Gunne and Zoë Brigley Thompson. New York: Routledge, 2010. 23–37.

———. *Reclaiming Difference: Caribbean Women Rewrite Postcolonialism*. Charlottesville: U of Virginia P, 2005.

Martin, Valerie. *Property*. New York: Vintage, 2003.

Mattison, H. *Louisa Picquet, the Octoroon: Or, Inside Views of Southern Domestic Life*. *Collected Black Women's Narratives*. 1861. New York: Oxford UP, 1988.

May, Vivian M. *Pursuing Intersectionality, Unsettling Dominant Imaginaries*. New York: Routledge, 2015.

Mayhew, Anna Jean. *The Dry Grass of August*. New York: Kensington, 2011.

Mayne, Judith. *Framed: Lesbians, Feminists and Media Culture*. Minneapolis: U of Minnesota P, 2000.

Mbembe, Achille. "The Aesthetics of Vulgarity." *On the Postcolony*. Berkeley: U of California P, 2001. 102–41.

McClintock, Anne. *Imperial Leather: Race, Gender and Sexuality in the Colonial Contest*. New York: Routledge, 1995.

McCullough, Kate. "'Marked by Genetics and Exile': Narrativizing Transcultural Sexualities in *Memory Mambo*." *GLQ* 6.4 (2000): 577–607.

McInnis, Jarvis C. "That 'the Land Would One Day Be Free': Reconciling Race and Region in African American and Southern Studies." *Mississippi Quarterly* 68.1–2 (2015): 15–20.

McInnis, Maurie D. *Slaves Waiting for Sale: Abolitionist Art and the American Slave Trade*. Chicago: U of Chicago P, 2011.

McLeod, Cynthia. *The Cost of Sugar*. 1987. Trans. Gerald R. Mettam. London: HopeRoad, 2013.

McPherson, Tara. "After Authenticity." *Creating and Consuming the American South*. Eds. Martyn Bone, Brian Ward, and William A. Link. Gainesville: UP of Florida, 2015. 309–23.

McRae, Elizabeth Gillespie. *Mothers of Massive Resistance: White Women and the Politics of White Supremacy*. New York: Oxford UP, 2018.

Means Coleman, Robin R. *Horror Noire: Blacks in American Horror Films from the 1890s to Present*. New York: Routledge, 2011.

Melancon, Trimiko C. "Towards an Aesthetic of Transgression: Ann Allen Shockley's *Loving Her* and the Politics of Same-Gender Loving." *African American Review* 42.3/4 (2008): 643–57.

Mellis, Delia. "Roots of Violence: Race, Power, and Manhood in *Roots*." *Reconsidering Roots: Race, Politics, and Memory*. Eds. Erica L. Ball and Kellie Carter Jackson. Athens: U of Georgia P, 2017. 81–96.

Memmi, Albert. "The Return of the Pendulum." Trans. Howard Greenfeld. *Dominated Man: Notes toward a Portrait*. Boston: Beacon, 1968. 165–81.

Miles, Tiya. *Tales from the Haunted South: Dark Tourism and Memories of Slavery from the Civil War Era*. Chapel Hill: U of North Carolina P, 2015.

Mitchell, Margaret. *Gone with the Wind*. 1936. New York: Warner Books, 1993.

Mittelhölzer, Edgar. *Children of Kaywana*. 1952. New York: Bantam Books, 1976.

Mohanty, Chandra Talpade. "Under Western Eyes: Feminist Scholarship and Colonial Discourses." *boundary 2* 12.3 (1984): 333–58.

Momsen, Janet Henshall. "Maids on the Move." *Gender, Migration and Domestic Service*. Ed. Janet Henshall Momsen. New York: Routledge, 1999. 1–20.

Monteith, Sharon. *Advancing Sisterhood?: Interracial Friendships in Contemporary Southern Fiction*. Athens: U of Georgia P, 2000.

Monteith, Sharon, and Suzanne W. Jones. "Introduction: South to New Places." *South to a New Place: Region, Literature, Culture*. Eds. Suzanne W. Jones and Sharon Monteith. Baton Rouge: Louisiana State UP, 2002. 1–19.

Moraga, Cherríe, and Gloria Anzaldúa, eds. *This Bridge Called My Back: Writings by Radical Women of Color*. Watertown: Persephone, 1981.

Morales-Franceschini, Eric. "Tropics of Abjection: Figures of Violence and the Afro-Caribbean Semiotic." *Journal of Postcolonial Writing* 55.4 (2019): 512–26.

Morgan, Jennifer L. *Laboring Women: Reproduction and Gender in New World Slavery*. Philadelphia: U of Pennsylvania P, 2004.

Morrison, Toni. *Beloved*. 1987. New York: Vintage, 2004.

———. *A Mercy*. New York: Alfred A. Knopf, 2008.

———. *Playing in the Dark: Whiteness and the Literary Imagination*. New York: Vintage, 1992.

———. *Tar Baby*. New York: Alfred A. Knopf, 1981.

Moseley, Rachel. "Glamorous Witchcraft: Gender and Magic in Teen Film and Television." *Screen* 43.4 (2002): 403–22.

Motz, Anna. *The Psychology of Female Violence: Crimes against the Body*. 2nd ed. New York: Routledge, 2008.

Nadasen, Premilla. *Household Workers Unite: The Untold Story of African American Women Who Built a Movement*. Boston: Beacon, 2015.

Naimou, Angela. *Salvage Work: U.S. and Caribbean Literatures amid the Debris of Legal Personhood*. New York: Fordham UP, 2015.

Nair, Supriya M. *Pathologies of Paradise: Caribbean Detours*. Charlottesville: U of Virginia P, 2013.

Nandi. *The True Nanny Diaries: A Novel*. Brooklyn: Bread for Brick, 2009.

Nash, Jennifer C. *Black Feminism Reimagined: After Intersectionality*. Durham: Duke UP, 2019.

Neroni, Hilary. *The Violent Woman: Femininity, Narrative, and Violence in Contemporary American Cinema*. Albany: State U of New York P, 2005.

Nesbitt, Nick. *Caribbean Critique: Antillean Critical Theory from Toussaint to Glissant*. Liverpool: Liverpool UP, 2013.

Newman, Louise Michele. *White Women's Rights: The Racial Origins of Feminism in the United States*. New York: Oxford UP, 1999.

Northup, Solomon. *Twelve Years a Slave*. 1853. New York: Penguin, 2013.

Oakley, Deirdre A., and James C. Fraser. "U.S. Public-Housing Transformations and the Housing Publics Lost in Transition." *City & Community* 15.4 (2016): 349–66.

Obejas, Achy. *Memory Mambo*. Pittsburgh: Cleis, 1996.

———. "Women Who Batter Women." *Ms.* 5 (1994): 53.

O'Callaghan, Evelyn. "Caribbean Migrations: Negotiating Borders." *Sex and the Citizen: Interrogating the Caribbean*. Ed. Faith Smith. Charlottesville: U of Virginia P, 2011. 125–35.

———. *Women Writing the West Indies, 1804–1939: "A Hot Place, Belonging to Us."* New York: Routledge, 2004.

O'Connell, Michael. "TV Ratings: *American Horror Story: Coven* Wraps with Series' Biggest Finale." *Hollywood Reporter* 30 Jan. 2014. Web. 27 June 2015.

Ombre, Ellen. "Shreds." "Flarden." 1992. *Words without Borders: The Online Magazine for International Literature*. Trans. David Colmer. Nov. 2005. Web. 21 June 2017.

Onstott, Kyle. *Mandingo*. 1957. Greenwich: Fawcett Crest, 1978.

Oostindie, Gert, and Alex Van Stipriaan. "Slavery and Slave Cultures in a Hydraulic Society: Suriname." *Slave Cultures and the Cultures of Slavery*. Ed. Stephan Palmié. Knoxville: U of Tennessee P, 1995. 78–99.

Painter, Nell Irvin. *Sojourner Truth: A Life, a Symbol*. 1996. New York: W. W. Norton, 1997.

Paravisini-Gebert, Lizabeth. "The Alienation of Power: The Woman Writer and the Planter-Heroine in Caribbean Literature." *The Woman, the Writer, and Caribbean Society: Critical Analyses of the Writings of Caribbean Women: Proceedings of the Second International Conference*. Ed. Helen Pyne-Timothy. Los Angeles: Center for AfroAmerican Studies Publications, 1998. 3–10.

"Part Two." *Roots*. History Channel. 31 May 2016. Television.

Patterson, Jennifer, ed. *Queering Sexual Violence: Radical Voices from within the Anti-Violence Movement*. Riverdale: Riverdale Avenue Books, 2016.

Patton, Stacey. "White Women Aren't Afraid of Black People. They Want Power." *Dame* 30 July 2018. Web. 26 Jan. 2019.

Pearson, Patricia. *When She Was Bad: Violent Women and the Myth of Innocence*. New York: Viking, 1997.

Perkins-Valdez, Dolen. *Wench: A Novel*. New York: Amistad, 2010.

Perry, Imani. *Vexy Thing: On Gender and Liberation*. Durham: Duke UP, 2018.

Pinto, Samantha. *Difficult Diasporas: The Transnational Feminist Aesthetic of the Black Atlantic*. New York: New York UP, 2013.

Portalatín, Aida Cartagena. "They Called Her Aurora (A Passion for Donna Summer)." 1986. Trans. Daisy Coco de Filippis. *Green Cane and Juicy Flotsam: Short Stories by Caribbean Women*. Eds. Carmen C. Esteves and Lizabeth Paravisini-Gebert. New Brunswick: Rutgers UP, 1992. 27–30.

Prince, Mary. *The History of Mary Prince, a West Indian Slave*. 1831. Ed. Sara Salih. New York: Penguin, 2000.

Rabinowitz, Paula. *American Pulp: How Paperbacks Brought Modernism to Main Street*. Princeton: Princeton UP, 2014.

Ramírez, Dolores Alcaide. *Violencia, Género y Migración en el Caribe Hispano: Reescribiendo la Nación*. New York: Peter Lang, 2011.

Randall, Alice. *The Wind Done Gone*. Boston: Houghton Mifflin, 2001.

Rhys, Jean. *Wide Sargasso Sea*. 1966. *Jean Rhys: The Complete Novels*. New York: W. W. Norton, 1985. 463–574.

Rich, Adrienne. "Conditions for Work: The Common World of Women." 1976. *On Lies, Secrets, and Silence: Selected Prose 1966–1978*. New York: W. W. Norton, 1995. 203–14.

———. "Disloyal to Civilization: Feminism, Racism, Gynephobia." 1978. *On Lies, Secrets, and Silence: Selected Prose 1966–1978*. New York: W. W. Norton, 1995. 275–310.

Rich, B. Ruby. *New Queer Cinema: The Director's Cut*. Durham: Duke UP, 2013.

Richardson, Bonham C. "The South and the Caribbean: A Regional Perspective." *The South and the Caribbean*. Eds. Douglass Sullivan-González and Charles Reagan Wilson. Jackson: UP of Mississippi, 2007. 3–20.

Richardson, Matt. *The Queer Limit of Black Memory: Black Lesbian Literature and Irresolution*. Columbus: Ohio State UP, 2013.

Richardson, Riché. *Black Masculinity and the U.S. South: From Uncle Tom to Gangsta*. Athens: U of Georgia P, 2007.

Roach, Joseph. *Cities of the Dead: Circum-Atlantic Performance*. New York: Columbia UP, 1996.

Roberts, Brian Russell, and Michelle Ann Stephens. "Introduction: Archipelagic American Studies: Decontinentalizing the Study of American Culture." *Archipelagic American Studies*. Eds. Brian Russell Roberts and Michelle Ann Stephens. Durham: Duke UP, 2017. 1–54.

Robinson, Zandria. *This Ain't Chicago: Race, Class, and Regional Identity in the Post-Soul South*. Chapel Hill: U of North Carolina P, 2014.

Rodríguez-Silva, Ileana M. *Silencing Race: Disentangling Blackness, Colonialism, and National Identities in Puerto Rico*. New York: Palgrave Macmillan, 2012.

Rody, Caroline. *The Daughter's Return: African-American and Caribbean Women's Fictions of History*. New York: Oxford UP, 2001.

Rollins, Judith. *Between Women: Domestics and Their Employers*. Philadelphia: Temple UP, 1985.

Rousseau, Nicole. *Black Woman's Burden: Commodifying Black Reproduction*. New York: Palgrave Macmillan, 2009.

Russ, Elizabeth Christine. *The Plantation in the Postslavery Imagination*. New York: Oxford UP, 2009.

Ryan, Tim A. *Calls and Responses: The American Novel of Slavery since Gone with the Wind*. Baton Rouge: Louisiana State UP, 2008.

Sankofa. Dir. Haile Gerima. Perf. Alexandra Duah and Oyafunmike Ogunlano. 1993. Mypheduh Films, 2003. DVD.

Sansay, Leonora. *Secret History; or, The Horrors of St. Domingo*. 1808. Ed. Michael J. Drexler. Toronto: Broadview, 2008.

Sargasso! A Caribbean Love Story. Dir. Michael Gilkes. 1991. Banyan Productions, 2007. DVD.

"Save Yourself." *True Blood*. HBO. 26 Aug. 2012. Television.

Scarry, Elaine. *The Body in Pain: The Making and Unmaking of the World*. New York: Oxford UP, 1985.

Scott, Anne Firor. *The Southern Lady: From Pedestal to Politics, 1830–1930*. Chicago: U of Chicago P, 1970.

Scott, Darieck. *Extravagant Abjection: Blackness, Power, and Sexuality in the African American Literary Imagination*. New York: New York UP, 2010.

The Secret Life of Bees. Dir. Gina Prince-Bythewood. Perf. Dakota Fanning, Jennifer Hudson, and Queen Latifah. 2008. 20th Century Fox Home Entertainment, 2009. DVD.

Seet, K. K. "Mothers and Daughters: Abjection and the Monstrous-Feminine in Japan's *Dark Water* and South Korea's *A Tale of Two Sisters*." *Camera Obscura* 24.2 (2009): 138–59.

Sharpe, Christina. *Monstrous Intimacies: Making Post-Slavery Subjects*. Durham: Duke UP, 2010.

Sharpe, Jenny. *Ghosts of Slavery: A Literary Archaeology of Black Women's Lives*. Minneapolis: U of Minnesota P, 2003.

Sharpless, Rebecca. *Cooking in Other Women's Kitchens: Domestic Workers in the South, 1865–1960*. Chapel Hill: U of North Carolina P, 2010.

Sheller, Mimi. *Consuming the Caribbean: From Arawaks to Zombies*. New York: Routledge, 2003.

Sherman, Delia. *The Freedom Maze*. Easthampton: Big Mouth House, 2011.

Shimizu, Celine Parreñas. "Master-Slave Sex Acts: *Mandingo* and the Race/Sex Paradox." *Wide Angle* 21.4 (1999): 42–61.

Shine, Ted. *Contribution*. 1968. *Black Comedy Classics: A Critical Anthology of Nine Plays, with Interviews and Essays*. Eds. Pamela Faith Jackson and Karimah. New York: Applause Books, 1997. 233–50.

Shockley, Ann Allen. *The Black and White of It*. Tallahassee: Naiad, 1980.

———. 2nd ed. Tallahassee: Naiad, 1987.

Shoemaker, Jan. "Ellen Douglas: Reconstructing the Subject in *Hold On* and *Can't Quit You, Baby*." *Southern Quarterly* 33.4 (1995): 83–98.

Silvera, Makeda. *Silenced: Talks with Working Class Caribbean Women about Their Lives and Struggles as Domestic Workers in Canada*. 1983. Toronto: Sister Vision, 1989.

Singh, Julietta. *Unthinking Mastery: Dehumanism and Decolonial Entanglements*. Durham: Duke UP, 2018.

The Skeleton Key. Dir. Iain Softley. Perf. Joy Bryant, Kate Hudson, and Peter Sarsgaard. Universal Studies Home Entertainment, 2005. DVD.

Smith, Jon, and Deborah Cohn. "Introduction: Uncanny Hybridities." *Look Away!: The U.S. South in New World Studies.* Eds. Jon Smith and Deborah Cohn. Durham: Duke UP, 2004. 1–19.

Smith, Lillian. *Killers of the Dream.* 1949. New York: W. W. Norton, 1994.

"Somebody That I Used to Know." *True Blood.* HBO. 29 July 2012. Television.

Soto-Crespo, Ramón E. "Archipelagic Trash: Despised Forms in the Cultural History of the Americas." *Archipelagic American Studies.* Eds. Brian Russell Roberts and Michelle Ann Stephens. Durham: Duke UP, 2017. 302–19.

———. *The White Trash Menace and Hemispheric Fiction.* Columbus: Ohio State UP, 2020.

Sparer, Joyce L. "Attitudes towards 'Race' in Guyanese Literature." *Caribbean Studies* 8.2 (1968): 23–63.

Spillers, Hortense J. "Mama's Baby, Papa's Maybe: An American Grammar Book." 1987. *Black, White, and In Color: Essays on American Literature and Culture.* Chicago: U of Chicago P, 2003. 203–29.

Spivak, Gayatri Chakravorty. "Three Women's Texts and a Critique of Imperialism." *Critical Inquiry* 12.1 (1985): 235–61.

Springer, Kimberly. "Divas, Evil Black Bitches, and Bitter Black Women: African American Women in Postfeminist and Post-Civil-Rights Popular Culture." *Interrogating Postfeminism: Gender and the Politics of Popular Culture.* Eds. Diane Negra and Yvonne Tasker. Durham: Duke UP, 2007. 249–76.

Stallings, L. H. "Re-Reading Ann Allen Shockley through Queer Queen B Eyes." *Obsidian III* 4.2 (2002–2003): 61–89.

Steele, Valerie. *The Corset: A Cultural History.* New Haven: Yale UP, 2001.

Stockett, Kathryn. *The Help.* New York: Amy Einhorn Books, 2009.

Stoker, Bram. *Dracula.* 1897. Ed. Glennis Byron. Toronto: Broadview, 1998.

Stryker, Susan. *Queer Pulp: Perverted Passions from the Golden Age of the Paperback.* San Francisco: Chronicle Books, 2001.

Subramanian, Janani. "The Monstrous Makeover: *American Horror Story*, Femininity and Special Effects." *Critical Studies in Television* 8.3 (2013): 108–23.

Sugar Hill. Dir. Paul Maslansky. Perf. Marki Bey, Don Pedro Colley, and Robert Quarry. 1974. 20th Century Fox Home Entertainment, 2007. DVD.

Sugg, Katherine. "Migratory Sexualities, Diasporic Histories, and Memory in Queer Cuban-American Cultural Production." *Environment and Planning D: Society and Space* 21 (2003): 461–77.

Sweeney, Carole. "The Unmaking of the World: Haiti, History, and Writing in Edouard Glissant and Edwige [sic] Danticat." *Atlantic Studies* 4.1 (2007): 51–66.

Tademy, Lalita. *Cane River.* New York: Warner Books, 2001.

Thomas, Deborah A. *Exceptional Violence: Embodied Citizenship in Transnational Jamaica.* Durham: Duke UP, 2011.

Thornton Dill, Bonnie. *Across the Boundaries of Race and Class: An Exploration of Work and Family among Black Female Domestic Servants.* 1979. New York: Garland Publishing, 1994.

Tinsley, Omise'eke Natasha. *Thiefing Sugar: Eroticism between Women in Caribbean Literature*. Durham: Duke UP, 2010.

Tinsman, Heidi, and Sandhya Shukla. "Introduction: Across the Americas." *Imagining Our Americas: Toward a Transnational Frame*. Eds. Sandhya Shukla and Heidi Tinsman. Durham: Duke UP, 2007. 1–33.

Tompkins, Kyla Wazana. *Racial Indigestion: Eating Bodies in the 19th Century*. New York: New York UP, 2012.

Trescott, Jacqueline. "An Emotional Preview of Haley's 'Roots'—'It All Came Alive.'" *Washington Post* 13 Jan. 1977: C1.

Trouillot, Évelyne. *The Infamous Rosalie*. 2003. Trans. M. A. Salvodon. Lincoln: U of Nebraska P, 2013.

Trouillot, Michel-Rolph. *Silencing the Past: Power and the Production of History*. Boston: Beacon, 1995.

Truth, Sojourner. *Narrative of Sojourner Truth; A Bondswoman of Olden Time, With a History of Her Labors and Correspondence Drawn from Her "Book of Life."* 1850. New York: Oxford UP, 1991.

Tuccelli, Jessica Maria. *Glow: A Novel*. New York: Viking, 2012.

Tucker, Susan. *Telling Memories among Southern Women: Domestic Workers and Their Employers in the Segregated South*. Baton Rouge: Louisiana State UP, 1988.

Udovitch, Mim. "Tarantino and Juliette." *Quentin Tarantino Interviews*. 1996. Ed. Gerald Peary. Jackson: UP of Mississippi, 1998. 166–82.

Van Wormer, Katherine, David W. Jackson III, and Charletta Sudduth. *The Maid Narratives: Black Domestics and White Families in the Jim Crow South*. Baton Rouge: Louisiana State UP, 2012.

Vásquez, Sam. "Violent Liaisons: Historical Crossings and the Negotiation of Sex, Sexuality, and Race in *The Book of Night Women* and *The True History of Paradise*." *Small Axe* 16.2 (2012): 43–59.

Vernon, John. "The Black Face of Freedom." *New York Times*. 29 Oct. 1995. Web. 24 July 2017.

Walker, Alice. *The Color Purple*. 1982. New York: Washington Square, 1983.

———. "The Revenge of Hannah Kemhuff." 1967. *In Love and Trouble: Stories of Black Women*. New York: Harcourt Brace Jovanovich, 1973. 60–80.

Walker, Christine. *Jamaica Ladies: Female Slaveholders and the Creation of Britain's Atlantic Empire*. Williamsburg: Omohundro Institute of Early American History and Culture; Chapel Hill: U of North Carolina P, 2020.

Walker, Kara. *Negress Notes*. 1995. Collage, ink, gouache, and watercolor on paper. Sikkema Jenkins & Co., New York.

Walker, Lisa. *Looking Like What You Are: Sexual Style, Race, and Lesbian Identity*. New York: New York UP, 2001.

Walker, Margaret. *Jubilee*. 1966. New York: Mariner Books, 1999.

Wallace-Sanders, Kimberly. *Mammy: A Century of Race, Gender, and Southern Memory*. Ann Arbor: U of Michigan P, 2008.

Wanzo, Rebecca. "Civil Rights Sentimental Fiction: Atticus Finch, *The Help*, and Archiving Political Feelings." Address presented at Black/White Intimacies:

Reimagining History, the South, and the Western Hemisphere Symposium, University of Alabama. Tuscaloosa, AL. 22 Apr. 2017.

———. "What Is the Liberatory Potential of *Bitch Planet*'s Exploitation Aesthetic?" *Hard Women, Hard Time: Bitch Planet Comics Studies Round Table (part three).* The *Middle Spaces* 13 Mar. 2018. Web. 26 Jan. 2019.

Washington, Margaret. *Sojourner Truth's America.* Champaign: U of Illinois P, 2009.

Wee, Valerie. "Patriarchy and the Horror of the Monstrous Feminine: A Comparative Study of *Ringu* and *The Ring.*" *Feminist Media Studies* 11.2 (2011): 151–65.

Weeks, Kathi. *The Problem with Work: Feminism, Marxism, Antiwork Politics, and Postwork Imaginaries.* Durham: Duke UP, 2011.

Weiner, Marli F. "Mistresses, Morality, and the Dilemmas of Slaveholding: The Ideology and Behavior of Elite Antebellum Women." *Discovering the Women in Slavery: Emancipating Perspectives on the American Past.* Ed. Patricia Morton. Athens: U of Georgia P, 1996. 278–98.

Wells, Jeremy. *Romances of the White Man's Burden: Race, Empire, and the Plantation in American Literature, 1880–1936.* Nashville: Vanderbilt UP, 2011.

White, Deborah Gray. *Ar'n't I a Woman?: Female Slaves in the Plantation South.* Revised ed. New York: W. W. Norton, 1999.

"Why the Public Perception of Crime Exceeds the Reality." *All Things Considered.* NPR, 26 July 2016. Web. 18 Mar. 2021.

Wide Sargasso Sea. Dir. John Duigan. Perf. Rowena King, Karina Lombard, and Nathaniel Parker. 1993. New Line Home Video, 2003. DVD.

Wide Sargasso Sea. Dir. Brendan Maher. Perf. Rebecca Hall and Rafe Spall. 2006. Acorn Media, 2008. DVD.

Williams, Heather Andrea. *Self-Taught: African American Education in Slavery and Freedom.* Chapel Hill: U of North Carolina P, 2005.

Williams, Linda. *Playing the Race Card: Melodramas of Black and White from Uncle Tom to O. J. Simpson.* Princeton: Princeton UP, 2001.

Williams, Sherley Anne. *Dessa Rose: A Novel.* 1986. New York: Quill, 1999.

Wilson, Harriet E. *Our Nig; or, Sketches from the Life of a Free Black, In a Two-Story White House, North. Showing That Slavery's Shadows Fall Even There.* 1859. New York: Vintage, 1983.

Winters, Lisa Ze. *The Mulatta Concubine: Terror, Intimacy, Freedom, and Desire in the Black Transatlantic.* Athens: U of Georgia P, 2016.

Wood, Marcus. *Blind Memory: Visual Representations of Slavery in England and America, 1780–1865.* New York: Routledge, 2000.

———. *Slavery, Empathy, and Pornography.* New York: Oxford UP, 2002.

Wood, Robin. *Sexual Politics and Narrative Film: Hollywood and Beyond.* New York: Columbia UP, 1998.

Yaeger, Patricia. "Circum-Atlantic Superabundance: Milk as World-Making in Alice Randall and Kara Walker." *American Literature* 78.4 (2006): 769–98.

———. *Dirt and Desire: Reconstructing Southern Women's Writing 1930–1990.* Chicago: U of Chicago P, 2000.

Young, Elizabeth. *Disarming the Nation: Women's Writing and the American Civil War.* Chicago: U of Chicago P, 1999.

Zimet, Jaye. *Strange Sisters: The Art of Lesbian Pulp Fiction 1949-1969*. New York: Viking Studio, 1999.

Zimmerman, Bonnie. *"Daughters of Darkness*: The Lesbian Vampire on Film." *The Dread of Difference: Gender and the Horror Film*. Ed. Barry Keith Grant. Austin: U of Texas P, 1981. 379–87.

Index

Note: Page locators in italics indicate figures.

12 Years a Slave (film), 17, 23, 37–43, *39*, 61, 86, 193n14

Abdur-Rahman, Aliyyah I., 82
abjection, 10, 20, 200n1, 200n4, 201n5; and bodily wastes, 143, 147; and desire, 170–71; and disposability of Black bodies, 146, 151–52; of monstrous-feminine, 143–55, 162–65, 173, 200n2, 200–201n4; of racism, 154; and same-sex desire, 164–65, 170–71; same-sex violence as, 158–61; of "unnatural" white characters, 150; white supremacy's reliance on, 147–49
abolitionist publications, 4–6, 81, 95, 185n3
Absalom, Absalom! (Faulkner), 8
Across the Boundaries of Race and Class (Thornton Dill), 104–5
Adams, Jessica, 2, 24, 185n2
Advancing Sisterhood? (Monteith), 105–6
"The Aesthetics of Vulgarity" (Mbembe), 155
African diaspora, 61, 166, 187n15, 195n12
agency, 1, 190n33; and "consent," 75, 98; enslaved women's, 18, 36, 53, 97–98, 189n27; public display of, 158–60; regimes act out through torture, 32, 38; and visual representation, 27, 189; white women's attempts to claim, 23, 32–36, 40, 47, 51, 53, 57, 74, 84, 86, 97–98
All Souls' Rising (Bell), 17, 45, 46–57, 61, 62, 88; agency through sadism in, 51–54, 57, 74; Enlightenment thought parodied in, 47–48, 54; failure of white women's attempts to claim power, 47, 51, 53, 57, 74; "insanity" mirrors plantation logics, 47–48, 51; and resistance by enslaved women, 53–55; sadism as reflection of plantation structure, 48–49; violence of male enslavers embodied by white women, 50–51; white male power in, 46–47
The American Anti-Slavery Almanac for 1840, 4–6, *5*
American Horror Story (television series), 20, 142–55; monstrous whiteness in, 144, 146; story line in 1830s, 144–47; story line in 2010s, 144, *145*, 147–49; violence of colonialism in, 142–43, 155. *See also* horror genre
Anatol, Giselle Liza, 164
Anderson, Bridget, 106, 198n6
Antebellum (film), 202n1
Aparicio, Frances R., 167
archive, 2, 45, 189n27, 191n34
audience: borders of, and horror film genre, 143; desires of, 16, 19, 22, 24, 37, 46, 59, 74, 92–93; discomfort elicited in, 47; enabled to see violent aspects of power, 88; expectations of women characters, 22–23, 29, 33, 37–38; false sense of separation from power structures, 182–83

Bailey, Carol, 156
Baker, Patrick L., 164–65
Ball, Erica L., 77
Baptist, Edward E., 32

Barbados, 76–77

Bell, Madison Smartt. *See All Souls' Rising* (Bell)

Beloved (Morrison), 67, 87

Benítez-Rojo, Antonio, 188n25

Ben-Ur, Aviva, 71–72

Bibb, Henry, 2, *3*

Bibler, Michael P., 80–81, 99

Bitch Planet (DeConnick and De Landro), 175–77, *176*

The Black and White of It (Shockley), 18–19, 75, 90–93, 107; cover designs, *92*, 92, *93*

Black freedom movements, 78

The Black Jacobins (James), 58

Black Subjects (Keizer), 10

Blaxploitation films, 24, 149

Blind Memory (Wood), 4

Bolles, A. Lynn, 121

The Book of Night Women (James), 17, 57–67, 74, 117, 124–25, 194n6; body as weapon in, 58, 64; Coulibre (fictional plantation), 61–62; instability of identity under plantation regimes, 52, 62; insurrection in, 65–66; internalization of violence in, 63–64; legitimate self-formation and violence, 64–66; "living beyond the sword," 45, 64–65; retributive violence in, 58, 62–66; skin-to-skin violence and identification with other, 58–59; white women's use of power in plantation context, 60–62

Breath, Eyes, Memory (Danticat), 156

Breines, Winifred, 105

Brickhouse, Anna, 186n10

Bridging the Americas (Coser), 118

Brontë, Charlotte, 123

Brooks, Kinitra D., 154

Brown, Kimberly Juanita, 15

Bullins, Ed, 199n13

Burfoot, Annette, 190–91n33

Burnard, Trevor, 57

Bush, Barbara, 62

Butler, Octavia, 32

Can't Quit You, Baby (Douglas), 109–10

Carby, Hazel V., 98

Card, Claudia, 168–69

Caribbean, 12, 188n25; exceptionality, narratives of, 103, 127, 130–32; exoticization and othering, 20, 103, 129–37; films set on plantations, 43–74; as origin of globalization, 46; silencing in, 121–22, 133; sugar trade, 68; U.S. tensions acted out in, 118, 120–21; white degeneration blamed on people of color, 50, 65, 194n6. *See also* circum-Caribbean

Cary, Lorene, 95

"catfights," 1, 172

Cather, Willa, 82

Centring the Periphery (Baker), 164–65

Chicago, 167, 202n14

Children of Kaywana (Mittelhölzer), 27–29, *28*, *29*

Childress, Alice, 115–16

Chopin, Kate, 30

Christian, Barbara, 15

"Circum-Atlantic Superabundance" (Yaeger), 46

circum-Caribbean, 14, 16, 188n20; continuum of violence in texts of, 19, 32, 46–48, 58, 62; Enlightenment and slavery linked in, 47–48, 54; as term, 11, 187n15, 187n16

civil rights activism (1950s and 1960s), 117

"civil rights sentimental fiction," 106–7

Cliff, Michelle, 200n20

Code Noir (1685), 48, 57, 147

Cohn, Deborah, 188n23

Collins, Patricia Hill, 15, 118–19

colonialism, 20, 189n28; and abjection, 142, 161; consent as discourse of, 75; forgetfulness of, willed, 166–67; as genocidal project, 49; in horror genre, 180–82; legacy of and domestic labor, 103, 121–23; neo-colonialism, 10, 13, 120–21; in pulp novels, 27; violence of, 142–43, 155; violent touch as threat to hierarchy of, 44–45; women's maintenance of structures of, 155–56, 159–63. *See also* plantation

The Color Purple (Walker), 116–17

consent, discourse of, 75, 97–98

Corregidora (Jones), 76, 156

The Corset (Steele), 33

Coser, Stelamaris, 118

Craft, Linda J., 166, 169, 202n15

Creed, Barbara, 143, 150–51, 153, 164–65, 173, 200n2, 200n4

Cuba, 166, 168

Cutter, Martha J., 6, 177, 185n4

Dalton, Anne B., 81

Danticat, Edwidge, 156

Davis, Cynthia J., 114, 115

Dayan, Colin, 47–48, 66, 70

decolonization, 10, 19, 58, 103, 167; of stereotypes, 140–41; violence of, 12–13

De Connick, Kelly Sue, 175

De Landro, Valentine, 175

de Lisser, Herbert G. *See Jane's Career* (de Lisser); *The White Witch of Rosehall* (de Lisser)

desire, 196n15; and abjection, 170–71; of audience, 16, 19, 22, 24, 37, 46, 59, 74, 92–93; dominant models challenged, 90–91, 101; plantation, as shorthand for unnatural, 24

Dessa Rose (Williams), 58, 196n12

deviant/"unnatural" behaviors and desires, 1, 24, 26–27, 33, 37, 76, 81, 150

Dirt and Desire (Yaeger), 12

"Disloyal to Civilization" (Rich), 104

disposability, of Black bodies, 48–49, 118, 121, 146, 151–52

Dispossessed Lives (Fuentes), 76–77

domestic labor, 18, 102–41, 199n13; adherence to social roles, 108–9; and capitalist expansion, 199n11; emotional labor, 118–19; globalized, 121–22; in Jamaica, 123–40, 199n17; migrant servants, 116, 121; militantly

violent servants, 115, 117; power structures in, 114–23, 197n1, 198n6; psychological exploitation in, 118; and silencing, 91, 97–98, 100–101, 103–4, 107–10, 114; speaking back, 114–17, 120, 123; white denial of violence in relationship, 112–14, 140. *See also* post-emancipation settings

domination, 15–16

Dominica, 122–24, 155, 163

Douglas, Ellen. *See Can't Quit You, Baby* (Douglas); *Hold On* (Douglas)

Douglass, Frederick, 11, 188n26

Down, Lorna, 156

Dracula (Stoker), 146, 165

Dragonard series (Gilchrist), 25, 26, 27. *See also* plantation pulp fiction

Drake, Sandra, 125

Due North, 177–79, *178*. See also *Insecure* (HBO series)

Duggan, Lisa, 165

Duigan, John. *See Wide Sargasso Sea* (film, 1993)

Edmonson, Belinda, 192–93n7, 199n16

Emancipation Act of 1833 (Britain), 123

emotional labor, 118–19

empathy, politics of, 177

Enlightenment thought, 66, 146; parodied in *All Souls' Rising*, 47–48, 54

enslaved people: depicted as awaiting white people's help, 4, 6; disposability of Black body, 48–49, 118, 121, 146, 151–52; as extensions of enslavers, 70; forced to enact violence against each other, 50, 62, 71; and French Code Noir, 48, 57; passivity stereotypes about, 2–6, *3*; resilience of, 53–54; as "things," 10, 48–49, 111, 113

enslaved women: identity in face of enslaver's violence, 45; and insurrection, 42, 44, 53, 65–66; passivity attributed to, 2–4, *3*; resistance by, 53–55, 58; retributive violence by, 17–18, 62–66 enslavers, women: attempts to claim agency, 23, 32–36, 40, 47, 51, 53, 57, 74, 84, 86, 97–98; domestic sphere as site of violence, *3*, 3–6; as enmeshed in sexual relations of slavery, 76–77; idealization of, 31; manipulation of plantation economies, 17, 23, 89; masculinized on pulp novel covers, 25, 28, *28*; power gained through sexual violence, 81–82; sadism of, 17–18, 23, 25, 28, 31–36, 44–58, 61–67, 71, 74, 193–94n1, 194n4. *See also* white women

Enszer, Julie R., 92

erotica, 18–19, 33, 91, 93, 196n14, 196n15

exceptionality, narratives of, 15, 42, 55, 76–77, 141, 144; and Caribbean women, 103, 127, 130–32; post-2016, 174–77, 180, 182–83; regional, 176–77

exploitation films, 16–17, 23–24, 36–37, 47, 192n2; Blaxploitation, 24, 149; reversals of racism in, 144; women-in-prison, 175

Falconhurst series, 25, *26*, 27. *See also* plantation pulp fiction

Fanon, Frantz, 13, 48, 58, 66, 201n5

Faulkner, William, 8

Faust, Drew Gilpin, 30

feminism, 85, 104–5, 189–90n30

film and television, 9; exploitation films, 16–17, 23–24, 36–37; independent filmmaking, 135–36; from pulp fiction, 25; set on Caribbean plantations, 43–74. *See also specific films and television series*

Fleischer, Richard. *See Mandingo* (film)

Francis, Donette A., 156

From Mammies to Militants (Harris), 104

Fuentes, Marisa J., 53, 76–77, 191n34

Fulton, DoVeanna S., 32, 58, 115

Garraway, Doris, 49

Garrigus, John, 57

gaze, 4, 6–7, 27, 37, 39, 82, 86, 95–96; male, 88, 159

Gebreyes, Rahel, 78

Get Out (film), 175, 179–82, *180*

Gilchrist, Rupert. *See* Dragonard series

The Gilda Stories (Gomez), 146, 165, 171

Gilkes, Michael. *See Sargasso! A Caribbean Love Story* (film, 1991)

Gilroy, Paul, 11–12

Girard, René, 194n2

Glissant, Édouard, 11, 186n13

globalization, 46, 186n10

Glymph, Thavolia, 24, 31

Goddu, Teresa A., 4, 6, 185–86n5, 186n6, 186n7

Goldman, Dara E., 167

Gomez, Jewelle, 146, 165, 171

Gone with the Wind (Mitchell), 8–9, 87

"goodness," narratives of, 15–16, 19, 168, 190–91n33

Green Cane and Juicy Flotsam (eds. Esteves and Paravisini-Gebert), 122

Grier, Barbara, 92–93

Guterl, Matthew Pratt, 188n20

Guyana, 27

Gwin, Minrose C., 8, 30

Gyssels, Kathleen, 47, 51, 193–94n1

Haiti, History, and the Gods (Dayan), 47–48

Haitian Revolution, 22, 46, 48, 54–56

Haley, Alex. *See Roots* (Haley, miniseries, 1977); *Roots* (Haley, novel)

Hancock, Ange-Marie, 189n30

Handley, George B., 185n2

Harper, Frances E. W., 58

Harris, Trudier, 104, 115, 117, 199n13

Hartman, Saidiya V., 12, 98, 188–89n26

Heffelfinger, Elizabeth, 131–32, 136

The Help (Stockett), 7, 106

Hendin, Josephine G, 190–91n33

The History of Mary Prince (Prince), 63. *See also* slave narratives

Hoe Duur Was de Suiker (book, McLeod), 67, 68, 71, 73

Hoe Duur Was de Suiker (film), 17, 18, 45, 67–74, 69, 194n7
Hold On (Douglas), 19, 103, 107–14, 115, 120, 126
Holland, Sharon Patricia, 196n15
hooks, bell, 104, 191n34, 191–92n35, 197n3, 199n15, 201n11
"Horror and the Monstrous-Feminine" (Creed), 143, 150–51, 153, 164–65, 173, 200n2, 200n4
horror genre, 142–73; "dangerous Blackness" in, 149; "haunting," 144; lesbian themes, 164–66; monstrous-feminine in, 143–45, 150–55, 162, 173, 200n2, 200–201n4; *soucouyant* myths, 159–60, 164. *See also American Horror Story* (television series); *Get Out* (film); *Memory Mambo* (Obejas); *Unburnable* (John)
Hurston, Zora Neale, 30, 194n8

idealism, 105
identification, 58–59, 128; psychological structures of, 11–12
identity: formation via acts of violence, 1, 10, 12, 14, 45, 96, 128–29; instability of in post-emancipation era, 125; instability of under plantation regimes, 17, 52, 62, 177; legitimate self-formation and violence, 64–66; loss of, 100; refusal to surrender, 53–54
The Illustrated Slave (Cutter), 6, 177, 185n4
"Images of Black Women in Afro-American Literature" (Christian), 15
imperialism, New World, 46, 185n2
Incidents in the Life of a Slave Girl (Jacobs), 81–82. *See also* slave narratives
Insecure (HBO series), 175, 177–79, 178
insurrection, 42, 44, 53, 65–66, 115
intersectionality, 14–15, 189–90n30
In the Castle of My Skin (Lamming), 142
intimacy, 2, 23–24, 38–39, 41; absent from sexual violence, 87–88; false,

7–8, 48, 66, 70, 112; monstrous, 10–11; and sadism, 44–46, 48, 51, 57, 66–70, 74
Iola Leroy (Harper), 58

Jackson, Kellie Carter, 77
Jacobs, Harriet, 81–82, 114
Jamaica, 57, 60–61, 122–24, 189n28, 199n17; domestic labor in, 123–40; racialized class status in, 123–27; "White Witch" tale, 144, 149–50, 164, 201n9
Jamaica Ladies (Walker), 57
James, C. L. R., 58
James, Marlon. *See The Book of Night Women* (James)
Jane Eyre (Brontë), 123, 128. *See also Wide Sargasso Sea* (Rhys)
Jane's Career (de Lisser), 123–24, 199n16
jealousy, 1–2, 34–39, 47, 50, 81, 86, 90, 177–78; within social expectations, 22–23; and social stability, 142–43
John, Marie-Elena. *See Unburnable* (John)
Johnson, Michele A., 123, 124
Johnson, Walter, 14
Jones, Edward P., 30–31
Jones, Gayl, 44; *Corregidora*, 76, 156; "The Machete Woman," 44, 53, 54, 56, 57, 60, 62–64, 74
Jones, Jacqueline, 198n6
Jones, Suzanne W., 84, 196n12
Jones-Rogers, Stephanie E., 31, 38

Kalisa, Chantal, 201–2n12
Keeling, Kara, 66
Keizer, Arlene R., 10
Kidd, Sue Monk, 198n7
Killers of the Dream (Smith), 111
Kindred (Butler), 32
King, Martin Luther, Jr., 112
King, Neal, 190–91n33
The Known World (Jones), 30–31
Kousha, Mahnaz, 118
Kristeva, Julia, 143, 200n1

"La Belle Zoraïde" (Chopin), 30
Laboring Women (Morgan), 76
La Fountain-Stokes, Lawrence, 202n14
Lambert, David, 189n27
Lamming, George, 142
LeBlanc, Amanda Kay, 154
lesbian fiction, 25–26, 195–96n6,
    196n12; interracial relationships,
    91–93; in post-emancipation Jim
    Crow setting, 76; silencing in, 91,
    97–98, 100–101; vampires and horror
    genre, 164–66, 170–71
Li, Stephanie, 193n14, 196n11
Like One of the Family (Childress), 115–16
Loichot, Valérie, 187n16, 188n22
Lord, Susan, 190–91n33
Lorde, Audre, 190n31, 197n3
Louisa Picquet, the Octoroon (Mattison),
    95. *See also* slave narratives
Lowe, John Wharton, 187n17, 194n3

Machado Sáez, Elena, 46, 59
"The Machete Woman" (Jones), 44, 53,
    54, 56, 57, 60, 62–64, 74
Maher, Brendan. *See Wide Sargasso Sea*
    (film, 2006)
Mammy (Wallace-Sanders), 112
mammy figure, 87, 112, 116–17
Mandingo (book, Onstott), 25, 86–87
Mandingo (film), 16–17, 23, 32–37, 35,
    62, 122, 192n2; critique of plantation
    system in, 36; low-budget knockoffs
    of, 32–33; reception history, 193n11
Mardorossian, Carine M., 127, 155, 160
Market Aesthetics (Machado Sáez), 46
Maroons, 54, 70, 73, 156, 163
marriage, 50, 69, 84, 98, 126, 157–60,
    195n10
Martin, Valerie. *See Property* (Martin)
Maslansky, Paul, 149
May, Vivian M., 14–15
Mbembe, Achille, 155
McCaughey, Martha, 190–91n33
McClintock, Anne, 191n34
McCullough, Kate, 166–67

McInnis, Maurie D., 4
McLeod, Cynthia, 67, 68, 71, 73
McQueen, Steve, 37, 193n14
mediated violence, 8, 16, 23, 44, 47, 63,
    81, 102
Memmi, Albert, 117
Memory Mambo (Obejas), 20, 142,
    165–73
A Mercy (Morrison), 85
"The Mistress and the Slave Girl"
    (Shockley), 18, 76–77, 90–99, 103–4,
    111
Mitchell, Margaret, 8, 9, 87
Mittelhölzer, Edgar, 27, 192n6,
    192–93n7
Momsen, Janet Henshall, 121
monstrous, the, 10–11, 20, 190n32,
    200n2, 200–201n4; "dangerous
    Blackness," 149; figures of, 20; racist
    culture as, 164; white supremacy as
    source of, 149–50
monstrous-feminine horror type, 143–45,
    150–55, 162, 200n2, 200–201n4; lesbian
    vampires, 164–65; reframing, 173
Monstrous Intimacies (Sharpe), 8, 10–11,
    186n14
Monteith, Sharon, 85, 105–6, 116,
    197n20
Morales-Franceschini, Eric, 200n1
Morgan, Jennifer L., 76
Morrison, Toni, 11, 82. *See also A Mercy*
    (Morrison); *Beloved* (Morrison); *Tar
    Baby* (Morrison)
motherhood, 11–12, 110, 119–20,
    190n33, 198n4
The Mulatta Concubine (Winters), 195n12

Naiad Press, 91–93
Naimou, Angela, 2
Nair, Supriya M., 121–22
Nandi, 116
*Narrative of the Life and Adventures of
    Henry Bibb, An American Slave* (Bibb),
    2–4, 3, 185n3, 185n4. *See also* slave
    narratives

Nash, Jennifer C., 189–90n30
Negress Notes (Walker), 2, 6–8, 7, 14
neo-colonialism, 10, 13, 120–21
Nesbitt, Nick, 12, 48, 65
Northup, Solomon, 38–43

Obeah, 60–61, 127, 133, 150
Obejas, Achy, 20, 142, 165–73
Ombre, Ellen, 197n21
Onstott, Kyle. *See Mandingo* (book, Onstott); *Mandingo* (film)
Oostindie, Gert, 71
Other, 12, 20, 45, 57, 103, 112
Our Nig (Wilson), 114–15
Out of the House of Bondage (Glymph), 24

Painter, Nell Irvin, 81
Patton, Stacey, 174
Pearson, Patricia, 190–91n33
Peele, Jordan, 179
Perkins-Valdez, Dolen, 95
Perry, Imani, 190n31
plantation: grotesque power structures of, 32, 83, 89–90; imaginaries of, 2, 10–11, 18, 174, 188n21; instability of identity under regimes of, 17, 52, 62, 177; logics, historical continuity of, 16–19, 31–32, 62, 76, 102, 155, 174, 179–80, 186n12, 187n16; and queer sexualities, 80–81; and retributive violence, 17–18, 62–66; as shorthand for unnaturalness, 24. *See also* plantation settings after 2016; post-emancipation settings; power structures
plantation pulp fiction, 24, 192n3, 192n4, 192n5; Dragonard and Falconhurst series, 25, 26, 27; hardcover-to-pulp trajectory, 25, 27; plantation erotica *vs.*, 90–91, 196n14; plantation mistress as staple of, 29
plantation pulp novel covers, 6, 9, 16–17, 76; depiction of scenes not in novel, 27–29, 29; differences between editions, 27–28, 28; gender-bending

images on, 24–28, 26; interracial sex implied, 25; light-skinned women on, 27–28, 28; taboo identities and activities, 23–24
plantation settings after 2016, 174–83; continuation of plantation logics, 174, 179–80; exceptionality in, 174, 175; horror genre, 180–82; jealousy theme, 177–78; melodrama/comedy genres, 177–79; science fiction/dystopian genres, 175–77
Playing the Race Card (Williams), 178
popular cultural representations, 2, 6, 10, 13, 16
Portalatín, Aida Cartagena, 102–3
post-colonial societies, 121–23, 143, 155, 163
post-emancipation settings, 10–12, 14, 102–41; segregated society, 19, 103–6, 113, 198n4; "sisterhood," narratives of, 19, 103–5, 119, 151; soft-focus conciliatory perspective, 105–6. *See also* domestic labor
power: complicity of in systems of, 19, 23, 36–37, 96, 151, 182–83, 191n34; controlling images, 15; hemispheric systems of, 11, 19, 46, 95, 118; historical contextualization of, 2, 9–13; through sexual violence toward enslaved people, 77, 81–82; torture's place in regimes of, 32, 38; white male, 17, 23, 30, 46–47, 50–51, 71–72; white women's as deviant, 17, 37, 55–56, 193n12; white women's use of in plantation context, 38–43, 60–62, 191n34
Powers of Horror (Kristeva), 143
power structures, 2, 10–15, 110–11, 178; Caribbean women's experiences of, 120–21; of colonialism, 163, 167, 185n2; critiques of silenced, 114–15, 129–31, 141; in domestic labor, 114–23, 197n1, 198n6; false sense of separation from, 182–83; feminist replication of, 19, 197n3;

power structures (*continued*)
   horror genre underscores fear of
   women's power, 151–52; sadism as
   reflection of on plantation, 48–49;
   sensationist violence as exposure of,
   33; speaking back to, 114–17, 120, 123;
   transnational, 121; white women's
   complicity in plantation, 12, 19, 23,
   36–37, 96, 151, 191n34
The Price of a Child (Cary), 95
Prince, Mary, 63
Property (Martin), 18, 76, 77, 82–90
Puerto Rico, 167
pulp fiction. *See* plantation pulp fiction;
   plantation pulp novel covers

queer sexualities, in plantation settings,
   80–81

Rabinowitz, Paula, 192n3
racist narratives, 15, 25, 105–7; and
   antislavery publications, 4–6, *5*; in
   horror genre, 20, 144, 148–49, 151,
   154–55
Randall, Alice, 87
Reclaiming Difference (Mardorossian),
   127
The Repeating Body (Brown), 15
repetition, 4, 10–12, 15, 47, 52, 75, 107–8
ressentiment, 117
"Rethinking the Nature of Work"
   (hooks), 104
retributive violence, 4, 13, 17–18, 58,
   62–66, 116, 119–20, 160, 163
"The Revenge of Hannah Kemhuff"
   (Walker), 199n12
Rhys, Jean, 19–20, 103, 121–40, 194n5,
   200n20
Rich, Adrienne, 104
Richardson, Matt, 146
Roberts, Brian Russell, 187n18
Rodríguez-Silva, Ileana M., 167
Rollins, Judith, 109, 117, 118
romance plots, 8, 18–19, 25, 45, 74, 93,
   103

Roots (Haley, miniseries, 1977), 24,
   76–78, 196n8; remake (2016), 18, 78
Roots (Haley, novel), 77
Russ, Elizabeth Christine, 2, 185n2,
   187n16
Ryan, Tim A., 8, 78, 81, 85

Sade, Marquis de, 48
sadism, 20; and agency, 40, 47, 51, 53,
   57, 74; agency attempted through,
   51–54, 57, 74; at heart of slavery, 48,
   55; and intimacy, 44–46, 48, 51, 57,
   66–70, 74; "living within/beyond the
   sword," 44, 45, 60, 62, 64–65, 68, 74;
   as structural, 32, 48–49, 65; as trope,
   31–32; of white enslaver women,
   17–18, 23, 25, 28, 31–36, 44–58,
   61–67, 71, 74; and white male power,
   46–47, 50–51, 71–72. *See also* horror
   genre; torture; violence
Saint-Domingue, 22; Code Noir of 1685,
   48, 57, 147
Sankofa (film), 66
Sansay, Leonora, 22–23, 32
Sapphic Slashers (Duggan), 165
Sapphira and the Slave Girl (Cather), 82
Sargasso! A Caribbean Love Story (film,
   1991), 128, 138–40, *139*
Scarry, Elaine, 32, 38, 51, 58, 175
Scenes of Subjection (Hartman), 12
science fiction/dystopian genres,
   175–77
Scott, Anne Firor, 33
Scott, Darieck, 201n5
*Secret History; or, The Horrors of
   St. Domingo* (Sansay), 22–23, 32
The Secret Life of Bees (Kidd), 198n7
self-emancipated people, 11, 54–57, 89
sensational violence, 17, 20, 36–38, 129,
   192n36. *See also* plantation pulp
   fiction; exploitation films
sentimental narratives, 19, 48, 103,
   106–7, 117, 119–20, 124
separation: false sense of, 182–83;
   mediation of violence with weapons,

16, 23, 24, 63; other people as intermediaries for violence, 23, 30–31; use of film shots to suggest, 35–36; violence as tool of, 2, 8, 16, 52, 63, 85, 109, 125–26, 169

sexual violence, 18–19, 74, 75–101, 195n3; cis perpetrators and victims prioritized, 75–76; consent, discourse of, 75, 97–98; contextualization of, 76, 91; indirectly hinted at, 79–82; intimacy absent from, 87–88; lack of remorse, 88–89; power enacted through, 77, 87–88; rape, 9, 15, 37–38, 40, 52, 59–61, 68, 73, 75, 82–83, 95, 98, 136–37, 142, 149; in *Roots*, 79–80, 80; silencing in sexual assault cases, 75, 195n3; between women, 79–80, 80, 155–56, 160–63, 170–71

Sharpe, Christina, 8, 10–11, 186n14

Sharpe, Jenny, 45, 74

Sheller, Mimi, 121, 189n29

Shimizu, Celine Parreñas, 193n12

Shine, Ted, 199n13

Shockley, Ann Allen. *See* "The Mistress and the Slave Girl" (Shockley); "Women in a Southern Time" (Shockley); *The Black and White of It* (Shockley)

Shoemaker, Jan, 108, 109, 112

silence/silencing: about structural violence, 114–15, 129–31, 141; about violence against domestic workers, 104, 107–10, 114; in Caribbean, 121–22, 133; in lesbian fiction, 91, 97–98, 100–101; and romance plots, 18–19; in sexual assault cases, 75, 195n3; as violence, 104, 141; witnesses, inaction of, 114–15. *See also* sexual violence

Silencing Race (Rodríguez-Silva), 167

Silvera, Makeda, 199n14

"sisterhood," narratives of, 19, 103–5, 119, 151

The Skeleton Key (film), 149

skin-to-skin violence, 16–17, 35–36, 38, 40, 44, 51, 153–54; and personal connection, 1, 8–9, 17, 24, 47, 58–59; social categories complicated by, 8–9, 16

slave narratives, 2–4, 3, 32, 38, 39, 41, 42–43, 58, 63, 81–82, 95, 185n3, 185n4

slavery: and Enlightenment thought, 47–48, 54; historical continuity with domestic labor, 114–15; plantation logics, historical continuity of, 16–19, 31–32, 62, 76, 102, 155, 174, 179–80, 186n12, 187n16; racialized sexual economies of, 18; and reproduction, 76; sadism at heart of, 48, 55; slave markets, 14; visual representations of, 4; westward expansion of, 32. *See also* enslaved people; enslaved women; enslavers, women; plantation; power structures

Smith, Jon, 188n23

Smith, Lillian, 111

social stability, and trope of rivalry, 142–43

Softley, Ian, 149

Soto-Crespo, Ramon E., 24, 27

soucouyant myths, 159–60, 164

South, 186n13, 187n19

The Southern Lady (Scott), 33

Speaking Power (Fulton), 58

Spillers, Hortense J., 82, 190n31

Stallings, L. H., 91, 95

Steele, Valerie, 33

Stephens, Michelle Ann, 187n18

Stockett, Kathryn, 105–6

Stoker, Bram, 146, 165

Stryker, Susan, 24

Sugar Hill (film), 149

sugar trade, 68, 71, 118

Sugg, Katherine, 166, 172

Suriname, 67; "hydraulic slavery," 71; Jewish enslavers, 194n7, 195n10; sugar trade, 68, 71; "Suriname marriage," 195n10

Sweeney, Carole, 162

Tademy, Lalita, 9
Tar Baby (Morrison), 19, 103, 117–21, 127
Taylor, Tate, 106
Their Eyes Were Watching God (Hurston), 30, 194n8
"They Called Her Aurora (A Passion for Donna Summer)" (Portalatín), 102
They Were Her Property (Jones-Rogers), 31
Thiefing Sugar (Tinsley), 65
"things," people of color as, 9, 48–49, 111, 113
Thomas, Deborah A., 12, 189n28, 201n9
Thornton Dill, Bonnie, 104–5
Tinsley, Omise'eke Natasha, 65
torture, 5–6; enslaved people forced to enact violence against each other, 50, 62, 71; graphic depictions of, 47; instruments of, 23–24, 31, 63, 161; as mainstay of plantation economy, 49; regimes act out agency through, 32, 38; as trope, 31–32; used to prove agency, 51–54; as verisimilitude of reality, 46. *See also* sadism
tourism, 121, 147, 188n20
trauma, 88, 107, 122; transgenerational transmission of, 155–57, 186–87n14; voice lost through, 162
Trouillot, Évelyne, 194–95n9
Trouillot, Michel-Rolph, 2, 55
True Blood (HBO), 165
The True Nanny Diaries (Nandi), 116
Truth, Sojourner, 81, 196n10
Twelve Years a Slave (Northup), 38, 39, 41, 42–43. *See also* slave narratives

Unburnable (John), 20, 142, 155–64

vampires: lesbian, 164–65, 170–71; *soucouyant* myth, 159–60, 164
Van de Velde, Jean, 17, 18, 45, 67. *See* Hoe Duur Was de Suiker (film)
Van Stipriaan, Alex, 71
Vásquez, Sam, 63, 194n6

Vastey, Baron de, 48, 54–55, 194n4
violence: abolitionist descriptions of, 5–6; of archive, 2, 191n34; in Bibb's engraving, 2, 2–4, 185n3; of colonialism, 142–43, 155–56, 159–61; contextualized, 9, 13, 18, 44, 59, 73–74, 76–77, 103, 122, 133, 137, 139, 191–92n35; of decolonization, 12, 13; decontextualization of, 17, 19, 59, 128, 129, 189n27; as everyday occurrence, 6, 15, 32, 123, 182–83; expressive, 190–91n33; familial, 191–92n35, 200–201n4; historical continuity of plantation logics, 16–19, 31–32, 62, 76, 102, 155; individuation of structural, 66, 130; internalization of, 15, 56–60, 63–64; legitimate, revolutionary, 48; "living beyond the sword," 44, 45, 64–65, 68, 74; "living within the sword," 44, 45, 60, 62; of male enslavers, embodied by white women, 25–26, 50–51; as male prerogative, 23, 30, 32–33, 37–38, 41, 43; mediated, 8, 16, 23, 30–31, 44, 47, 63, 81, 102, 144; public display of, 3–4, 95, 142; reciprocal, 13, 58, 117; retributive, 4, 13, 17–18, 58, 62–66, 116, 119–20, 160, 163; sensational, 17, 36–38, 129; silence as, 104, 141; social order upheld by, 17, 113, 163, 165; structural, 66, 70, 102–3, 122; surfeit expenditure, 46, 169; as tool of separation, 2, 8, 16, 52, 63, 85, 109, 125–26, 169; two-way, 19, 43, 117–24, 126–27, 129, 140; victim/perpetrator boundary, 155; between women, as common to patriarchal colonial structures, 155–56. *See also* sadism; same-sex violence; sensational violence; sexual violence; skin-to-skin violence; weapons
voyeurism, 83, 86, 92, 95–96, 175, 185n4

Walker, Alice, 116–17, 199n11
Walker, Christine, 57

Walker, Kara, 2, 6–8, 7, 14
Wallace-Sanders, Kimberly, 112
Wanzo, Rebecca, 106–7, 116, 120, 175
Washington, Margaret, 196n10
weapons, 49; blade associated with slave insurrections, 53; body as, 38, 41, 58, 64; mediation of violence with, 16, 23, 24, 63; white women's use of, 33–34, 40
Weiner, Marli F., 31
Wench (Perkins-Valdez), 95
White, Deborah Gray, 22
whiteness, monstrous, 144, 146
white supremacy, 8, 16, 147–50, 174
The White Witch of Rosehall (de Lisser), 149–50, 164
"White Witch" tale, 144, 149–54, 164, 201n9
white women: complicity of in systems of power, 12, 19, 23, 36–37, 96, 151, 191n34; denial of violence by, 30, 106, 112–14, 140, 191n34; failed motherhood, 119–20; "goodness," narratives of, 15–16, 19; honor, notion of, 77; "keeping her hands clean," 30–31, 40, 41, 42, 106; post-2016 depictions of, 174; as property through marriage, 84; as "pure," 33; racial segregation, support for, 198n4; "white feelings," 106–7, 116, 120. *See also* enslavers, women

Wide Sargasso Sea (film, 1993), 128–29, 133–37, *135*; colonial context of, 129–34; decontextualizing perspectives in film adaptations, 129–34; skin color in casting choices, 136
Wide Sargasso Sea (film, 2006), 128–33, *132*, 140
Wide Sargasso Sea (Rhys), 19, 103, 121–40, 194n5, 200n20; colonizing perspective in film adaptations, 129–31, 134; filmic adaptations of, 19–20, 128–40, 150; as post-colonial text, 122–23
Williams, Linda, 178
Williams, Sherley Anne, 58, 196n12
Wilson, Harriet E., 114–15
The Wind Done Gone (Randall), 87
Winters, Lisa Ze, 195n12
"Women in a Southern Time" (Shockley), 18, 75–77, 90–93, 99–101, 103–4
"Women Who Batter Women" (Obejas), 168
Wood, Marcus, 4, 185n3, 185n4, 193n10
Wounds of Returning (Adams), 24, 185n2
The Wretched of the Earth (Fanon), 13, 48, 58, 66
Wright, Laura, 131–32, 136

Yaeger, Patricia, 12, 46, 188n23

Zimet, Jaye, 25
Zimmerman, Bonnie, 164

Made in United States
Orlando, FL
27 September 2022

22837525R00150